PRAISE FOR H

M000314762

"You can feel the heat, the danger, and the bullets whizzing by like angry bees. . . . You shudder at each wounded Ranger and narrow escape. . . . You know what's coming next and your eyes mist. *HEART OF A RANGER* masterfully and artfully transitions between all aspects of Ranger Ben Kopp's life, service, death, and legacy . . . author Bill Lunn leaves no facet out."

—CSM JEFF MELLINGER, US ARMY RANGER (RETIRED)

"Captivating . . . I could not put *HEART OF A RANGER* down until the very last page. This is such a beautiful story of love . . . love between a mother and her only son and love between that son and his brothers in arms. The love of a Ranger's heart beats on and the love continues in a way no one could imagine."

—CANDY MARTIN, NATIONAL PRESIDENT, AMERICAN GOLD STAR MOTHERS INC., CHIEF WARRANT OFFICER FIVE, US ARMY (RETIRED)

"Bill Lunn's *HEART OF A RANGER* is a beautifully told story about a young hero and the woman he rescued, a woman he never met. A gut-wrenching but utterly inspiring account of hope through unspeakable loss, the book deftly weaves both Ben Kopp's brutal combat with the Ranger Regiment in Afghanistan and the life of transplant recipient Judy Meikle back in the US. With a reporter's keen eye for detail, *HEART OF A RANGER* reads with the intensity of a thriller, and I can unequivocally recommend it to all."

—MARK GREANEY, #1 *NEW YORK TIMES* BESTSELLING AUTHOR OF *GUNMETAL GRAY*

"Beautifully written, an inspiration to all. . . . To read *HEART OF A RANGER* is to feel in a million ways all that is good in humanity."

—SUSAN GUNDERSON, CEO, LifeSource ORGAN AND TISSUE DONATION

"*HEART OF A RANGER* is a powerful piece that clearly identifies with the most recent generation of warriors. For love of country and family, this book gives you an insight into what it takes to serve as a Ranger, and who the heroes are who sacrifice it all so that we may live in peace."

—CAPT. FLORENT GROBERG (RETIRED),
2015 MEDAL OF HONOR RECIPIENT

"Bill Lunn beautifully crafted this work of narrative prose in a way that simultaneously captures the essence of who Ben Kopp was and the nature of his chosen profession as a Ranger. *HEART OF A RANGER* is not merely a hero's story; it's a testament to the indomitable will of the human spirit."

—MARTY SKOVLUND, JR., AUTHOR OF
*VIOLENCE OF ACTION: THE UNTOLD STORIES OF THE
75TH RANGER REGIMENT IN THE WAR ON TERROR*

"This is the kind of story that should be required reading in schools around the country. Ben Kopp embodied the kind of values that are the very definition of honor . . . *HEART OF A RANGER* gives us a deep look into what true heroism looks like. . . . A truly important read."

—CHUCK HOLTON, AUTHOR, WAR CORRESPONDENT AND FORMER
ARMY RANGER WITH BEN KOPP'S UNIT

"Often, the heart of a warrior is passed on from one generation to the next. This book is different. *HEART OF A RANGER* will tell you the incredible true story of how Ben Kopp's heart gave America freedom and gave one woman a new life."

—MAJOR JEFF STRUECKER, RANGER CHAPLAIN (RETIRED)

"Read *HEART OF A RANGER* and aspire to live a life worthy of the enduring legacy of this American soldier. Rangers lead the way, and Ben Kopp led the way in life and as he faced death. His Ranger heart beats on and his legacy lives on in all who knew him."

—PETE GEREN, SECRETARY OF THE ARMY, 2007 – 2009

HEART
OF A
RANGER

The True Story of Cpl. Ben Kopp,
American Hero in Life and Death

Alex,
Thank you
for your service.
to our country. I
hope this book inspires
you!

Bill P___

WISE
CREATIVE • PUBLISHING
Ink
2022

ISBN 13: 978-1-63489-067-0
eISBN 13: 978-1-63489-068-7

Library of Congress Catalog Number: 2017938937

Printed in the United States of America
First Printing: 2017
21 20 19 18 17   5 4 3 2 1

Cover and interior design by James Monroe Design, LLC.

This book is also available in an electronic version.

Wise Ink, Inc.
837 Glenwood Avenue
Minneapolis, Minnesota 55405
wiseinkpub.com
To order, visit itascabooks.com or call 1-800-901-3480.
Reseller discounts available.

For Dad and Mom, William J. Lunn Jr. and Joan M. Lunn:
You made all things possible.

I love those who can smile in trouble, who can gather strength from distress, and grow brave by reflection. 'Tis the business of little minds to shrink, but they whose heart is firm, and whose conscience approves their conduct, will pursue their principles unto death.

—LEONARDO DA VINCI

AUTHOR'S NOTE

In the early fall of 2011, I was sitting at my desk at KSTP-TV in St. Paul, Minnesota, reading my hometown news, the *Winnetka Talk*, online. I discovered the story of a suburban Chicago woman who had received a heart transplant. The heart came from a soldier who had been mortally wounded in Afghanistan. Reading a bit further, I learned the soldier was a native of Rosemount, Minnesota. I immediately recalled the news of Ben Kopp's death in the summer of 2009, but I didn't know the extraordinary circumstances that preceded and followed it. As a news anchor and reporter covering military and veterans' issues, I immediately reached out to Ben's mother, Jill Stephenson, to see if I could do some sort of follow-up. Jill agreed, and I traveled to Chicago to meet Ben's heart recipient, Judy Meikle. I interviewed Judy and Jill at Judy's Winnetka home. While Jill held it together during our on-camera interview, I fought tears the whole time. *How can this woman be so strong? How can she possibly deal with such an earth-shattering tragedy?* I was awestruck as I felt Ben's heart beating inside Judy's chest. Our television news story, which aired that November, was well received and nominated for an Emmy Award.

In the years that followed, when people asked me, "What's the most compelling news story you've ever covered?" I would always respond with the same answer: the story of the brave Army Ranger from Minnesota whose heart ended up in the chest of a woman from my hometown. Sometimes I got choked up just repeating the facts.

In the fall of 2014, I was flying with my wife to Fort Benning, Georgia, to visit our son, who was going through Army basic training.

At the time I was very much aware Fort Benning was where Ben Kopp spent much of his short Army career. On the plane, I turned to my wife and said, "I'm going to ask Ben's mother about turning his story into a book."

A few days later, Jill agreed to have lunch with me in downtown Minneapolis. As soon as I presented my idea, she replied, "I've been praying for six months that someone would approach me with this."

I don't know if I've ever been the answer to anybody's prayers, but what followed was an odyssey into the life of Ben Kopp, a young man who squeezed more into his twenty-one years than most do in a full lifetime.

One further note. In keeping with the operational security requirements of Special Operations forces, the names of some Rangers have been altered to protect their identity.

FOREWORD

The day my son was born, I looked into his baby blue eyes and promised I would love him with all my heart. I told him I'd do the very best I could to prepare him for the world; I would aspire to teach him all that was needed to face life with a sense of courage and purpose.

I had eighteen years to make good on this promise. It seemed like an eternity, yet as life always does, it went by too fast. I suddenly found myself saying goodbye to my only child as he left home to join the Infantry of the United States Army. Ben had reaped what I hoped he would. I was confident he had the tools he needed to go confidently into the world without me. I had fulfilled the promise I made looking into his innocent eyes all those years ago.

Little did I know that three years later, I would be saying goodbye to him again. This time, I learned that while I believed I had been preparing him, he had in fact been preparing me. I had guided him and given him all the love I had in my heart. When his time on earth was through, he gifted it all back to me, and then some.

In Steve Jobs's 2005 commencement speech to the Stanford University graduating class, he talked about how trusting that the dots of his life would connect to his future had made all the difference in his life, never letting him down. As I reflect back on the events of Ben's life, I see how the dots connected and weaved through the years. As a small boy, he would relentlessly question his great-grandfather about his service in World War II. He was punished for horsing around in middle school, but used that punishment years later for his benefit. He played football all four years in high school, and then left for the Army one month after graduation. Each of these things would represent a thread in the beautiful tapestry that would become his legacy, making a difference in the lives of countless people.

I never imagined I would lose Ben, and I am sure he never imagined his life would end before his twenty-second birthday or that someone would find his life interesting enough to write a book about it. I had no idea either. Neither one of us had a clue who Ben would ultimately become—he simply followed his heart and went boldly where his gut told him to go. Knowing where his convictions and passions came from, it's not a surprise he chose the road he did. In fact, anyone who knew Ben from middle school onward never questioned his post-high school plan to join the Army.

As a parent, there is a level of pride our children give us in their growing-up years with the many firsts and accomplishments they achieve. We then keepsake these achievements on paper or in our hearts and minds. My heart swelled, as any mother's would, sharing these things with Ben—and then he burst open the skies when he died. When he signed his name to join the Army, he was committed to fight for the life and liberty of his fellow man, and knew this might include giving up his own. Three and a half years later, when he made that ultimate sacrifice, he saved lives on and off the battlefield, in life and in death. His final act of courage caused a ripple effect, the end of which is nowhere in sight. He continues to live in the hearts of so many (literally, in one case) and will surely save future lives by influencing strangers to act in the same way he did.

The enormous sense of pride and love I feel because I am Ben Kopp's mother goes way beyond what I ever imagined was possible. I continue to learn from his example of what it means to be truly self-less. Not a day goes by that I don't feel a sense of gratitude for all I have received because Ben lived, and because, for reasons I don't understand, I was chosen to be his mother. I will spend the rest of my life paying this forward in his honor. As I count my blessings, I can only hope I give enough and live long enough to make him as proud of me as I am of him.

—JILL STEPHENSON, BEN KOPP'S MOTHER

PROLOGUE

Helmand Province, Afghanistan – July 10, 2009

Ben's heart raced. He and his squad of about a dozen Army Rangers hustled across the unforgiving landscape of southern Afghanistan. They hoped to rescue a recon team of six pinned down by enemy sniper fire. The Rangers stopped on the edge of a crop field, and Specialist Ben Kopp pulled a belt of machine gun ammo out of his pack. He fed the lead round into the Mk 48 he and Private Sean Scappaticci were setting up overlooking the field.

Somewhere in front of them were two Ranger snipers, three Ranger reconnaissance (RECCE) guys, and a combat photographer. Their operation—to nab a high-ranking Taliban leader alive—had gone to hell in a hurry. Gunfire flew from multiple directions. Their ground assault force was split into four smaller groups in the area intelligence had assured them that a high-ranking Taliban leader was hiding. The special operators had traveled overnight deep into Taliban territory in Garmser District, dangerously deeper than any American or British troops had been in years, if ever.

About one hundred meters in front of the rescuers, the recon team huddled face down in a shallow depression. They'd been pressed body to body in the hole for more than an hour. Enemy sniper fire tore up the dirt around them; the shots were so close the exploding earth peppered their faces.

Ben's squad couldn't see them. His leaders, Captain Krueger and Sergeant Benson, scanned the field and radioed the recon group asking them to show some sign of their location. The pinned-down snipers and recon guys responded and quickly flashed a brightly colored panel, revealing their location to the rescuing Rangers. But the quick flash also gave up their position to the enemy, intensifying the small arms fire around their hole.

The rescuers were set up now. About a dozen Rangers armed with M4s, grenade launchers, and two machine guns simultaneously opened with a vicious barrage. Private Scappaticci let his machine gun rip in the direction of the enemy fire coming from some small buildings and compounds about five hundred meters in the distance. Ben fed the belt of brass ammo into the weapon and felt it roar, watching the tracer rounds just a few feet off the ground disappear in the distance.

About a third of the way across the field from Ben's position, white smoke exploded then billowed, a smoke grenade to cover the recon group's exit. Ben watched as the six Americans rose from their hole and began sprinting toward safety, still under fire. The white smoke swirled and dissipated in a crosswind, leaving the retreating Americans exposed to enemy fire. The recon team galloped, weighed down by their gear, enemy fire chasing them. Ben's heart beat faster watching the six in a life-or-death dash as friendly machine gun fire covered their exit.

Ben carried so much into this deployment: the inspiration of his great-grandfather's World War II service, the fear and anxiety over his own mortality, the heaviness of losing one of his Ranger friends two months earlier. The twenty-one-year-old from Minnesota had expressed some of his fears to his mother just before leaving for Afghanistan. This was the kind of moment he'd warned her about. The tough kid and only child of a single mother knew this deployment would be different. But there was no time for those thoughts now.

As Ben looked out through the haze of smoke grenades, the six in the recon group dashed toward their location wearing looks of anguish. They finally crossed the threshold to safety, joining the other Rangers. They gasped for air knowing they had just cheated death. Ben locked eyes with one of the arriving snipers, Sergeant Nick Irving. Irving's look said it all: *You just saved my life. Thanks, bro!* Ben gave him a confident nod in return, then a glimpse of his notoriously crooked smile. Nick forced a smile back.

For the recon group—Nick, his spotter Mark Pendleton, and the four others—standing in safety felt as if they'd just experienced a miracle. They owed their lives to Ben and the rest of that Ranger squad. They had escaped what minutes earlier they thought would be certain death. It had gotten so bad Sergeant Irving had even considered taking his own life, not wanting to give the satisfaction to the Taliban. Danger for Army Rangers is an expected part of their life. But this day was different. For Ben Kopp and the Third Platoon Rangers of Charlie Company 3/75, more peril—even tragedy—lay just a few meters ahead.

Chicago, Illinois – October 2008

The news for Judy Meikle was earth shattering. *Will I survive another year?* The heart beating in her chest was failing, and no doctor in the world could fix it. The word her cardiologist had just used, *transplant*, kept ringing in her head. As she sat in the Chicago hospital, the statistics hit her too: eighteen people nationwide die every day waiting for a transplant.

As Judy thought about her diagnosis, it struck her that someone else would have to die for her to get the heart she needed. She would be the beneficiary of their tragedy. *Who are they? What are they doing right now?* The thought was overwhelming. She began to feel guilt. *If you're praying for a heart transplant, are you praying for someone to die?*

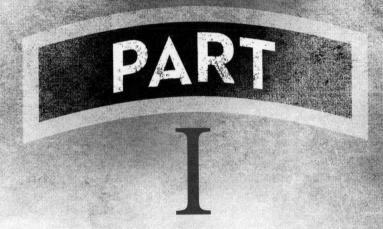

PART

I

Wood Lake, Minnesota – Summer 1995

By the time Ben Kopp was seven years old, his favorite thing to do was visit his great-grandfather's cabin in north central Minnesota. The drive with his mom seemed to take forever, about three and a half hours northwest to Wood Lake in the Fifty Lakes area.

Pulling into the driveway always brought a sparkle to Ben's blue eyes. He was a round-faced boy with a mop of blond hair. Jill Stephenson had spent time at the cabin when she was a girl and knew the woods and waters would be good for her energetic son. Jill, twenty-seven, was a single parent and Ben her only child.

From a young age, Ben craved the attention of a strong male figure, and his great-grandfather, LeRoy Rogers, fit the bill perfectly. LeRoy was raised in Michigan during the Great Depression. He was a hard worker, and after his Army service in World War II he got a job with the post office delivering mail by foot. He was a quiet, confident man, the kind of person who wouldn't take anything from anybody. Those who spent time around LeRoy developed a quick respect and admiration for him. Now in his seventies, the deep lines of experience cut across his kind and knowing face. Jill and Ben's frequent visits to the cabin created a bond between the boy and his great-grandfather.

LeRoy and his wife, Marian, whom Ben called Granny, had a post-Depression sensibility and were frugal and independent. LeRoy loved to show his grandkids and great-grandkids the ways of the woods, and Ben was especially willing to learn. LeRoy never went to town to buy worms. Instead he would take Ben around the grounds of the cabin to dig for them. Ben loved the smell of fresh earth as they dug and sifted for fishing bait.

To Ben and the other kids in the family, Leroy was known as Ay-Yi. He earned the nickname by continually singing the Mexican song "Cielito Lindo," which included the line, "Ay-yi-yi-yi . . ." Ay-Yi strolled around his property singing just about anything from the forties and fifties, including country songs. Ben watched him as he sang and saw a man who always seemed to be in a splendid mood.

Ben often followed Ay-Yi around the property, looking for new adventures and soaking up any advice, stories, or insight Ay-Yi had to share. LeRoy taught Ben how to use tools and how to mix the gas and oil for the lawn tractor and boat motor. Ben was thrilled by the whir of the engines and the smell of the exhaust. Before long, Ben got to use the riding mower and could pull-start the motor in the boat.

All the kids loved the gentle Ay-Yi, but Ben was fixated on him. In return, Ay-Yi was the only family member who called him Benji. The two were inseparable. When Ben arrived at the cabin, Ay-Yi was always the first person he'd look for.

"Hey Benji, what's up?"

"Nothin', Ay-Yi," Ben replied.

Ay-Yi found Ben's reply funny and laughed. Ben loved his great-grandpa's laugh, noting that the old man laughed a lot.

One time, Ben was watching Ay-Yi sitting by himself. His great-grandfather, who was deep in thought, suddenly broke into a hearty cackle.

"Why do you laugh so much?" Ben asked.

"Better than crying," Ay-Yi replied. Ben thought that made pretty good sense.

Another time, Ay-Yi caught Ben crying. LeRoy thought Ben was overreacting and was very direct with his great-grandson. "Be quiet, Benji," he said, "until you really have something worth crying over."

Ben wiped away the tears and looked up at his great-grandfather, seeing his shiny bald head reflecting the sunlight. Ay-Yi sat down next to Ben and told him about a time in his own life when things had been tough. Ben was always mesmerized by Ay-Yi's stories, and hearing them made him forget what he was crying about in the first place.

Ben trailed Ay-Yi everywhere and watched him do all sorts of jobs. He also asked questions constantly: "Where did you get those? How did you get those? How did you do that? What was that like?" Ben wouldn't be denied. He always pinned Ay-Yi down until he got a

Ben with his great-grandparents, LeRoy and Marian Rogers, at the family cabin near Fifty Lakes, Minnesota. Ben and LeRoy developed a fast bond. LeRoy, a World War II veteran, was an inspiration for Ben to later join the Army.

satisfactory answer to his little boy curiosities.

"Don't ask him so many questions," Jill finally warned her son, trying to protect LeRoy from the inquisition.

Ay-Yi would have none of it. "Nonsense!" he said to Jill. "Questions mean he's smart."

Ben's favorite thing to do with Ay-Yi was to go fishing. They headed onto the lake in Ay-Yi's small aluminum boat. The elder taught Ben all the tricks, like how to adjust his bobber depending on the depth they were fishing, how to cast farther, how to tie line onto the hook, how to undo snarled line, and how to troll using the boat's motor. They would often return to the dock after dark with a stringer full of fish, walleye and northern pike, but mostly sunfish.

Ay-Yi would hand Ben a big blue bucket to store their fish in overnight. Sometimes a heron would show up and help itself to breakfast from their bucket. Ben was perfectly happy to share his catch and liked to watch the heron from a cabin window. Ay-Yi nicknamed the heron Oscar. Sometimes Ben caught sunfish by himself off the dock and deliberately left them in the bucket for Oscar. Ben loved to watch Oscar eat the fish, especially when he saw the giant lump in the bird's long throat while the fish was going down.

Ben and LeRoy cleaned anything that was left, Ay-Yi keeping close watch as Ben gutted and filleted the fish. Even though Ben could see the pile of fish guts building in front of him, he was sure not to react in front of Ay-Yi. When Ben made a mistake filleting the fish, Ay-Yi was patient, knowing his great-grandson was learning. They took the cleaned fish inside where Granny fried them for dinner, the skins of the sunnies crackling in the pan. That smell of fish frying was heaven to Ben. He loved to eat them, especially with a side of his favorite vegetable, green beans.

Inside the simple cabin, Ben discovered oddities that fascinated him. One morning, he noticed a curio case hanging on a wall. There were several brightly colored objects inside, and Ben's natural curiosity led to more questions. "What's that?" he asked his great-grandfather.

"Those are my medals," LeRoy replied.

"Medals for what?"

"I earned them in the war."

"Where did you get them?"

"I served in the Army."

LeRoy looked at the case, which displayed a Purple Heart and several other military medals. He grabbed a small black-and-white picture near the case and handed it to Ben, who examined it closely. It was Ay-Yi, only much younger. He was in an Army uniform. On the picture was a note: "Anzio Beachhead American Cemetery, May 1944."

Ben felt something in his heart stir as he looked at the picture. This Army stuff was about as exciting as anything he'd ever seen or heard. He wanted to know more, and the ever-patient Ay-Yi obliged him with battle stories from World War II.

Minneapolis, Minnesota – December 1941

The news broke on KSTP radio across the Twin Cities of the Japanese bombing at Pearl Harbor. The nation was suddenly at war. National Guard soldiers like LeRoy Rogers knew their lives were about to change. After learning of the attack LeRoy, who had turned twenty-three the day before, reported to the armory in Minneapolis. He was told his unit—the 135th Infantry Regiment, which was part of the 34th Infantry Division—would soon be shipping out. A few months later, he and Marian were married at Fort Dix, New Jersey. Days later, LeRoy boarded a ship for Northern Ireland.

After months of training and preparation, on November 8 and 9, 1942, Operation Torch began, with LeRoy's 34th Infantry landing on the beaches of North Africa. By February, the 135th had dug in near Sbiba for the Battle of Kasserine Pass, matching wits with General Erwin Rommel, the "Desert Fox." A ferocious battle unfolded that by some estimates resulted in 2,500 Allied deaths.

By February 8, 1943, LeRoy and his 135th Infantry moved from Algeria into Tunisia. Sergeant Roger's job was to supply ammunition to troops on the front, including mortar rounds, artillery shells, and rifle ammo.

One time, during what they thought was a break in battle, LeRoy and some of the others in his company were playing cards. As the game wore on, they heard the tell-tale sound of incoming artillery. They all ducked into their foxholes. The blast was frighteningly close. LeRoy felt the earth shake. Then big chunks of dirt and other rubble rained down on him. When the dust cleared, the men climbed from their holes and brushed themselves off. They checked on each other only to find one of the card players lifeless on the edge of his hole, the back of his head blown off.

LeRoy sometimes shared the bad news with Marian. He wrote home to her nearly every day he was gone. He mentioned that she'd met one of the casualties, back at Fort Dix, when they'd gotten married.

March 1942

The other chaplain in the chapel who you asked about was the one who was killed. Bill was his name. He was a fine fellow. Chaplain Larson is now our head chaplain in the regiment and is now a captain.

Lee

LeRoy and his company spent a lot of time in their foxholes. He pinned a picture of Marian at eye level. Her sweet face made the terrors of war a little more tolerable and reminded him that he needed to make sure he got home in one piece.

On the morning of April 26, 1942, LeRoy's 135th got orders to relieve the 168th Infantry to the west of a strategic rise in the Tunisian topography. That rise had been labeled Hill 609. The 135th was ordered to make a diversionary attack in support of the main attack on the German stronghold. It was a key strategic point the Germans held, one that allowed them both a good view of American troops and a perfect launching point for artillery.

Many strategies were considered, even bypassing the hill altogether. But in the end, General Omar Bradley ordered the 34th Infantry to take the hill. During the Battle of Hill 609, LeRoy wrote home.

April 28, 1943

Harp and I are working together again. His job is ammo. My job is to get it transported. From here I can follow the path of the enemy shells in the air as they are landing about a mile from here. A fellow gets used to it all. We're in no danger here as long as the shells keep landing where they have been.

Lee

Leroy Rogers and the 135th Infantry Regiment got a bit of a break in the summer of '43. But they were planning and training for a new advance. By early fall, they would turn their attention to the Italian front.

On September 15, 1943, LeRoy and the rest of the 135th's Service Company were aboard a British transport ship and headed for the Italian coast. The Germans held the hills in the areas above the Italian beaches near Salerno. As the Allied Forces invaded, vicious fighting broke out. The battle lasted for days, the Allies launching an attack only to be driven back by a German counterattack. By September 21, LeRoy and the 135th Infantry were ashore at Paestum. Once the beach was won, the 34th Infantry Division began the drive toward Avellino and continued the attack on Benevento. By September 30, LeRoy and the 135th were ten kilometers east of Montemarano.

On October 18, LeRoy and his service company were in Ruviano. The conditions that autumn into the winter of 1943 were challenging. The rain was incessant, turning mountain roads into muddy quagmires where Sergeant Rogers' supply truck would get stuck. Rivers like the Volturno and the Rapido swelled, and the soldiers were often soaked and cold. LeRoy offered Marian a slice of his routine.

November 1943

It is cold and rainy all the time and you are tired and sleepy 'cause the darn artillery keep pounding all night and you couldn't sleep (I can but most of the fellows can't!). . . . You hold your mess cup out for black coffee and step forward when it is filled, to have a cook slap a spoonful of hash or stew into the mess kit. A piece of bread (if they have it) is slapped on top of it with margarine for butter. . . . And then you look around for a clear place on the ground . . . you find it and take off your steel helmet and use it as a seat and commence to devour the eye-appealing tasty breakfast.

Lee

They had to cross the Volturno River under high water conditions. One challenge LeRoy and his company faced was that the river divided the fighting front from the ammo supply dump. On one cold and rainy morning, LeRoy climbed into the truck and started out for the dump, which was several miles away. LeRoy felt the warmth in the cab coming from the engine. It felt good after a long, cold night in a tent. Crossing the river was complicated by the fact that the Germans had blown up all the bridges. The only option was a makeshift pontoon bridge the Army Corps of Engineers had built. LeRoy knew the crossing would be the most exposed they would be to enemy fire. The Germans would have a good view of them from the hills above. As the truck pulled up to the banks of the raging Volturno, an MP put his arm up, stopping them.

"They're shelling the bridge; you're proceeding at your own risk," the MP warned.

LeRoy found the warning absurd as they had orders to pick up and supply ammo, and really didn't have a choice in the matter.

"Well, what the hell do you expect us to do? Fly over?" LeRoy replied.

As they rolled slowly over the bridge, the structure bobbed and weaved with the current and weight of the big truck. The shifting motion gave them an uneasy feeling. LeRoy said a short silent prayer, asking God to protect them from the German artillery rounds. When they cleared the bridge, Sergeant Rogers and the driver found deep mud on the roads, which were virtually washed out. The supply truck struggled through the mud, nearly getting stuck a few times before finally making it to a better road.

When they reached the ammo dump, they found a group of Italian civilians waiting to load the truck. They were supervised by American soldiers guarding the cache. As soon as the truck was loaded, LeRoy and his partner started back. They plowed through the mud again, the truck now loaded with ammo. They needed to cross the pontoon bridge over the Volturno again. They could've waited for the blanket of darkness to shield them, but LeRoy and the driver decided to keep going. As they started across the bridge, German shells came whistling in, exploding in the river nearby.

"If we get hit, they won't even find our dog tags," said Rogers.

The driver nodded in agreement. They were loaded down with 81mm high-explosive mortars. Despite the shells bursting frighteningly close, they rolled slowly over the precarious bridge. LeRoy wasn't worried about the shells; he didn't usually worry in situations like this. Many of the guys he served with talked about the possibility of not coming back. But LeRoy always felt he would make it. Marian was his inspiration. The truck cleared the bridge and rambled up toward the front, where American mortars were waiting.

Meanwhile, the 34th Infantry was ordered to move back out to sea and up the coast to flank the Anzio beachhead. On March 27, 1944, the 34th relieved the 3rd Infantry Division at Anzio. The plan was to get behind German lines to the south. But the fighting at Anzio was severe, and the Allies didn't take control of the coastal town until May 23, 1944.

Ben's great-grandfather, Sergeant LeRoy Rogers, at Anzio Cemetery in Italy during World War II. Rogers, part of the 34th Infantry Division, completed tours in North Africa and Italy, supplying ammunition to soldiers on the fronts.

Sergeant LeRoy Rogers walked up the beach and into Anzio Cemetery. There were Allied graves as far as he could see; white crosses lined up in formation like the men once did who lay beneath them. The earth was still fresh and piled above the grass at each grave. LeRoy held his steel helmet in his right hand and his left hand in his pocket. He turned, pausing briefly for a photograph, a serious look on his face.

But as fall and early winter arrived in 1944, Sergeant Rogers received orders that his service was complete. He felt both satisfaction and relief. He had seen the terrible realities of war. Friends he had known from Minnesota had died right beside him. He missed his darling Marian terribly. Two years and eight months after kissing his new bride good-bye, he was on his way home.

Wood Lake, Minnesota – 1995

When Ay-Yi was finished telling war stories, Ben looked at him in silent awe. LeRoy could tell he was thinking about something. "What is it, kid?"

"When I grow up, I want to join the Army too," Ben announced.

Ay-Yi locked eyes with Ben. "Kid, you don't join the Army because someone else did. You do it because you want to. When that time comes, your gut will tell you, and you'll know."

Ben nodded. He trusted Ay-Yi, and trusted his advice. He filed it away, not realizing how handy it would be one day.

Rosemount, Minnesota – 1998

Three years later, Ben was so restless at school his teachers told Jill they weren't sure what to do with him. He got teased over his last name, which at the time was Burud, his mom's maiden name. Kids would call him "Ben Rude" or "Ben Be Rude," which angered Ben, setting off numerous fights and trips to the principal's office. Jill finally decided she and Ben needed a fresh start.

During the summer of 1998, just before Ben entered fifth grade, they moved from St. Louis Park about twenty-five miles southwest to Rosemount. There, Jill and Ben found a quiet working-class community about twenty minutes south of St. Paul. Jill also changed Ben's last name to Kopp, his father's last name.

Even in a new town, Ben still managed to find trouble. On one occasion in sixth grade, he was serving detention at Rosemount Middle. He pushed a garbage dumpster down a school hallway and could hear the cackling voices of girls his age coming from the library just ahead. As he walked past the door he noticed a group of girls passing a video camera around. He locked eyes with one of them, a tall blond girl named Jenny Boll. She grabbed the camera and zoomed in on Ben's backside. When the others leaned in to see what she had found in the viewfinder, they exploded in a burst of giggles. Ben kept walking, wondering what the fuss was all about.

Ben made friends quickly in Rosemount. His circle included Tyler Nelson, Kyle Hildreth, Adam St. Marie, and Colt Hale. One thing Ben loved about Rosemount was that they lived on the edge of woods, farm fields, and other rural lots. There were lots of places the boys could find adventures. Ben especially liked riding bikes and making jumps, lighting fireworks and bonfires, and shooting BB guns.

On one summer day in 2001, Ben (now thirteen), Tyler, and Adam gathered at Ben's house. They were planning an all-out war with their BB guns in the woods just a few blocks away. The boys marched out of the house heading west, weapons in hand. The woods would give them good hiding places and provide the perfect setting for what they hoped would be an epic battle. They passed a dozen or so houses on the way, then stepped over some railroad tracks that ran along the edge of the woods. What they didn't know was that someone was watching them.

When the boys entered the woods, each claimed territory to

defend, and the war was on. They each had their own style of combat. Ben liked hiding and picking off his targets like a sniper. Tyler and Adam preferred to stalk through the woods and sneak up on their enemies.

As Ben lay in the brush, he thought about his great-grandfather, and what it must have been like fighting in World War II. He remembered Ay-Yi's curio case, full of medals, and thought of the valor on the battlefield. Ben was still daydreaming when he heard a car come screaming to a halt a short distance away. He jumped up and saw Tyler and Adam running. To his shock, they were being chased by a police officer.

"Freeze! Get down on the ground!"

Too scared to stop, the boys kept running through the woods. They eventually reached an industrial area, where more squad cars pulled up. Officers cornered them in a parking lot and ordered the boys to drop their weapons and get on the ground. They were surrounded by flashing blue lights and a squadron of police cruisers.

Employees from nearby businesses came out to see what the commotion was about. The teenage fugitives surrendered willingly, and the officers placed the boys in a squad car. Their families later learned that an anonymous neighbor had reported them, telling police he had seen three "men" with rifles heading toward the woods. The boys were driven home by police and handed over to their parents.

Their run-in with the law did little to discourage them. Not long after, they were in the same woods. Ben had upgraded and now bragged that he had the most powerful weapon in the neighborhood. It was a combination BB/pellet gun that could be pumped up to deliver a fairly serious wound. Tyler meanwhile had the classic Red Ryder BB gun, nostalgic, but lacking in ballistic advantage.

Ben was in sniper mode again. Through the nettle and other patchwork undergrowth, he could see Tyler creeping along out of range. Ben started to move slowly in his direction, staying low, concealing himself in the vegetation. Ben crawled to a more open part of the woods and now could see Tyler walking away from him. Ben rose to his feet. He checked his gun to make sure it was fully pumped. He looked down and pressed the safety to the off position. He had Tyler dead to rights. Tyler was about to "die" and there was nothing his friend could do to save himself. Ben then started running at Tyler, his gun up, ready to fire. Either Ben stepped on a stick or Tyler had a sixth sense, because Tyler spun around just in time to see Ben bearing down on him. Ben, knowing his element of surprise was now gone, opened his mouth, stuck his tongue out, and screamed, trying to intimidate his opponent. Tyler, fear flashing through him, quickly drew the Red Ryder to his cheek and pulled the trigger. Ben dropped to the ground and let out a scream as though he'd been shot with a real gun. Ben rolled around on the ground, holding his face. Tyler was worried now that he'd shot Ben in the eye.

"You shot my tongue off!" Ben said, slurring his words while holding his mouth.

Ben let out a few choice words not normally in the working vocabulary of most thirteen-year-olds. He then looked up from the dirt and the weeds and gave Tyler an angry gaze. Once the pain subsided Ben got up; he was sticking his fingers into his mouth to make sure his tongue was still there. It was, but he could feel a lumpy wound. Tyler had hit him square in the tongue.

Over the next few days Ben felt that his tongue was not healing right. There was a lump, and it wouldn't go away. Jill began to notice that something was not quite right about her son. There was something that was agitating him.

"How did your tongue get swollen?"

"I have a BB in my tongue," he replied casually.

"What? How did that happen?" Jill inquired. "Were you sticking something on your tongue, and they tried to shoot it off?"

"No!"

He explained the story of Tyler's lucky shot. Jill said she was taking him to the doctor to get checked out. After an x-ray, they realized there was indeed a BB embedded in Ben's tongue. The wound had nearly healed, and at this point the doctor said it would do more damage to cut it out, so they decided to leave it there.

Years later Ben would show girls the bump on his tongue and learned to use it to his advantage.

"It makes me a better kisser," Ben would tell the girls.

Fifty Lakes, Minnesota

By the end of March 2001, Jill was dealing with what she knew would be a tough situation for her son. The cancer LeRoy had been battling for several months had progressed, and the prognosis was grim. The body that had once carried him off landing ships to battle the Nazis in both Africa and Italy was giving out. Jill thought it would be good for Ben to see Ay-Yi one more time, so they headed northwest from the Twin Cities to the cabin on Wood Lake.

They found Ay-Yi in surprisingly good spirits. He was still healthy enough to sit at the kitchen table in his wheelchair, and they spent a pleasant afternoon recalling family gatherings and good times on the lake.

Jill rose to leave, not wanting to overstay their welcome. Ay-Yi turned to Ben. "Come back again soon, kid," he said. "We'll go fishing."

Ben smiled at the thought of fishing with his great-grandfather again. It was almost that time of year. The fishing opener—a day celebrated like Christmas in Minnesota—was only five weeks away. But Jill knew what Ay-Yi meant. He probably wouldn't make it to Minnesota's opener in May. He was just trying to give Ben some hope. A few days later, Jill got the call. On April 4, LeRoy finally succumbed.

The funeral was three weeks later in Minneapolis. LeRoy's grandkids were asked to share their favorite stories about Ay-Yi. Since Ay-Yi had meant so much to Ben, Jill asked if he'd be willing to speak.

"Every time I think about a story it hurts too much," Ben said. "I can't do it."

When the funeral ended, Marian handed Ben something. It was the picture of Ay-Yi at Anzio Cemetery, the same one he'd shown Ben years before. Ben put the picture in his wallet. He would carry it with him always.

Ben was crushed by his great-grandfather's death. That pain would last for months, long enough to carry over into one of the darkest days in American history.

Rosemount, Minnesota

Ben landed his first job in the summer of 2001. One of the teachers had put the word out at school about a job detasseling corn. Ben took the job, and while most kids were sleeping in, he would get up at six and catch a bus to different fields in the area—Hastings, Coates, Rosemount, Cannon Falls, and Welch. Each person was assigned a row of corn. Ben had to pluck the tassel off the female plant. It made his hands raw, and it was hard work. They started the summer with a team of about fifty and finished the season with just fourteen, Ben among them. Seven dollars an hour plus occasional bonuses was good money for a thirteen-year-old.

That same summer, Richard Rivera moved from Colorado to Rosemount. Richard was Puerto Rican, the child of military parents, and had already moved a few times in his young life. When one of the neighborhood kids had a party, Richard showed up hoping to make some new friends. He couldn't help but stare at the one kid who seemed entirely out of place.

Ben Kopp came through the door wearing a big white cowboy hat, cowboy boots, a flannel shirt, and an oversized belt buckle. There before everyone was a thirteen-year-old suburban Minnesota cowboy. Rivera was perplexed but thought, *This guy must be pretty confident to come here dressed like that.* No one else was wearing boots or a hat or

Ben (right) with his pal Richard Rivera (left). Both would later join the Army, but in different capacities. Rivera would warn Ben about the dangers of his job as a Ranger, urging him to transfer to a different Army unit that was less dangerous.

anything resembling Western wear. The outgoing Richard decided to investigate.

He approached Ben cautiously. "Hey, I'm the new guy next door, Richard Rivera. Are you from Texas?"

"Hell no!" answered Ben, a little agitated by the question. But they ended up talking. Richard asked him about his taste in music.

"Country," Ben replied definitively, consistent with his clothing choice. Richard told Ben that he preferred hip-hop and music with a Latin flare. Despite this difference, they quickly realized they had many things in common: Ben and Richard lived in the same area, less than a mile apart. They were both industrious, and they were both children of single moms. The two soon became close friends.

As school started in early September of 2001, no one could know that what was about to happen to the United States would change the course of thousands of lives. The families of the victims of the 9/11 attacks would surely be impacted in a terrible and tragic way. But young men and women all over the country would be inspired to do something about those attacks, and Ben Kopp would be among them. On the day of the terror attacks on the World Trade Center, Pentagon, and flight 93, Ben was furious. Jill watched her son acting in a way she had never seen him behave before. He took the attacks personally. All he could think about was his great-grandfather and his sacrifice—it was as if the terrorists had killed LeRoy Rogers that day. To Ben the attacks were a mockery of his great-grandfather's service during World War II.

Jill and Ben watched the news reports in his bedroom. As they did, the eighth-grader became increasingly angry, clenching his fists and pacing around the house. After a couple of days of news coverage, Ben couldn't take it anymore. He made a solemn vow: "I'm gonna join the Army. I'm gonna become an Army Ranger. I'm gonna find Osama bin Laden, and I'm gonna kill him myself!"

Hearing this gave Jill mixed feelings, because she knew her son meant it. She looked at Ben and saw the serious and determined expression on what had always been a sweet little boy's face. She felt the direction of her son's life changed in that instant, and that her son would carry through on the promise. The September 11 terror attacks had ripped the scab from the pain of his great-grandfather's death. There was a conviction in Ben now that Jill had never seen before. It was a key turning point in his life and in the lives of so many other young men and women across the country.

Rosemount Middle School

One day in eighth grade, Ben's science class was working with some finely calibrated scales. Ben and another boy were recording measurements, but something happened, and by the time they'd finished their experiment, the scale was broken.

The teacher insisted they would have to pay for it. Ben and his lab partner were sent to see the assistant principal, Mrs. Mary Thompson. She served as Rosemount Middle's disciplinarian and was quite familiar with young Ben Kopp, calling home to talk to his mother "at least once a week." Ben was a handful for Mrs. Thompson. He walked the halls of Rosemount Middle with a "smirk on his face and glint in his eye." Mrs. Thompson was never quite sure what he was thinking or what he was up to. And unlike nearly every other kid in the school, she knew that Ben wasn't afraid of her.

Knowing the boys had to pay some sort of price for breaking an expensive piece of science equipment, she mulled over the punishment.

"You'll have to do some form of community service," she told them.

Ben had never heard the phrase "community service" before, but it stuck in his head. Mrs. Thompson assigned them to do twenty-four hours of community service—a month of Saturdays working with the custodians to clean the school.

Ben was actually excited about his penance. He longed for older male figures in his life. Here were a couple of guys he'd seen around school each day with big key rings on their belts and access to all doors and closets. Behind those doors, Ben found heavy cleaning equipment, chemicals, and other tools. To him, this was adventure and fun, not punishment. They let him and his friend run the various cleaning machines. Ben vacuumed carpets, polished floors, washed windows, and took out the trash.

Ben also liked the lingo the men used, the stories they told, and the way they razzed each other. The two custodians told stories about their big weekends and shared schemes on how they'd get rich. Even when they were just talking between themselves, Ben listened, soaking it all up. He never complained about his punishment, and he did such a good job the custodians offered him a job working with them over the summer.

Rosemount High School

By high school, Ben had transformed into a handsome young man with closely cropped hair, a chiseled jaw, and a sly, crooked grin. His eyes and smile would've made Ben a lousy poker player—he always looked like he was up to something.

Ben had also developed a taste for adventure that often walked on the edge of trouble and, like most boys his age, had a growing interest in the opposite sex.

In the winter of their freshman year, Ben and Tyler went to a dance competition at a rival high school. Tyler's older sister, Desirae, was competing for Rosemount High School, and Ben and Tyler thought this would be a prime location for girl watching. The two were wandering around the gymnasium when they bumped into Brittney Doran, a pretty, green-eyed brunette about their age.

Brittney was second of three sisters. Like Ben, she was strong willed, arguing even the smallest of points with her parents. She attended nearby Eastview High School in Apple Valley, and she had an obvious crush on Tyler.

She gazed at Ben's friend with her bright smile and green eyes. The pounding dance music blared behind them as they chatted and flirted. The situation was a bit awkward for Ben as Brittney focused all her energy on Tyler.

Days later, Brittney invited Tyler and Ben to her house to hang out with her and a friend. The boys came over, and they all got to know each other better. Brittney was still very much interested in Tyler, but as the days progressed, Tyler didn't show much interest in return. Ben, meanwhile, was chatting her up, and it dawned on Brittney that Ben was pursuing her. They started talking on the phone and via instant messenger. After a few weeks, Ben finally worked up the nerve to ask Brittney out on a date, a first for both.

They went to a movie. Their early dates were a bit awkward. Jill would drive while Ben and Brittney sat on opposite sides of the backseat. On one particular date night, Ben asked Brittney to scoot over. When she did, he put his right arm around her. She liked it, but thought, *This is just about the cheesiest thing ever.* Ben's mom didn't seem to notice, or if she did, pretended not to.

Ben and Brittney's relationship blossomed. Instead of hanging out with his friends all the time, Ben now focused his attention on Brittney. The feeling was mutual—Brittney once rollerbladed four miles to Ben's house just to see him. Their tempestuous relationship would be the backdrop for much of Ben's high school career.

Ben loved a good prank. One day in the cafeteria during lunch his friend Kyle Hildreth pulled a plastic spool of clear monofilament fishing line out of his backpack. Kyle taped the end of the line to a penny for weight and then taped the penny inside a potato chip bag. He and Ben ran the fishing line down an aisle between tables in the cafeteria. They put the chip bag in the middle of a walkway. One of the cafeteria ladies, a Russian woman of about sixty, was sweeping the floors. She came upon the chip bag and swept it into her pile of debris. But when she turned around for a second, the boys gave a yank on the line, pulling it a few feet out of the pile. The woman turned back around and saw the bag had mysteriously left the pile. *A gust of air?* A perplexed look came over her face. She moved to get the bag, but as she laboriously bent over and reached down for it, they pulled the string again. Now she knew she was being played. She stood up and started looking around, a scowl bursting across her face. But there were so many kids at the tables that the boys blended in. Ben and Kyle and the others seated with them were trying to control their laughter. The woman again turned toward the chip bag on the floor, this time using the broom to collect it. Kyle pulled the string, moving the bag a couple more feet. Now the woman raised her broom and hit the bag as though she were killing a rat, pinning it to the floor. She reached down and grabbed the fishing line and started pulling it, knowing her tormentors were on the other end of the line. But the boys had a whole spool containing a couple hundred yards of line. She pulled and pulled but couldn't make any headway. They laughed again as the snarled line built up in her hands.

By now Ben and Kyle were laughing so hard they gave themselves away. One of the school administrators, seeing the poor woman's anguish, came over to assist her. She pointed to the boys and he escorted the traumatized lunch lady to their location. Ben and Kyle's faces were still red from laughter, but they calmed down quickly and put on a straight face. At the administrator's urging, they both told the woman they were sorry. She then turned and walked away, but the administrator stayed.

"Boys," he started, Kyle and Ben looking up at him, knowing he was about to nail them for their deed. "That's the funniest thing I've seen so far this year. Now don't let it happen again."

Josh Maldonado was an overweight, nerdy kid with glasses who roamed the halls at Rosemount High School with kids of similar social status. He became a natural target for bullies. Deep down, Josh was very sensitive and the teasing hurt. Josh was five seven and an unfit 220 pounds. The complexion on his round face was dark, revealing his Latino heritage. Maldonado had been born in Honduras and had moved to the United States with his mom at age four. He lived in Rosemount with her and his stepdad. Maldonado was a whiz with computers and had mastered the art of making fake IDs before he could drive. That skill got him an introduction to the "cool kids" crowd, of which Ben was a leader.

Despite their very different social statuses, Ben accepted Josh from the beginning. One day Ben saw Josh getting harassed in the hallway. He later pulled the perpetrator aside and said, "Hey, he's cool. Don't do that anymore."

Because of Ben's friendship and protection, Josh's life at Rosemount High School became peaceful and it remained that way through graduation. One simple act by Ben Kopp had taken care of that. Nothing more needed to be said.

Maldonado observed in Ben an innate sense of cool and an

outward confidence. Ben had a swagger and students at Rosemount High School respected him. Not only did Ben step up for Maldonado, Ben would get in the way of anyone who would give any of his friends a hard time. Ben was not the type of guy to start a fight, but had already built a reputation as a tough guy. The reason others were intimidated by Ben was not his size, about five nine and 155 pounds early in high school. It was his track record that he would never back away from a fight no matter whom he was up against. Someone pushing Ben Kopp to see what his limits were knew they were going to get a brawl. Ben's rep grew to where people knew that if you pushed his buttons, you better be able to back yourself up.

Ben's best friend in high school was still Tyler Nelson. They had similar interests and seemed a natural pairing. Josh, meanwhile, became best friends with Richard Rivera, and the foursome would often get together. Richard was everything Josh wasn't—a high school playboy, skilled with the ladies, and muscular, with the ability and confidence to start a conversation with just about anyone.

Cars and Trucks

Ben, now fifteen and without a driver's license, decided it would be a good idea to take his mother's Chrysler Concorde for a joy ride. Jill was out for the evening and was not expected back for a few hours. The car was parked in the driveway outside Ben's townhome on 156th Street. He hopped into the driver's seat, Tyler climbing in shotgun, and Adam St. Marie jumping in the back. Ben backed out of the driveway. A couple of turns later, the teenagers were on the wide-open drag strip of County Road 46.

"How fast do you think it will go?" Tyler asked.

"I don't know. Let's find out," Ben suggested.

Ben pushed the pedal to the floor, throwing their heads back. As the engine roared, the green Chrysler picked up speed. Their wide eyes fixated on the speedometer, 65 . . . then 75 . . . 85 . . . soaring above 90 miles per hour. The car was still accelerating, past 100 . . . then 110. The car then leveled off; the boys caught the needle on the odometer. They had just hit 116 miles per hour. Ben pulled his foot off the gas, and the boys' heads whipped forward as the car decelerated. They roared in thunderous delight at what they had just done. They had hit 80 miles per hour on their snowmobiles, but now they had found a new thrill. They continued to joy ride the deserted streets on the rural edges of Rosemount, just southeast of town.

The adrenaline and excitement distracted them from the time. After some hairpin turns and screeching tires, Ben decided they needed to get his mom's car back home. He turned north onto Chippendale then onto 156th Street and pulled into his driveway.

Ben strutted from the car with pride, the keys dangling from his right hand. He opened the front door then froze in fear. There sat his mom on the stairs, waiting for them. Tyler and Adam followed Ben in. To Jill, they "looked like they were going to shit their pants." She gave a sly chuckle knowing they knew they were busted. She would deal with Ben alone, and now stared past him at his friends.

"I'm going to give you two a pass," she said. "I trust that you will tell your parents and then call me and tell me when you do, otherwise I'm going to call your parents and tell them myself."

Tyler and Adam nodded in agreement with the plan and left. They both called her that night to tell her that they had told their parents. Tyler had not.

Ben Kopp liked fast cars and loud trucks, and his teenage years were transported on a combination of pavement burners and mud runners. When Ben turned sixteen, he was ready with a pile of cash earned by shoveling driveways and performing other odd jobs around the neighborhood. He'd also sold his snowmobile.

Ben had been thumbing through the local *Autotrader* magazine and found a truck in his price range. Jill drove him about an hour north to Taylors Falls along the St. Croix River. Ben got out of his mom's car and circled the black 1985 Chevrolet Scottsdale 1500. The single cab pickup already had been "lifted" about four inches and was sitting on a set of thirty-three-inch mudding tires. Ben shook hands and paid cash for the truck. He hopped in and followed his mom back to Rosemount.

Brittney Doran was the love of Ben's life. Their relationship was the backdrop of most of Ben's high school career. Ben would think about Brittney often and even had dreams about her during the last weeks of his life.

Driving his own vehicle for the first time, Ben couldn't keep the smile off his face. Having his own truck gave him a sense of freedom and independence. Jill didn't pay a dime and looked at her son and what he had pulled off and was suddenly very proud of him. He had set a goal, saved his money, researched it, and located just what he was looking for. He couldn't wait to show it off to friends.

Ben had a rule about his truck. No one was allowed to drive it but him. He didn't let his friends, and he didn't let Brittney. Despite that, she and Ben spent a lot of time together in that truck. The Chevy had a cassette deck, and the lovebirds played their favorites, George Strait, Tim McGraw, and Garth Brooks. They'd blast country music and sing along. Ben and Brittney went to the homecoming dance together their junior year and had pet names for each other. Ben referred to Brittney as "Pretty Girl" and she called him "Teddy Bear" or "Benny Boo." She loved his confident monosyllabic laugh. He'd squint and let out a "huh" like *I got this, I'm Mr. Cool.*

Brittney Doran loved Ben Kopp with all her heart. Halfway through high school, she was convinced they would be together forever. But their relationship was starting to show its cracks. Brittney had a jealous streak, especially when other cute girls were around Ben. Girls seemed to gravitate toward him, and that really bothered her. She was in love with his softer side, the one few people ever got to see. While Ben could be rough and wild around his friends, he spoke to her in a gentle and very comforting way when they were alone. She always felt safe and protected around him. She felt like she was his entire world and he was hers and nothing could break them apart.

Football Team

By the time Ben was in high school the only sport he was still involved in was football. Ben did not have the physical tools to be a great player, as he was always a little smaller than the rest of his friends. By the time they were upperclassmen, Tyler Nelson was at least six feet tall. Ben, stretching himself, might have been five foot ten. Ben also was not

Ben wore #44 for the Rosemount Fighting Irish. Ben wasn't the fastest, biggest, or strongest on the team, but teammates say he played with the most heart.

among the fastest kids on the Rosemount High School Fighting Irish football team. But Ben had a secret weapon that many other players did not. He had heart. What he lacked in physicality, he made up for with grit, determination, and guts. Ben had a motor on the playing field, and it always seemed to be in overdrive. He tried harder on the field and in the weight room than most of the other guys.

Ben wore number 44 on his navy blue "Irish" uniform and played along with his pals, Tyler Nelson and Richard Rivera. In practice, when Rivera had the ball as a running back, it was very often Ben who was tackling him.

Coaches weren't exactly sure where to play Ben. They tried him at guard and his tenaciousness made him a good blocker, but he was too small for the offensive line. They made him a defensive end, and he would respond with tackles and big plays. Again, the position didn't fit his body type. They tried him at linebacker, where he was also undersized, but his aggressiveness helped him settle in to that slot. He was hard hitting, knocking guys down. And from the linebacker position he was a leader, watching over the rest of his teammates and barking out orders.

On the Rosemount Fighting Irish football team there were faster guys, there were bigger guys, and there were stronger guys. But there was not another player on the team who had more heart than Ben Kopp.

Jenny

Jenny Boll, the laughing sixth-grader with the video camera, was now a striking young woman, tall and blond. She and Ben were close—Jenny called Ben her best friend.

Jenny and Brittney were also friends, but Brittney's jealous streak and Jenny's good looks made for some friction. The arrangement caused a lot of angst between Ben and Brittney.

Jenny and Ben lifted weights together. Ben always went out of his way to make her feel welcome and comfortable in an atmosphere dominated by the guys.

Ben's mom worked in corporate banking and would occasionally travel. Ben found this to be the perfect time to have people over to the house. During his junior year, he texted Jenny and told her to come over after she got off from work at Applebee's. As she walked up Ben's driveway she saw that Ben and some of his buddies were sitting inside

Jenny Boll called Ben her best friend. Ben encouraged Jenny to lift weights and work out with the guys. Ben stood by Jenny while she struggled with addiction issues and was her inspiration to finally overcome them.

the garage drinking beer. Ben had a boxing heavy-bag hanging in the garage and liked to host his friends for boxing matches. That's exactly what they were doing when Jenny arrived. Ben was a little tipsy from the beer and was laughing heartily. Jenny was tired from work and feeling a bit crabby as she walked up. Ben grabbed a pair of boxing gloves and ran up to greet her.

"Put the gloves on, Jenny! Put the gloves on! Let's box!"

"No," Jenny replied, not in a party or boxing mood. She pushed the gloves away and continued to walk toward the garage to find a place to sit down.

"Put 'em on! Come on!" Ben pleaded with her.

Jenny shrugged, knowing that a determined Ben Kopp was not going to stop pestering her. She grabbed the gloves and started to put them on, Ben helping her pull the big mitts over her hands. He then guided her over to the heavy-bag in the corner of the garage and told her to hit it a few times. Jenny made a few feeble punches on the bag and quit, embarrassed that everyone was watching her.

"Come on! I'm tired. That's enough," Jenny said, her shoulders sagging in protest.

"No, come on!" Ben encouraged her. "Hit me real quick."

Ben stuck his face forward taunting her with a target. As Ben urged her to throw a punch, they were drifting out of the garage and onto the driveway.

"No, Ben, I'm not gonna hit you," Jenny said in retreat.

"Come on! Just hit me one time!" he said with a smirk.

Ben began playfully pushing her, chuckling and trying to get her to take a swipe at him. Jenny started laughing at his persistence. She loved his enthusiasm, and she knew there was only one way to get him to shut up. She cocked her right arm and exploded with her fist right into the middle of his face. Ben backed up then leaned forward, dropping his hands to his knees. He stood stunned for a moment and shook his head. He looked up at Jenny then slowly lifted his hand to his nose. He felt a warm stream oozing from his nostrils and looked down at the crimson trickle that had run onto his fingers. He burst out laughing.

"Oh my God! You made me bleed!"

"Oh my God! I'm sorry!" Jenny pleaded. "You made me do it!"

Ben's nose was ringing; his blood was now collecting in splotches on his white t-shirt. He quickly recovered, gathered his wits, and suddenly found this very funny. He started to laugh harder and then could not stop laughing. His friends, first stunned by what they had seen, now followed his lead in a chain reaction of laughter. Ben turned to Jenny and, still holding his nose and wiping blood with his left hand, gave her a high five with his right. Ben had always encouraged Jenny to get in touch with her more physical side. The two had been lifting weights together and it was clear Jenny's work in the weight room was paying off.

Ben loved physical challenges, especially those that were man-to-man. At one of his beer-fueled garage gatherings, he and his pals were pushing each other around and challenging each other to various tests of physical strength. While Josh Maldonado watched, Ben got into a wrestling match with a kid who was much bigger by several inches and about forty pounds. They had a vicious duel, wrestling to a draw. By the time they were done, they were both spent.

"Holy shit, Ben. That was amazing," Maldonado said afterward.

Deep down Ben was proud of himself for the effort, but on the outside he pretended like it was nothing.

Jill was not aware of Ben's little beer gatherings and had strictly warned Ben that his friends could not drink at the house. Ben, like most teenagers, was open to experimenting. He had tried other forms of alcohol but never really liked them. He had decided that beer was his thing. He rarely, if ever, drank anything else alcoholic. Jill would lecture her son, reminding him of his age, and asking him not to drink. Ben developed a standard reply that he would continually deliver very slowly and deliberately.

"But mother . . . beer . . . is delicious."

Ben's competitive streak extended even to his girlfriend. One warm, sunny summer day Ben, Brittney, and Jill were in a rowboat on Wood Lake at the family cabin. Jill was so happy to be with the two of them. She adored Brittney. They were right in the middle of the lake, just floating around and enjoying the day, when Ben bet Brittney that he could beat her in a swim race back to shore. Brittney looked at the shoreline, about a half mile away.

"Alright, let's go!" she said.

She jumped into the water. Jill laughed hysterically as the teenagers splashed fearlessly. Ben knew he could beat her and didn't mind that she had a bit of a head start. She had a floating seat cushion and could easily rest on it and swing her arms and kick. She moved along efficiently. Ben meanwhile was wearing a life jacket. The life-saving device dragged in the water, slowing his progress. She looked back as she approached the shore and realized she was winning. She couldn't believe it. She now feared the wrath of what Ben would be like the rest of the day after losing to her. When Ben got to shore in second place he showed no reaction. He didn't want her to know it bothered him to lose the race. He did have a smirk on his face and let out a smug little laugh, "Huh, huh, huh." As if to say, *You just wait. I'll eventually get you for that.*

In the spring of 2005, Brittney got into a fight with her mom and ran from the house. She ended up at a nearby church and called Ben. He came to pick her up. She climbed into his truck and curled up in a ball on the floor. As they drove off, Ben looked in the rearview mirror and recognized the car behind them.

"Brittney, your step-dad is following us. What do I do?"

"Just keep going!"

He did, stopping at a Holiday gas station. Brittney's step-dad pulled up behind them. He got out of his car to confront her.

"Brittney, get in the car!"

"No!"

Ben drove off, taking Brittney to his house where she spent the night. In her mother's eyes, there was too much drama surrounding Brittney's relationship with Ben. She saw her daughter often cry over it. For her part, Brittney thought her parents didn't like Ben and considered him a bad influence, which she thought was unfair.

The summer before Brittney's senior year, her mom hatched a plan. Saying she was tired of all the drama with Ben, she sent Brittney to Florida to visit her dad, "just for the summer." But when Brittney got there, her dad told her it was a one-way ticket, and she wasn't going back to Minnesota.

"I have to get back! I have a boyfriend. I have friends!"

"Nope, you're staying here," he told her.

Ben and Brittney tried to make it work, talking on the phone long distance, but the plot to break them up had done its damage. The one thing her parents didn't bank on was that in August Brittney turned eighteen. She was now an adult and realized she could legally make decisions for herself. She flew back to Minnesota just in time for her senior year.

Bigfoot

Ben spent the summer of 2005 adjusting to life without Brittney. While they tried to maintain a long-distance relationship, it was hard. He was now spending more time with his friends, including Richard Rivera. One day in July, Ben picked up his phone and called him.

"Hey Richard, you wanna do something crazy?"

"What do you wanna do today, Ben?" Richard said, suspicious of another Ben Kopp scheme that could get them into trouble. Richard, like Ben, had a future in the Army and didn't want to do anything to screw it up.

"I've got some EZ Go golf cart keys," Ben started. "Master keys. They'll work on any cart."

"Okay, and?"

"I know this golf course. They leave their golf carts out at night. We could go get a few carts and drive them all over," Ben suggested.

"Where did you get those keys?" Richard asked.

"Don't worry about where I got the keys. I'll pick you up."

Ben picked up Richard, then they went to gang headquarters, Josh Maldonado's house. Josh insisted on driving.

"What are we gonna do with the golf carts?" Josh inquired, just getting briefed on the plot.

"I don't care, I just wanna go joyride," Ben replied.

They hopped into Josh's Jeep Grand Cherokee. After a short drive, they parked in a cornfield across the street from the golf course. It was now close to midnight.

"Ben, are you sure there won't be anyone there?" Josh asked.

"Yeah, dude. Golf courses close at dusk, then they leave because they've gotta be back early in the morning."

Ben handed his friends keys, and they each jumped on their own cart and took off into the darkness. They did donuts, skidding out and tearing up patches of fairway. They played chicken, driving the carts at one another. And they explored the golf course under the cover of night. They knew a course manager lived on one of the fairways, so that added to the danger.

"Hey, follow me," yelled Ben.

They convoyed across the course. Ben, who worked at an automotive shop, knew enough to remove the speed governor. That allowed the carts to go about twenty miles per hour. They drove through sand traps and played smash-up derby. They hollered and laughed at the top of their teenage lungs.

During one particularly intense crash, Josh flew out of his cart and into Ben's. Ben's cart was now laboring at less than ten miles per hour, so he jumped into a cart with Richard. Ben took over as driver.

"Go over there," Ben suggested. He was pointing to a wood line, away from homes on the course, where they would be less likely to be detected. It was very dark as they approached. Josh was catching up, and as he closed the distance, they all spotted a moving silhouette on the course that appeared to be nine or ten feet tall.

"Is that a deer?" Richard asked.

"That's not a deer," Ben replied.

"What is that?" Richard said.

Ben's heart pounded at the sight of it, but they kept driving toward the massive moving object.

"Dude, let's go," Richard urged. "I think that might be the guy," meaning the golf course manager.

"That thing is too big," said Ben. He brought the cart to a halt.

"Let's go! That guy is gonna come out with a shotgun and kill us!" Richard protested.

"Screw him," Ben said "Let's follow it."

Ben floored the pedal and the cart lurched forward, carrying them toward the creature. They got about forty yards away, and it started to run. They chased it, pushing the cart as hard as they could, but they couldn't gain ground. They watched the creature running on two legs with a strange gait. They were certain it wasn't human; it ran with stiff, swinging legs, the way a running back high-steps as he enters the end zone. It also seemed to have white and black fur.

Before they could get another good look, the behemoth was gone. They brought their cart to a stop. Their hearts were pounding; their eyes were wide.

"Dude, what the hell was that?" Ben asked, turning to Richard.

Josh was just pulling up behind them. Richard turned to see Josh slamming on the brakes, a look of bewilderment on his face.

"Dude, we just saw Bigfoot!" Richard announced.

"I thought I saw something out there running like that," Josh said, adding that he saw the creature bound across an entire putting green in just a few steps. Josh looked back at Richard and Ben and saw something he'd never seen on his friends faces before—fear. It was the only time Josh had ever seen Ben or Richard scared. "That was incredible!" Ben declared.

The trio conferred for a moment. They concluded it was too tall to be a human. Josh looked for footprints and found nothing. Now they thought they had seen a ghost.

"Let's go," Ben said at last.

They made it to Josh's Jeep. It was now about 2:00 a.m. The whole ride home they couldn't wrap their heads around what they had seen.

"No one is ever gonna believe us," Ben said.

They drove to Josh's house and did a follow-up meeting in his garage. They called up the computer, trying to find more information. They looked up what they could on ghosts, large mammals, and Bigfoot. They concluded they had seen Bigfoot. They couldn't find anything else even close. As Ben said, "We're the only ones who know there's a creature out there that no one else has ever seen."

Blue-Collar Ben

Ben and Richard always had jobs and worked for their own money. During his high school years, Ben made pizzas at the Pizza Man in Rosemount, manned the counter at the Apple Valley Holiday gas station, and did odd jobs at a nearby horse farm. Ben's work ethic had become the center of who he was. For Ben and Richard, their dedication to their jobs created a bond between them. But it also divided them from other kids, who seemed entitled and completely dependent on their parents.

"They don't know what it is to work," Ben said.

"They also don't know what they're gonna do with their lives," said Richard, knowing he and Ben were planning military careers.

On a hot day in July 2005, Ben was working at Jim Cooper's Goodyear Tires on County Road 42 in Burnsville. He was rolling and stacking tires in the parking lot, unaware he was being watched. Behind the wheel of a government vehicle just a few dozen yards away was Staff Sergeant Andrew Antolik, an Army recruiter. Sergeant Antolik was on what he referred to as ODA duty, or "out driving around," looking for recruits. He hadn't had much luck that day. As a recruiter, he was always ready for rejection.

He watched Ben stacking tires—here was a young man who was athletic, fit, and appeared to be a hard worker. He thought, *This kid doesn't want to be stacking tires the rest of his life.*

The sergeant pulled into the parking lot and drove up to where Ben was pushing a tire. He rolled down his window. "Hey, have you ever thought about the Army?"

"Well, yeah, I have," replied Ben, surprised someone was asking. He noticed the man was wearing an Army uniform.

Sergeant Antolik had asked that question hundreds of times before. The standard answer was, "Uuuuuuh, no," coupled with a look that said, "Get away from me." Ben's answer caught him off guard. "Oh? Okay then," he replied.

A good military recruiter can spot a kid who won't waste his time. Right off the bat, Ben reminded Antolik of himself. He caught the teen's sly grin. He noticed the dirt and grease on his hands and the sweat on his brow and shirt and concluded Ben was the kind of kid who wasn't afraid to get his hands dirty. After a couple of minutes of chatting, Antolik realized the young man in front of him wanted something bigger and better for his life and wanted to achieve that through the Army. They made plans to meet again to talk about getting Ben signed up.

Senior Year

As Ben started his senior year of high school, he was even closer to realizing his dream. Joining the Army was something he'd first thought about at the age of seven, when his great-grandfather shared stories of serving in World War II. Ben was now seventeen, old enough to sign up with a parent's written permission.

He looked at signing with the Army the same way a blue chip high school football player looks at committing to a top university.

"Mom, if you don't sign this for me now, I'm just gonna do it myself in January," he said, referring to his eighteenth birthday. Jill knew this was her son's dream and destiny, so she agreed to sign the application.

Richard Rivera was also signing up. The friends liked to discuss their futures.

"Man, I'm gonna go Airborne Ranger," Ben declared. "I'm gonna do some crazy shit."

Richard was a bit more conservative. "I want to join so I can get trained in something useful, something I can use when I get out."

"Dude, that's for pussies," Ben taunted.

When it came time to make it official, Sergeant Antolik went to Ben's home. He sat at the kitchen table with Ben and his mom, and they signed all the paperwork. That was it. Ben's destiny was sealed. He now had a path for his life. It was his dream come true—joining the Army during wartime and fighting for his country like his hero, LeRoy Rogers.

Richard signed up for the Army reserves. He would be heading for basic training at Fort Knox, Kentucky, the following summer. Ben, who'd declared an interest in the infantry with the goal of being a Ranger, would go to Fort Benning, Georgia.

Ben was already getting some insight into what life at Fort Benning would be like. His friend Eric Pittlekow, who'd graduated Rosemount High School the year before, was just getting back from basic training at Fort Benning. Eric and Ben had known each other in high school, but they hadn't been close. Eric was a wrestler and Ben a football player. Ben would seek advice from upperclassmen like Eric in the weight room, but that had been the extent of their relationship. Now that they were bonding about their Army aspirations, their friendship started to take off.

Ben picked his friend's brain about what the training was like and what he would need to do to succeed.

"I want to be a Ranger," Ben said.

"That's really awesome," Eric replied.

"I'm looking forward to all that camaraderie and brotherhood," Ben said.

"You know, becoming a Ranger means you're going to go through a lot more training than most guys," Eric said. "I can't give you much advice on that, but you can always call me up, and I'll tell you whatever I know."

Ben appreciated Eric's offer of help. Eric would one day be there for Ben in a way neither could imagine.

Ben and Brittney were trying to get their relationship off the ground again as they started senior year, but Ben was focused on his future in the Army.

"Well, what's going to happen with us?" Brittney asked.

"I really don't know," Ben said. "But I know I want to be with you."

The thought of Ben joining the Army scared Brittney. To make matters worse, things had grown awkward between them. They had both seen other people while she was in Florida over the summer. They agreed that too much damage had been done. They loved each other, but they decided to break up.

Graduation?

Ben's future was set. He'd signed with the Army and was set to go to basic training. He also had a contract that gave him the opportunity to *try* to become a Ranger. Having his future predetermined made Ben a little lazy second semester, and he started sleeping in on school days. Jill would call him on her way to work to make sure he was up, but he often wouldn't answer.

One morning Jill called him twenty-five times, then declared she'd had enough. She confronted her son face-to-face.

"That's it. I quit!" she announced in a voice of growing frustration. "It's your choice now. I'm not responsible for getting your butt out of bed. You're eighteen years old. This is a choice for you."

Ben endured the scolding, knowing his mother was right. To get into the Army, he had to have a diploma. The United States Army wouldn't accept a GED.

"Choose it or not," Jill said. "It's up to you, Ben. Be grateful you're not in the Army yet, because when you are, it's going to be some big drill sergeant standing over you, and he's not going to be nice."

To make matters worse, Ben suddenly learned he was in serious jeopardy of not graduating.

One of the school counselors, Laurie Martin, had called Ben down to the office and told him that he was a full six credits short, and there was virtually no way he could make that up in time.

She told Ben that he had two or three options to earn his diploma and that she would commit to working with him. She connected Ben with Patty Matos at Dakota County Technical College (DCTC). At a time when most seniors were slacking, Ben worked hard, spending extra time at DCTC making up the credits. Despite passing at DCTC, he got some more bad news just a couple of weeks before graduation.

"I've done all I can," Patty told him. "You've got one credit left, and you're going to have to find it on your own."

Ben slumped in his chair after hearing the news. His Army Ranger dreams would be shattered. *Where in the world can I earn one more credit just weeks before graduation?*

"Think about any person, any teacher in this community you've ever done a favor for," Patty said. "Any type of community service you've done where you can call on someone and say, 'Hey, I'm in a jam, can you help me out?'"

Ben drove the short route home from DCTC, mulling over her words. He wasn't sure how his mom would take the news, and he had no idea how to find that credit. He had worked so hard taking the extra classes. His mom had warned him, and now he had to face her and eat crow.

"Mom, I need one more credit to graduate."

Jill thought about all the times he had slept in, all the times over the last four years she had pushed her son to work harder in school. She did the best thing a mother of an eighteen-year-old could do, telling Ben he was on his own.

"This is your show here, pal. You've got to figure it out."

But Ben was unsure what to do. *How do you get a credit where one doesn't exist?* He walked downstairs to his bedroom and lay on his bed. Patty Matos had used the phrase "community service." Those words kept taking him back to the same place. Four years before, when he'd broken that scale in science class, Mrs. Thompson had used the same phrase to describe his punishment. While Ben could be a rascal and drive teachers to their breaking point, he was also very charming. He'd kept in contact with Mrs. Thompson, popping in every now and then to say hello. He decided he needed to pay her one more visit.

He walked into Rosemount Middle and sat down before the woman once charged with keeping him in line. Ben explained the situation, his dream of joining the Army, and how much getting his high school diploma meant to him. He reminded her of that month of Saturdays when he performed "community service." He looked her in the eye and asked if she would give him one more credit.

Mrs. Thompson thought about it. She could've exacted revenge on behalf of all the teachers Ben had aggravated. But she didn't. Instead, she told him she would give him a single credit for his efforts all those years ago.

Ben was overjoyed. Against all odds, it now appeared he would graduate from high school after all.

Graduation Day

On the morning of high school graduation, Tyler Nelson bought a 1978 Pontiac Firebird. Tyler called Ben and begged him to come over and see his new ride. Graduation was the last thing on their minds as they worked under the hood, tuning the carburetor.

Ben, perhaps a little jealous of Tyler's new toy, had a vision of his own spectacular car he would one day drive. "One day I'm gonna have a sixty-nine Camaro," he said. "And one summer day, I'm gonna have 'Renegade' by Styx cranking. The windows will be down, and I'll be sitting at a stoplight. It's the beginning of the song, kind of mellow."

Tyler nodded, chuckling at Ben's silliness.

"Next to me there's a minivan with a guy and his wife," Ben continued. "I'm checking her out. She looks over and thinks to herself, *Man, I wish I was in that guy's car.* Then the song kicks in, and I floor it and take off."

Tyler nearly fell over laughing. He looked at Ben and shook his head. Ben just stood there smiling. It was easy for these closest of friends to get caught up in their dreams and stories. But then they looked at the clock and realized they needed to be at school for the graduation ceremony in twenty minutes. They looked down at their clothes—they were both covered in dirt and grease from the Pontiac's twenty-eight-year-old engine. They threw their graduation gowns on, grabbed some cans of Busch Light, and headed out to kiss high school good-bye.

Ben and close friend, Tyler Nelson, on the day of their graduation from Rosemount High School in June of 2006. The duo had been working on an old car when they realized they were running late to the ceremony.

They ambled into the ceremony a bit late, joining their class of about five hundred. When it was Ben's turn to walk across the stage, Jill watched with incredible pride.

"Benjamin Stephen Kopp," rang the voice over the loudspeaker.

After the ceremony, Jill found her son and gave him a big hug. "Ben, I'm so proud of you. You graduated by the hair on your chinny chin chin."

"No, Mom, that one fell out, and I grew another one."

They both laughed heartily, something that was hard to do just a few weeks before when Ben was scrambling to find that last credit. Now it was the anticipation of his departure that started to take its toll on Jill.

Shipping Out

In the last months before Ben left, Jill could hardly look at him without getting choked up. She'd look at her son and think, *How did you go from being five to being eighteen? What's going to become of my life?* She was thirty-nine years old, and her only child was leaving to see the world. He would be gone for at least four years.

Jill wasn't only worried. She was also very excited for Ben, knowing he was pursuing a dream he'd had since he was a little boy. She was proud he'd charted his course at a young age and was now acting on that.

Ben had grown into an independent young man. She knew that she needed to let go. She told herself that she needed to trust God that Ben would be taken care of and that she herself would be taken care of. With the days ticking down until Ben shipped out, Jill now required one thing from her son—a hug. It had to happen every night before he went to bed. Ben, whose mind was squarely on becoming a soldier, would protest by saying, "Mother!" But then would compassionately give in to her demand. Ben grew more excited with each day that brought him closer to his shipping date. He was finally going to get that uniform. He knew he wouldn't be able to see his friends or family much, so he made time to see everyone before shipping out.

Days before leaving for basic training, Ben went to Tyler's house. They were sitting on the Nelsons' backyard deck with Tyler's older sister, Desirae. Tyler was heading off to college at Minnesota State Mankato, where Desirae was already a student. They talked about their futures and what they wanted to accomplish.

"You guys go to college to better yourself to make this world a better place," Ben told them. "I'm going to the Army to better myself and to make the world a better place."

Desirae was impressed with Ben. He'd matured a lot over the past year, and she saw he was on a mission and clearly believed in what he was doing.

The morning of July 6, Ben's alarm rang at 3:00 a.m. He didn't really need it; in his excitement, he couldn't sleep anyway. His recruiter picked him up to make sure he caught the bus that would take him to Minneapolis–St. Paul International Airport. All Ben took with him were the clothes on his back, his duffel bag, and fifty dollars cash.

Ben had been spending a lot of time with Jenny, and she promised to see him off at the Eagan strip mall, the bus's departure point. But Jenny had fallen in with the wrong crowd, and her life was a mess. She was struggling with addiction issues.

Ben stood waiting in the parking lot off Pilot Knob Road. He scanned the streets in the early morning darkness, looking for any sign of Jenny. Most of the recruits were already aboard the bus for the fifteen-minute ride to the airport. Ben's heart sank when he realized she wasn't going to make it. *Where is she? She promised she'd be here!*

Just as he was about to climb aboard, a car pulled into the lot. It sped up to the bus and parked, and Jenny jumped out.

"I'm sorry, I'm sorry," she said.

Ben didn't say anything, and she started to cry. His luggage was already on the bus. The diesel engine was rumbling, and Ben could smell the fumes. Jenny looked Ben in the eye and he looked right back at her.

"I promise I'll get my life together and get right," she said.

"I know you will," he replied.

They hugged, and Ben turned around and headed for the bus. Jenny watched him climb aboard and find a seat among the other recruits. They were nearly all recent high school graduates, and most had nervous looks on their faces.

Ben looked out at Jenny through the window. She was watching as the bus pulled away. Jenny felt a mix of feelings. There was guilt, worry, and sadness that her best friend was going away. There was also disappointment in herself. Ben had always been unwavering in his support for her, and on his big day, she was barely holding it together. She had two groups of friends, and neither had been true to her. One was pulling her in the wrong direction. The other, her friends from high school, had turned their backs on her because of her addiction struggles. And then there was loyal Ben, who'd always stood by her.

As the bus rolled away, Ben's mind turned to his friend Eric Pittlekow, whose unit had just deployed to Iraq. They'd exchanged a few e-mails over the last few days. Eric told Ben what life was like deployed in Baghdad. Ben pored over every word, envious that Eric was in the thick of a war zone. It wouldn't be long before Ben was there too.

PART

II

Fort Benning, Georgia

It's a ninety-minute bus ride from Hartsfield-Jackson International Airport in Atlanta to Columbus and Fort Benning. For many of the baby-faced recruits who arrive at the Army's infantry training center in southwestern Georgia, it's their first time on a plane and their first time away from home. The journey can be daunting for a prospective infantry soldier. Unlike other soldiers, recruits who choose infantry normally commit to complete basic training and the follow-up training for their infantry specialty.

While "basic training" is a common Army term, the technical term at Fort Benning for infantry soldiers is One Station Unit Training (OSUT). It's about three and a half months from beginning to graduation.

The first step for Ben and the other recruits was reception. It's a time to get gear and uniforms and learn about what awaits them in OSUT. Drill sergeants prevail, but at reception they're dialed back from the intensity recruits will soon face. For Ben, reception lasted eleven days, an eternity of waiting to get down to the real business of Army training.

On July 17, Ben and the other recruits loaded up on another bus at Fort Benning for the short ride to the Sand Hill area of the base, where OSUT was about to begin. Ben fidgeted in his seat, craning his neck to look out the front window to see what awaited them. He was nervous. He double-checked to make sure he had all his belongings. So many thoughts were running through his head. He was fulfilling his life-long dream to become an American soldier. His Army career was now right in front of him. He knew he would be good at it, but he wanted to get through the first few days and didn't want to stand out for doing something stupid.

As they pulled up at Sand Hill, Ben could see the drill sergeants in their wide-brimmed, brownish-green hats wearing ACUs (Army Combat Uniform) waiting to greet them. He watched the recruits ahead of him grab their bags and get off. He could hear the drill sergeants barking the moment the recruits' feet hit the ground.

"Get your shit and get off the bus!"

As Ben stepped off the bus, his duffel bag caught on something and ripped, splitting open. He quickly grabbed the flaps, struggling to keep his new gear and clothing from spilling onto the grass, but it was too late. The bag broke open, and his things went everywhere.

The drill sergeants, like sharks smelling blood, came at him and ate him alive. He was less than a minute into OSUT and was already off to a bad start. He wanted to run and hide. He couldn't even tell his mom about it—his first letter home was a form letter letting her know he'd arrived. The Army had written on that form letter home, *Don't worry about me. There are twelve drill sergeants whose only job is to see that my needs are met daily.* That line likely brought little comfort to any mother. Ben had filled in only "Mom" at the top and "Kopp" at the bottom.

Despite the rough start, within days Private Kopp was adjusting. He didn't mind the food at the dining facility, or DFAC. The chicken thighs were pretty good, the hamburgers seemed boiled, he dreaded the brussels sprouts, broccoli, and spinach. He was usually so hungry, he'd eat it all anyway. He was always relieved when they served good clean protein along with his favorite veggie, green beans. But they barely had time to eat, often less than five minutes. There was little to no talking at mealtime, and they had to keep their boots on the floor and heels together.

"You don't have time to taste!" the drill sergeants would yell, hurrying them along.

The hardest thing for Ben was getting out of bed at five most mornings and being outside for PT (physical training) by five thirty. Ben wasn't an early riser by nature. He once slept through a wake-up call, and the drill sergeants dumped him out of his bunk. That didn't happen again.

Ben didn't mind the running and workouts. He loved singing the songs in cadence while the young privates ran or marched with their drill sergeants. Ben was already in good shape, so the initial demands of basic training weren't overwhelming. Still, Ben was amazed at the conditioning of some of the drill sergeants, who ran alongside them holding conversations without breaking stride or gasping for air. Meanwhile, other privates huffed and puffed. That fitness disparity was discouraging for some, but for Ben, it was a motivator. He thought that if those drill sergeants could achieve that level of fitness, he could too. Ben was always hungry for strong male role models, and he had plenty of that now in these drill sergeants.

Ben was also adapting to the intense heat and humidity. It was July in southwestern Georgia. The Minnesotan had never felt oppressive heat like this before, and there never seemed to be a breeze. They were also conditioning all the time. Ben wrote home saying, "I've never sweat so much in my entire life."

There were other challenges for the young soldiers and their families. While some of their peers were heading off to college, Ben and the others were experiencing something very different. Parents can visit their freshman college students and call, text, or e-mail anytime. That isn't the case during OSUT at Fort Benning. Cell phones are surrendered on arrival. Computer privileges and e-mail don't exist. It's old school; written letters only, something recent high school graduates growing up in the age of smart phones and social media aren't used to. That's why the "mail call" is so anticipated during basic training.

When it was time for mail call, new privates sat in a yoga position and anxiously waited for their names to be called. The presiding drill sergeant would throw their mail at them. If they fell out of their positions, they had to do push-ups.

One of the rules at Fort Benning is that new recruits can't receive care packages. The responsibility for communicating this falls on the young soldiers. One private didn't make that clear to his mother, who kept sending goodies. The private must've really liked Reese's Pieces, because they arrived by the boxful. To make his point, a drill sergeant made the private line up individual Reese's Pieces along opposite walls in the room. He then made the private relay back and forth and eat every single candy. When he was finished, the drill sergeant had a message for the platoon: "Now, tell your mothers to stop sending you candy, soldiers!"

"Yes, drill sergeant!" they all answered in unison.

The care packages stopped.

Drill sergeants have a way of saying the word "private" as though it were a dirty and disgusting word. While many of the young privates feared the drill sergeants, Ben was starting to see through their hardened exteriors. He realized there was a method to their madness. He wrote to his mom, "You can see it in the eyes of each drill sergeant that they only mean well and are bettering you by the day. They are turning us into the infantrymen that this country expects."

Toward the end of basic training, when the privates received phone privileges for a day, Ben told his mom about one particular drill sergeant. "He's the meanest, baddest motherfucker I've ever met in my life. But I love him like a mother."

By mid-August, Ben was honing his M16 rifle skills. He also took a turn firing fully automatic machine guns, an AT4 antitank weapon, and an M203 grenade launcher, telling his mom, "It was pretty badass." His company also had to walk into a gas chamber. They entered wearing their combat gear, including gas masks. As part of their training, they had to take off their masks and adjust their equipment while inside. When he did it, Ben's eyes and skin started to burn. Snot and tears streamed down his face, and he started to cough. Pure hell. After about twenty seconds with the masks off, they got the okay to bolt from the chamber. Fresh air never felt so good.

The day arrived when it was time to throw hand grenades. Ben could hardly contain his excitement. Not everyone would get the chance. The privates had to qualify with a nonexplosive grenade and show the drill sergeants they could hurl the explosive far enough so that none of their own guys got hurt. When the platoon assembled on the grenade range, Ben couldn't believe what he was seeing. It was only a matter of getting the grenade over a concrete wall and far enough away that it could detonate safely, but some of the privates simply couldn't throw. In a land where baseball is the national pastime, some of the privates had clearly never developed any throwing skills as children. *They must've been soccer players*, Ben thought. The non-throwers had to stand and watch as the other privates, standing behind a concrete enclosure under the watchful eye of their drill sergeants, got to hurl the real thing. Growing up, Ben was a standout catcher on the baseball field, and he had a good arm. When it came time for him to throw the dummy grenade, he qualified easily.

Ben's days were spent training with his company. His night-time routine included more pushups, sit-ups, a shower, and about ten minutes of Bible study by flashlight before going to sleep. When the lights went out, Ben thought about the cabin on Wood Lake and all the good times he'd had there with Ay-Yi, Granny, and his mom. Other times he'd fantasize about eating an entire pizza by himself while watching movies in an air-conditioned room.

He wondered how Brittney was doing. He'd written to his mom and asked her to send pictures of the two of them together "so he could show them off to the guys." Even after Jill sent some, he asked for more. He knew in his heart that he would always love her. Brittney also sent pictures of herself, which Ben was thrilled to get. He wished fervently that Brittney would come with his mom to his graduation day, and in a letter he urged his mom to bring her along, even offering to pay for the trip.

On the last day of September, as they lined up in the early morning for PT, it was forty-one degrees. Even Ben, a hearty Minnesotan, felt cold. He wrote to his mom the next day, "I guess hell *can* freeze over."

By the last week of OSUT, Ben was a squad leader. They were now facing field training exercises, a week of outdoor training. During that week, the young soldiers eat "meals ready-to-eat" (MREs), take no showers, get very little sleep, and do night maneuvers. They end exercises by packing up their patrol base and marching roughly twelve miles in full combat gear back to a big celebration at Honor Hill. The drill sergeants call this hike "The Bayonet March."

Ben and his squadmates carried litters (military stretchers) and water jugs. When they arrived at Honor Hill, they celebrated with a big bonfire. Each drill sergeant talked about how infantrymen impacted the outcome of different wars in US history. The young privates then received their "blood rifles," a crossed rifles pin worn on their collars. They're called blood rifles because some drill sergeants punch the pin just below the privates' collarbone, breaking the skin and drawing blood, a rite of passage.

Ben, Jill, and his grandma Mimi on graduation from OSUT at Fort Benning in October of 2006. After three months on base, Ben couldn't wait to go out to eat and order his own food.

Ben graduated from basic training/OSUT at Kanell Field within Fort Benning on Friday, October 19, a hot day in Georgia. Jill was there to see her son for the first time in fourteen weeks, the longest they'd ever been apart. Ben's grandmother, Mary "Mimi" Barnes, and Jill's niece, Ashley, were also there. Brittney didn't come.

They first attended Ben's "turning blue" ceremony, when infantry soldiers are presented with blue cords, which distinguish them from other Army soldiers. Jill had hoped to attach Ben's cord, as many other parents did, but in the end it was a drill sergeant who did the honors, pinning it over Ben's right shoulder on his dress uniform.

The next day was the full graduation. Jill beamed with pride. At the ceremony, Ben was part of a combat demonstration team that came through the trees of Kanell Field through the haze of smoke grenades. At the end of the ceremony, he was finally free to leave the base for the first time. "Get me out of here, I don't want to see this place," Ben begged Jill and Mimi.

Ben had a big appetite after more than three months of MREs and dining facility food. His family took him to TGI Fridays in Columbus. "This is the first time in three months I've gotten to look at a menu and choose what I eat," he said, celebrating his newfound freedom.

After his visitors left, Ben returned to Fort Benning to complete Airborne School, a three-week course. It was then time for the greatest test of his life: the Ranger Indoctrination Program, or RIP. His performance in the program would determine if he became a Ranger or not. Most who try, fail. For Ben, failure wasn't an option.

Ranger Indoctrination Program

Ben had a Ranger contract going into the Army that gave him no guarantees. It basically meant that upon the successful completion of OSUT, he would get the opportunity to become a Ranger. There are strict physical training standards for the Ranger Regiment and no one was getting into the Ranger Indoctrination Program until they could show they were fit enough to be a Ranger. Ben, along with about 330 other soldiers, most of them recent basic training graduates, showed up for the initial PT. Ben was feeling pretty good about himself. RIP was the initial training and elimination process for enlisted soldiers hoping to join the 75th Ranger Regiment. At the time, it was a grueling three-week test designed to separate those who would go on to careers in the regular Army from those who would become elite Rangers.

Since the holidays were approaching, the decision was made to put the RIP class off until January. Ben's dream of becoming a Ranger would have to wait about eight weeks.

Ben was starting to make friends with some of the other guys in his RIP class. One of them, Ryan McGhee, was a star football player from Fredericksburg, Maryland. He was a big kid and a jokester who made everyone laugh. Another of Ben's new friends was the clean-cut Shane Harris, a recent high school graduate from tiny Carlinville, Illinois.

Erick Innis was the son of military parents. His father had been a Green Beret, and his mother was in the Air Force. He grew up moving from base to base and had attended four high schools in four years graduating in Virginia Beach. At five-foot-five, he was self-conscious about his height, but he had an affable personality, was a good story-teller, and could make anyone laugh. He was also, it turned out, a natural wingman for Ben.

Morgan Garrett was twenty-three years old, a little older than the rest. He hailed from the East Texas town of Atlanta. He'd already been a Ranger in 3rd Battalion's Charlie Company but had decided to leave to attend college. After more than a year away from his company, he missed the camaraderie and decided to return. Despite his status as an E-5 sergeant, he had to suck it up and go through RIP all over again, a blow to his ego. He was an experienced Ranger who'd already been deployed to combat zones, and now he would be training with a group of privates fresh out of basic training. It also meant, in some respects, that Morgan was a marked man. Because of his experience and rank—he was the highest enlisted man in the RIP class—more would be expected of him. And the cadre let him know he would be looked to as one of the leaders of the class.

Ben's RIP training finally got under way on January 2, 2007. South Georgia may seem like a mild climate, but when the winter rains fall, it gets cold and very damp. For Rangers in training, who might be outside for days at a time, the conditions can become quite challenging.

Physical training includes a five-mile run, road marches, rope training, and a water survival test, among other activities. In addition, Ranger recruits learn map reading and land navigation, Ranger history, airborne operation, and combat lifesaving. They must also memorize the Ranger Creed:

> *Recognizing* that I volunteered as a Ranger, fully knowing the hazards of my chosen profession, I will always endeavor to uphold the prestige, honor, and high esprit de corps of my Ranger Regiment.

> *Acknowledging* the fact that a Ranger is a more elite soldier, who arrives at the cutting edge of battle by land, sea, or air, I accept the fact that as a Ranger, my country expects me to move further, faster, and fight harder than any other soldier.

> *Never* shall I fail my comrades. I will always keep myself mentally alert, physically strong, and morally straight, and I will shoulder more than my share of the task, whatever it may be, one hundred percent and then some.

> *Gallantly* will I show the world that I am a specially selected and well-trained soldier. My courtesy to superior officers, neatness of dress, and care of equipment shall set the example for others to follow.

Energetically will I meet the enemies of my country. I shall defeat them on the field of battle, for I am better trained and will fight with all my might. *Surrender* is not a Ranger word. I will never leave a fallen comrade to fall into the hands of the enemy, and under no circumstances will I ever embarrass my country.

Readily will I display the intestinal fortitude required to fight on to the Ranger objective and complete the mission, though I be the lone survivor.

RIP candidates have to be intimately familiar with Ranger history and the origin of the familiar phrase, "Rangers lead the way," which originated during D-Day. While landing at Omaha Beach, troops were pinned down under heavy machine gun fire. They were having trouble making advances toward the cliffs ahead where the Nazi machine gun positions were entrenched. General Norman Cota walked under heavy machine gun fire over to Major Max Schneider.

"What outfit is this?" the general asked.

"Fifth Rangers!" was the answer from the major over the roar of gunfire and planes whizzing overhead.

"Well, goddamn it then, Rangers lead the way!" came Cota's reply.

The phrase is so entrenched in Ranger culture that RLTW is really all that's necessary for a Ranger to understand. For Rangers, it means you are the first guy in and the closest guy to the enemy. If somebody is going to get killed, it's going to be you because you're first out of the airplane and you're first on the beach. On D-Day someone was going to have to clear a hole, clear the wire, and get up the cliffs to pave the way for the rest of the invasion force. And as it turned out on that day, Rangers led the way.

RIP candidates also learn the regimental motto, "Sua Sponte," a Latin phrase that translates to "of their own accord." For Rangers, it means they are performing at their own will. They have volunteered for the Army, volunteered for Airborne School, volunteered for Ranger School, and volunteered for service in the 75th Ranger Regiment.

Ben and Erick Innis were becoming fast friends and would often partner up for drills and other tests. Erick was bright and articulate with an immediately likeable quality.

For Ben and Erick, much of the Ranger training took place outdoors under damp and cold conditions. Because Ben was from Minnesota, he rarely complained about the cold. Ben was trying to show toughness, and it wasn't hard for him to put that image out to the others.

On one finger-numbing day with rain alternating in light and heavy waves, the Ranger candidates were challenged with a timed land navigation, or "land nav" exercise. The test was to negotiate dense woods using maps but no GPS. The cadre had left a series of words and numbers at various waypoints along the plotted route. It was up to the two-man teams to navigate through the Georgia pines and record the words and numbers to prove they'd correctly found the waypoints.

Ben was dealing with acute tendonitis of the Achilles tendon in both ankles. He struggled to walk, let alone run. The conditions were especially challenging as they were fighting through the muck underfoot. That red Georgia clay would "damn near pull our boots off with every step," Erick remembered.

Erick saw Ben fighting back tears from the intensity of the pain. Private Innis knew he could easily complete the land navigation on his own, but he decided he and Ben were going to finish this together. If they got kicked out, so be it. "Come on, man!" he shouted. "It all boils down to this. You need to suck it up, Ben."

Ben grunted and willed himself forward. The pines overhead filtered the rain, leaving a cold mist on their faces that mixed with the snot running from their noses. At last they found their final plot point and rushed back to the finish as fast as they could. As they emerged from the woods cold, soaked, and tired, they each had a sinking feeling they'd run out of time. Their despair turned to delight when they realized they completed the operation with a minute to spare.

During what is known as Marksmanship Week, the Ranger candidates focus on using their weapons. After getting used to the M16 during OSUT, Ben and his friends now had to learn how to use a new rifle, the M4 carbine. Its smallish, 5.56-millimeter round can be fired individually or on full automatic. Like everything else during RIP, the candidates were being tested, and speed mattered.

Toward the end of the week, as part of a timed drill, the Ranger candidates had to go to the arms room and take out their weapons. They then needed to get back to the barracks and gather on what was referred to as "the blacktop," an old basketball court in front of the RIP barracks. The cadre gave them just minutes to get it done. The RIP candidates scrambled out of the arms room and tried to get into formation. Ben, with his injured ankles, was moving slowly and holding up others. On the way out of the arms building, Sergeant Morgan Garrett walked behind Ben. As a leader, it was Garrett's responsibility to make sure all the Ranger candidates made it back in the allotted time. Time was running out, and they were now in danger of not meeting the designated cutoff.

"Hurry up, let's go!" Garrett barked at Ben. "We don't have much time!"

"What do you want me to do?" Ben replied, limping and half turning to face Garrett.

Garrett, feeling the pressure of the clock and the greater expectation of leadership on his shoulders, reached forward and shoved Ben to the side. Ben stumbled into the side of a pickup truck as Garrett passed him. Ben picked himself up and limped to the finish, making it back just in time.

Several days passed, and word began to spread of a "fight" between Private Kopp and Sergeant Garrett. By the time the story got back to the cadre, it had become greatly exaggerated. One version suggested that Garrett had beaten Ben up, another that he had punched Ben. The RIP instructors conducted their own investigation and confronted Sergeant Garrett.

"It's unacceptable to put your hands on one of your subordinates," an instructor told him.

Morgan Garrett's Ranger indoctrination was over. Sergeant Garrett was kicked out. His plan to come back as a Ranger had ended. The development was crushing—he was not only dropped from the course but forced to wait six months before attempting another comeback. "I acted unprofessionally," he would later admit. "I really acted like an ass. It's not something I'm real proud of."

Ranger indoctrination had started with about 330 soldiers taking physical training tests. Of those, 135 passed and were allowed to continue with the indoctrination. Ben's RIP finished with a graduating class of sixty-four newly minted Rangers. Among them were Ben's new friends Shane Harris, Erick Innis, and Ryan McGhee.

The feeling was glorious to Ben. He was barely nineteen and he'd already achieved his dream of becoming an Army Ranger. He had earned the coveted tan beret that only Rangers wear. But there was little time to rest. Ben Kopp's greatest challenges were still ahead.

Ranger Barracks

Ranger candidates who successfully survive indoctrination are assigned to a battalion and company. The Ranger Regiment has four battalions. The 1st is based at Hunter Army Airfield in Savannah, Georgia; the 2nd at Fort Lewis near Tacoma, Washington; the 3rd Ranger Battalion is based at Fort Benning in Columbus, Georgia; the Regimental Special Troops Battalion is also based at Fort Benning.

When young Rangers reach this stage, they might think the worst is over. Nothing could be further from the truth. Once Ranger privates get to battalion, they must prove themselves all over again.

By a stroke of good luck, Ben and Erick were both assigned to the same unit, 3rd Ranger Battalion, Charlie Company, Third Platoon. Shane would be close by; he was assigned to the Second Platoon within Charlie Company. Ryan McGhee was assigned to Bravo Company.

A Ranger company during wartime of 2007 was composed of three platoons totaling ninety to 110 Rangers. Ranger platoons and companies are generally smaller than their regular Army counterparts. Platoons become very tight—enlisted Rangers often call their fellow soldiers "brothers." As far as the enlisted men and NCOs (noncommissioned officers), there isn't a lot of turnover in Ranger companies. However, commissioned officers within the Ranger Regiment generally transfer in and out of other Army assignments.

When new privates get to battalion, they're under the watchful eye of everyone who outranks them. They're regularly "smoked" (the Army term for hazing), but many believe that treatment is what makes good Rangers. Their inferior status lasts until the privates go to Ranger School, generally within six to eighteen months. Because of that, privates desperately want to get to Ranger School as soon as possible to earn their Ranger tab—a small patch that reads "Ranger" and is affixed to their shoulder. It shows they've joined the upper ranks.

Upon arriving at battalion, Ben had to complete some paperwork. One questionnaire asked: "Why did you volunteer to become a Ranger? What does being a Ranger mean to you?" Ben wrote, "I want to be a more elite soldier. I want to be the best. Being a Ranger is my entire life. I expect to move faster and fight harder than any other soldier."

Normally this time would've been an opportunity for Ben and Erick to meet the more experienced soldiers in their new unit. But that wasn't possible since Charlie Company was deployed to Iraq. At the height of the Global War on Terror, nearly all Ranger companies were on rotating deployments. The country had been at war for more than six years, and most of the Rangers in 3rd Ranger Battalion were already veterans of multiple deployments.

Freshly minted Ranger. Ben, new to Ranger battalion,
sports the Ranger's distinctive tan beret.

One thing that reassured the pair was that Charlie Company
hadn't had a fatality for as long as anyone could remember. But days
after Ben graduated from RIP, the company suffered a devastating
loss. Sergeant James Regan, a twenty-six-year-old from Manhasset,
New York, died on February 9. An IED detonated near his vehicle
while his platoon was on patrol in northern Iraq. His death hit Charlie
Company hard, both in Iraq and back at Fort Benning. One of their
own, who had left just months earlier, was coming home in a flag-
draped casket.

Ben also learned his assignment to Charlie Company would be an even greater test than he'd expected. This was Morgan Garrett's former company. Garrett had a lot of friends anxiously awaiting his return. On the day Ben finished RIP, Sergeant Garrett was still hanging around Fort Benning. His friends were curious about why he was kicked out. Garrett told them, but he didn't mention Ben's name. As he stood in the barracks talking with a couple of the other sergeants, Ben walked in.

Garrett looked at Kopp like he was seeing a ghost. He was surprised to see Ben in his old barracks, a place he'd once called home. The new privates had just arrived. They were being assigned to their quarters and getting settled in.

Garrett's friends kept up the questioning.

"Is it one of these guys?" one of the sergeants asked Garrett, referring to the new privates who had just walked in.

Garrett glanced at Ben, then said, "No, it's not." Garrett lied, trying to protect Ben from what he knew would be extra hazing.

Ben realized this was a tough draw for him. When the privates got their bunks in order, Garrett walked outside and motioned to Ben to follow him. When they were safely out of earshot of the others, he turned to Ben. "Look, I'm not gonna say anything to anyone about this," he started in his East Texas drawl. "As long as your buddies don't rat you out, you're gonna be fine."

Ben nodded but didn't say a word.

"Just do what you're supposed to do here," Garrett advised.

"I will." Ben shook his head and walked back into the barracks, and Garrett left.

A bit later that night, as the new Rangers were still getting settled, one of the company's staff sergeants addressed them. "I heard one of your classmates got my friend kicked out," he said. He looked around, waiting for someone to give up the name.

The privates remained silent. Everyone knew the sergeant was talking about Ben, but no one dared say a word. They were all trying not to make a mistake. Shane Harris, like everyone else, thought the best course of action was to bite his tongue.

Ben raised his hand. "Yeah, it was me."

The sergeant stared at Ben in stunned silence. He couldn't believe what he was hearing. *Who would have the balls to admit this?*

The next day, Garrett returned to the barracks and learned that Ben had admitted he was the one connected to Garrett's dismissal. Garrett again approached Ben. He knew Kopp would be set up for failure if he didn't try to do something.

"I wasn't going to tell anyone it was you," Garrett started. "But you stood up, and you're owning it. It might cost you some heat, but I'll talk to my friends."

What could Ben say? He appreciated the gesture, but he knew some of Garrett's friends in the company were looking for any excuse to come after him. No matter what Garrett said, it was probably too late. But Garrett made good on his word. He told his friends that what happened in RIP was his fault and urged them not to take it out on Ben. No one listened. Ben caught hell regularly. If he was a minute late, it cost him. If he was nine minutes early, it cost him. Any slipup and Ben seemed to get smoked worse than anyone else.

Garrett's buddies let Private Kopp know how they felt.

"You're responsible for getting a good Ranger kicked out. You'd better become a good Ranger to take his place," barked Sergeant Jeramy Smith.

Ben didn't take the sergeant's words as an insult or a threat but a challenge. He wanted nothing more than to become a good Ranger, and he set his mind to it. He and the other new Rangers spent the next few days waking at 6:00 a.m., working out, and doing chores.

As Charlie Company got closer to its return from Iraq, Ben and the rest of the untested Rangers grew nervous. Despite what they'd accomplished, they still felt like boys among men. The soldiers coming back had been in battle. They had killed people. They had seen death and had even seen one of their own die. They weren't likely coming home to make friends with rookie Rangers, some of whom were still teenagers. As one remembers it, "We were scum to them. We were all very afraid."

The day finally arrived for Charlie Company's Third Platoon to return from Iraq. As the battle-hardened Rangers flooded back into Fort Benning, many had the same question Ben had already been dealing with: "Who's the one that got Garrett kicked out?"

Ben raised his hand again. He would always fess up and take his medicine. Nearly everyone above the rank of private and below mid-level sergeant seemed to have it in for him, often making him do push-ups and mountain climbers. Some wanted Ben to quit. Morgan Garrett was a popular guy, and they'd expected him to be there when they returned from deployment.

Meanwhile, the new guys in the company watched Ben get abused. Shane found it particularly painful to watch. He didn't think Ben could survive the current level of hazing. *I'm sure glad I'm not going through that, because I don't think I'd make it,* he thought. Ben was in a truly unenviable position.

Shane shared his worry with some of the other privates in the company. "He's gonna break," he said.

The other young Rangers nodded in agreement. They stuck together the way gazelles cluster when lions are prowling. But as the days pressed on and the hazing got worse, Ben refused to crack. He'd always stand up for himself, be held accountable, and take his punishment.

In the long run, Ben's ability to take the abuse played in his favor. As Shane observed, "When you can't break someone, you eventually develop respect for them." After about six months, the tide against Ben started to turn. Many, including his initial detractors, grew to respect him. He had been through one of the worst starts in the battalion anyone could remember, but the hazing had a positive impact on Ben. The wild and sometimes cocky kid from Minnesota now seemed to be maturing.

Panama City, Florida

The fledgling Rangers finally got a break. They had a pass for a few days, and the timing couldn't have been better. It was March, and spring break was in full swing on the Gulf Coast. Panama City, Florida, was less than two hundred miles from Columbus. Five young Ranger privates—Ben, Erick, Shane, and a couple of others—piled into a car and made the trip.

When they arrived in the spring break Mecca, they found just what they were looking for: thousands of college students partying hard. The beer flowed freely, and pounding hip-hop music emanated from every bar and beachside motel they passed.

The Rangers cruised the strip looking for a suitable place to stay. For five Army privates who'd spent some of the last sixty days sleeping in the dirt, "suitable" meant "affordable." They eventually found a motel after spotting a large group of college girls unpacking their cars in the parking lot.

After checking in, Ben used his always-dependable charm to find some girls who were twenty-one to help him buy beer. Back at their room, the group decided to split up. Erick and Ben had heard there might be a wet t-shirt contest at a place along the beach. If they couldn't find that, they would surely find some other party. The other three Rangers were convinced that if they started drinking in their room, the party would grow. Erick and Ben disagreed and split for the beach.

Not finding much excitement on their patrol, Erick and Ben returned a couple of hours later. As they approached their motel, they couldn't believe their eyes. On the balcony just outside their room was a big party—girls, beer, and music, everything they'd looked for on the beach.

When Ben and Erick reached their room, the bash was in full swing. The newcomers gave the other three a look of disbelief—*How did you guys pull this off?* In reality, it wasn't surprising that a bunch of college girls would suddenly show up at the room of five Rangers,

Teenage Rangers Ben and Erick Innis on their first trip to Panama City in the spring of 2007. It was a welcome break after finishing the grueling Ranger Indoctrination Program.

all of whom had spent the last four months getting into the best shape of their lives.

When Erick woke the next morning, he didn't feel well. His head hurt, and he had a hard time opening his eyes. When he finally cleared the sleep from his vision and focused on the ceiling, he rolled his head to the side. Just inches from his face was a sound-asleep and buck-naked Ben Kopp.

Erick screamed, "You're naked right there!"

That awakened Ben, who looked down at himself in shock.

"Why am I naked?" Ben screamed, still lying in bed, craning his neck up off the pillow to view himself. Ben jumped up in a panic looking for something to put on. He spotted his pants lying across a chair and grabbed them but found they were drenched. "What the hell? Why are my pants soaking wet?"

Fearing his phone and wallet were ruined, Ben pulled them from the pockets, but somehow they were dry. His head ached as well, but he smiled. His wet pants and dry wallet were a mystery. They all had their theories. The best they could come up with in their fogginess was that Ben jumped into the Gulf to avoid a jealous boyfriend.

The next evening, armed with cans of beer, the Ranger squad patrolled the main drag. They were all underage, but they weren't too worried about being confronted by the police for drinking in public. "It's spring break," one said. "They're not gonna hassle anyone."

Moments later, an unmarked squad car pulled up and two uniformed police officers got out. Three of the Rangers stopped, but Ben and Shane kept walking.

One cop ran up and grabbed them by the wrists. "Sit down!" he ordered.

We're gonna get kicked out of Ranger battalion before we even have a chance, Harris thought. Just then, the coolheaded Innis spoke up. "We're Army, 3rd Ranger Battalion." This ploy could've gone either way. Either the cops now had the fuel they needed to bust them and notify their company, or the admission would distinguish them from the dime-a-dozen college kids the cops were used to dealing with.

The police officers talked to each of them individually, then conferred with each other.

"They're all military," the older cop said. "They're all Rangers. Let's cut 'em loose."

"That's fine with me," agreed the younger officer.

After a three-minute talk on how not to get into trouble in Panama City, the officers let them go. "Hope you guys have a good weekend," the older cop said.

"Thanks, officers," the Rangers said in unison.

The next afternoon Ben was alone, relaxing on their motel balcony and soaking up the Florida rays. He looked down and noticed a disheveled man, decades older than the other nearby college-aged kids, wandering the parking lot. The man's leathery skin was toughened by years in the sun, and his long, fraying gray hair was unkempt. He looked like he'd been drinking all day, if not all his life.

The beach-comber looked up at Ben, saw the beer in his hand, and locked eyes with him. "Throw me a beer!" he called.

"You want one?" Ben asked. He thought the last thing this guy needed was another drink, so he dropped an empty. The hollow silver can pinged against the concrete deck and rattled around before spinning to a stop.

The man wasn't having it. The man's trained ears told him that the offering was of no worth.

"Why don't you give me a full one?" he shouted indignantly.

Someone else several stories above Ben's balcony had been watching the exchange. Whoever it was fulfilled the man's request and launched a full beer. But the man's focus was on Ben and not the incoming twelve-ounce grenade. It hit him squarely on the head, knocking him to the ground and drawing blood.

By now Shane, hearing Ben's conversation, had wandered onto the balcony to see what was going on. Arriving just in time to see the beer hit the beachcomber, he assumed it was the work of Ben Kopp. Shane looked at his friend in disbelief.

"I didn't do it!" Ben said, putting up his hands in defense.

"What just happened?" Shane asked.

"I swear to you, I threw an empty. I didn't do that," Ben repeated, a serious and sudden sobriety in his voice.

On the ground below, the thirsty vagabond was down for the count. The two Rangers now turned their attention upward, scanning the balconies for the sniper. They saw nothing. Whoever had thrown the beer so accurately had vanished into the safety of their room just as quickly. Shane and Ben went back inside too, then decided they should go check on the guy. They went downstairs and found hotel security bandaging the man's head before they escorted him off the property.

The Rangers stayed in Panama City for another night. But after a second minor run-in with the law, they decided it was best to leave town and head back to the confines of Fort Benning.

Baldwin, Wisconsin

Jill Stephenson's fortieth birthday was fast approaching, and she wanted to do something big to ring in the milestone. In May of 2007, she decided skydiving was about as big a challenge as she could think of. She ran the idea past Ben; not only did he like it, he figured out a way to get home from Fort Benning to help her celebrate. Jill was so excited to share this moment with Ben, but what really struck her as funny was that she felt absolutely no fear about jumping out of a plane. It was comforting to her that her Army Ranger son was going with her.

When the day arrived, Jill and Ben drove to Twin Cities Sky Diving in Baldwin, Wisconsin, about forty minutes from Rosemount. But as they pulled into the parking lot, all the confidence Jill had felt days before was gone. She was suddenly terrified.

"I'm not going in," she told her son, sitting in the car in the parking lot. "You go ahead and jump, Ben."

"Mom, come on."

"No, you go ahead. I'll stay on the ground and watch."

Ben wouldn't take no for an answer. He loved his mom with all his heart. She had raised him by herself. She had given everything to him. He wasn't going to jump out of a plane for her birthday without her. After a standoff, Ben persuaded Jill that she would be fine, and he would be right there with her. They got out of the car and walked inside.

Despite Ben's graduation from Airborne School, where he'd completed five solo jumps and earned his Parachutist Badge, he and Jill would be doing tandem jumps, each tethered to an instructor. They sat through what felt like hours of instruction and were then paired with jump instructors. Jill chuckled seeing Ben's jump partner. "Scooter," a female instructor, was no taller than five two. She had a mop of blond hair and the presence of a drill sergeant. Responsible for the lives of everyone she jumped with, she made it clear she wouldn't take crap from anyone, and that included a cocky nineteen-year-old Army Ranger.

Ben suited up in a navy and bright green jump suit. They walked out toward the aircraft. Scooter had a few more tips for Ben, suggesting he put his hands up. Ben went through the motions with her, but the look on his face suggested her instruction was below his level of expertise. They climbed aboard the 1968 Dehavilland DHC-6-200 Twin Otter. The turbo props roared to life, and Ben and Jill smiled at each other. Jill was still afraid, but she knew her only two options were to strap herself to something in the plane and refuse to jump or just go along with the plan.

Once airborne, Scooter warned Ben not to mess with his goggles. Minutes later, Ben fidgeted with his eyewear, and Scooter slapped his hand. *She's worse than a drill sergeant*, Ben thought. *At least drill sergeants can't touch you.*

When they reached thirteen thousand feet, Ben got up and Scooter told him to sit on her lap. Ben cringed, but he sat down, and she buckled him to her. They were over the jump zone now.

Jill and her instructor went to the open aircraft door. Ben watched as his mom disappeared into the blue. He and Scooter readied to jump next. Ben, again, didn't listen to her instructions on how to get into a seated position at the door; she now had to force him to squat. Scooter gave a push and out they went. As they free fell, Ben smiled, stuck out his tongue, and gave the double thumbs-up. This was different from his jumps at Fort Benning. At jump school the chute was pulled immediately for him at low altitude, about a thousand feet. There was virtually no free fall.

But today, Ben, a natural thrill seeker, loved the feeling of free falling, which felt to him like floating. Seconds later, Scooter pulled the cord and they slowed to a drift. The Wisconsin countryside was now clear and beautiful. Ben looked out over vast farm fields surrounded by thousands of trees, recently lush after spring rains. It was such a perfect day—blue sky, growing cumulus clouds, and sunshine. Ben looked up at his chute—it was rectangular with multicolored blue panels, shades from navy to those that matched the sky.

Ben looked down and was suddenly troubled. The videographer, his chute also now deployed, was quite close to them and drifting closer. It was starting to make Ben feel uneasy. *He's getting too close,* Ben thought. During his airborne training, Ben had learned that two deployed parachutes too close together could result in a number of problems. First, they could get tangled, causing one or both to fail. Second, a parachute too close below could "steal" air, causing the chute above to perform erratically and possibly fail. That's exactly what seemed to be happening. The camera guy was drifting nearly right below them. His chute was coming right at Ben. Ben grew livid. A second later, the guy's chute rubbed on Ben's leg. Ben attempted to kick him away. Seeing this, Scooter wrapped her legs around Ben's to stop him. Ben let out of flurry of choice words, telling Scooter they needed to get away from the guy as quickly as possible. They did, much to Ben's comfort. About a minute later, Scooter and Ben touched down safely in a big field.

"You scared him," Scooter announced to the camera guy. "You should've heard the words he was saying."

Ben was just happy to have the jump completed, his feet on the ground, and most of all, to be disconnected from Scooter. They were celebrating his mom's birthday, and he didn't feel like getting in the guy's face about it at this point.

"Go see your mom," Scooter suggested.

This time Ben complied with her order and found Jill nearby. When Ben got home, his friends were in disbelief that the two of them had gone skydiving together. But Ben and his mom weren't like most mothers and sons.

Fort Bliss, Texas

In late July 2007, Ben Kopp and Charlie Company arrived at Fort Bliss for training. They'd traveled there for a "train-up," an intense training period in conditions that mirrored their upcoming deployment. Since they would be based in Baghdad, Charlie Company was here in Texas training in the desert heat.

Ryan Lundeby (left) with Ben during a treacherous hike in the mountains near Fort Bliss. Lundeby saved Ben from slipping over the edge of a cliff, a bonding experience that began what became a close friendship.

Their training took them into the mountains of southeastern New Mexico for some grueling marches. On one of those mountain hikes, they wore full-body armor and carried heavy packs. Ben felt great; he enjoyed the spectacular scenery of the high desert as he walked along a trail on the edge of a 1,500-foot cliff. It was like nothing he'd ever seen back in Minnesota.

The Rangers moved along the precarious cliff edge. Ben looked down and was in awe of the drop. As they marched down the narrow, uneven path, Ben hit loose rock and started to slip. He desperately grabbed for anything he could, but he was slipping over the edge.

Ryan Lundeby was nearby and saw Ben struggling. Lundeby dove grabbing Ben, preventing him from going over the edge. As Ben hung there, still in danger, Lundeby pulled him back to safety.

Ben got up and brushed himself off. Either he didn't realize he'd just had a brush with death, or he didn't want to call attention to himself; for whatever reason, he didn't say a word to Lundeby. The march continued without incident, and the platoon eventually returned to their quarters for a break.

Later that day, the Rangers visited VFW Post 812 in El Paso. They were enjoying a couple of beers with some of the local veterans and swapping war stories. The reality of what happened on the edge of that cliff hit Ben. He realized he would've died had he fallen. He knew something needed to be said, and he approached Lundeby, who was a little taller than he was. Lundeby was a native of Modesto, California. He and Ben lived on the same floor at Fort Benning.

"Thank you for saving my life," Ben said.

"What're you talking about?" Lundeby replied, brushing off the gesture.

"Dude, you saved my life," Ben insisted. "Thank you." And with that another block was laid in one of Ben's developing friendships.

During their training at Fort Bliss, news broke out of Minneapolis that a major interstate bridge over the Mississippi River had collapsed. There were multiple fatalities, and the video coming over TV news reports was horrific. Ben was very concerned because his mom worked in downtown Minneapolis and often crossed that bridge. He desperately wanted to get a hold of her to see if she was okay. Normally during the training, cell phones were off limits. But leadership decided to let Ben check on his mom. He talked with her briefly and confirmed she was safe.

It eventually came time for a bonding experience known as the "Meet the Hooah Story." This was a chance for guys in the platoon to share stories with each other, and the stories could be about anything under the sun. It could be a soldier's most embarrassing moment, like peeing his pants during basic training. It could be sexually explicit. It could be truthful, or it could be a complete lie.

Ben decided to tell a story from a Tucker Max book he'd read. The book was adult themed and quite explicit. "Hi, I'm Ben Kopp," he began.

As he continued, a chorus of boos drowned him out. That's part of the game—everyone gets booed. Ben regurgitated the vulgar story as though it were his own. Undeterred, Ben forged on, telling his fellow Rangers about the time he and two of his high school buddies chased after Bigfoot on a golf course, swearing it was true. That story was met with quite a bit of skepticism. Ben also shared that his uncle by marriage was WWE professional wrestler Sgt. Slaughter. Half the platoon didn't believe that either. But it was a claim that would one day be proven true, and under the most difficult of circumstances.

The Blue Book

The official name is the Emergency Notification and Casualty Assistance Booklet. But in the Army, it's more commonly referred to as "the blue book." Rangers are required to complete a blue book (which, despite the nickname, isn't blue) before their first deployment. It's an opportunity to list their final requests in case they die. Ryan and Ben completed their blue books together. Despite the heavy topic, they were lighthearted, not believing death would come for either of them on the battlefield. A few of Ben's answers included:

Type of funeral: *Military*

Active-duty military person who I want to escort my remains: *The rest of my squad*

Location to be interred: *Viewing and wake to be in home-town, buried in Arlington*

Music you want played at the funeral procession: *Mother will decide*

Personal effects I want buried with me: *Can of dip and a case of beer*

Scripture you want read: *Something honorable and heroic*

Special requests: *I want a flyover with Black Hawks over the funeral*

Do you want to be an organ donor? *Yes*

If yes, which ones? *Any that are needed*

Charlie Company was getting ready to deploy to Iraq. This would be Ben's first deployment, and he was nervous and excited. Lundeby had deployed once before, so Ben naturally looked up to him. As their deployment approached, one Ranger officer warned the newcomers, "War is going to happen, but it can be very painful. Be careful what you wish for, because you just might get it."

The night before Ben's company was set to depart for Iraq, he made one last call to his mom. Jill could hear the anxiety in his voice, which only added to her worry. She'd been anticipating this call since he'd signed up for the Army, but in the moment, words escaped her. Jill could feel herself getting emotional. She heard Ben take a deep breath and blow it out hard. She didn't want her emotional state to change his.

"I love you. I'm so proud of you, Ben. Be safe. A lot of people care about you and support you. And say your prayers."

"All right, Mom," Ben said. "Love you too."

After they hung up, Jill jotted down some words:

What does a mother say to her only child who has volunteered to proudly serve his country? "Go get 'em, kid, kill 'em all? Anybody comes at you, kill 'em, take no prisoners, just shoot 'em dead?" This isn't how I raised my son to react to conflict, but in situations he may find himself in, it's exactly how I want him to react.

First Iraq Deployment, October 2007

A big C-17 sat on the tarmac at the Fort Benning airfield. Gear was being loaded, and the Rangers from Charlie Company were preparing to board the aircraft. Rangers travel light; most of their gear is packed in advance. The Rangers would jump on the aircraft with only their weapons and assault packs.

The guys who'd done multiple deployments had the long overseas trip down to a science. They brought aboard thin air mattresses and poncho liners—pieces of synthetic fleece that could easily double as a blanket. Rangers called this a "woobie." Once aboard the cavernous C-17, medics would hand out Ambien to anyone who wanted it. Some Rangers would find a spot on the floor of the aircraft, stretch out, and try to sleep the eight-plus hours to Ramstein Air Base in Germany. Others read, listened to music, or watched movies on portable DVD players.

During the war, Baghdad International Airport was simply called BIAP. Ben's platoon was assigned quarters on the edge of the huge base. Their quarters in Iraq were reasonably nice, either rigid tents or small cabins. Their bathrooms were connected to their dwellings, and they had a shower. They also got hot chow whenever they wanted. And while they were in a walled-off compound, they were on the edge of a Baghdad neighborhood. They could hear the call to Muslim prayer several times a day from loudspeakers outside the base walls. While returning from ground operations they mingled with Iraqi children, their sweet faces a reminder of innocence in a place that now seemed so hostile.

Ben Kopp had been dreaming of this deployment for years and had been training for it for fifteen months. But all the training in the world could not equal the reality of combat. Ben was finally getting a crack at the real thing. He was very excited to earn his stripes as a Ranger. For Ben and his buddy Erick Innis, also on his first deployment, this would be their biggest test to date as Rangers.

Ben was immediately assigned to combat search and rescue (CSAR) duty. CSAR teams were multibranch, multilevel groups; they included Air Force members, Rangers, some enlisted guys, some NCOs, and an officer. CSAR teams often flew around in a Black Hawk in the areas where another group of special operators was working. If something went wrong or the special ops team needed backup, the CSAR team would land and assist. They were also called in to pull security during rescue operations for downed aircraft.

Rosemount, Minnesota

Knowing her son was in a combat zone was difficult at first. All Jill knew was that Ben was somewhere in Iraq. He couldn't tell her anything else.

Within a few days, she inadvertently learned his whereabouts. Jill had joint access to her son's bank account. One morning she noticed he had made some cash withdrawals at a Baghdad ATM. That small bit of information brought her comfort. Every time she saw another withdrawal, she knew where he was and that he was okay.

Occasionally, Ben would call on the phone. The calls were short, and Jill always knew it was him because the incoming call would come up either as "unknown" or a series of zeroes. He couldn't tell her much about what they were doing, only that they were working at night and sleeping during the day. Three weeks into her son's deployment, she felt a sense of despair, writing down her thoughts in a journal.

> I feel so broken. I feel like I could cry a river. . . . I'm just thinking of the danger and the fact that it's so dangerous, there can be no contact. I feel so alone in this. I don't know anyone who understands, and I just want to be hugged. This is the hardest thing I've ever gone through, and I just find myself tearing up without warning.

Baghdad

Charlie Company was part of a greater task force in Iraq. They were targeting Shiite extremists and other radicals who were being backed by support from Iran. (That support wasn't necessarily from the Iranian government but from networks within that country.) Charlie Company was staying very busy and had what they called a high mission rate. It wasn't uncommon to undertake multiple missions within twenty-four hours.

Ben wrote home, telling his mom that one thing he really liked about the deployment were the Iraqi kids. They had very little in life and as a result were overjoyed by anything the Rangers showed them or gave them. The kids would hang around just outside the base and weren't the least bit afraid of the American soldiers. The Rangers' flashlights amazed them, and their faces lit up whenever Ben clicked his on and off. They also loved when the soldiers shared a piece of gum or a sucker.

Seeing these kids smile made Ben's day. He wrote home requesting care packages, including—among other things—items to give away to children:

Gum (for the Iraqi kids)
Peanut butter
Oatmeal
Beef jerky
Swedish Fish
Chocolate
Cookies
Copenhagen

Jill sent Ben a package every few weeks, as did her sister.

After a couple of months on CSAR duty, Privates Innis and Kopp worked their way onto their platoon's main assault force. One night near Baghdad, Ben and Erick were up well before dawn preparing for an operation.

Fall and winter nights in Baghdad can get surprisingly cold, and it wasn't unusual to find Rangers hanging around the helicopter exhaust to take advantage of the heat. On this night, the clear desert air had dropped into the thirties Fahrenheit. Ben and Erick lay next to each other in the darkness on the concrete landing area near the Black Hawk, waiting for the mission to commence. Ben had a Redman chew pressed into his cheek. He pulled out the green and red foil pouch and offered some to Erick.

Erick had never chewed before, but with the cold and his nerves, this seemed like a good time to try. After a brief tutorial from Ben, Erick grabbed a hunk of the shredded tobacco and wedged it into his mouth. He felt the juices from the mass start to build. The tobacco made his salivary glands go into overdrive, and he couldn't keep up with spitting it out. Ben told him not to swallow no matter what, but a rush of tobacco-infused saliva flowed down Erick's throat.

It was now time to load into the chopper. Rangers travel a variety of ways; on this night, the platoon was packing into a few of the UH-60s. Ben and Erick loaded into the Black Hawks with several other guys. The ride was a bit more acrobatic than most because the pilots banked and weaved at low altitude to avoid enemy fire. Erick had had enough. His first experience with chewing tobacco wasn't going well, and this rollercoaster ride was stirring the pot in a very bad way. Fortunately, he was seated near the partially open door. If he could get his head out, he could let go of the swirling mass in his stomach.

As he leaned forward, Erick felt an uncontrollable rush in his guts. Whatever it was flew from his mouth in a torrent, most of it out the side of the helicopter. But the ejection hadn't gone as well as he'd hoped. The air rushing in the chopper's door carried about half of his stomach contents back inside the chopper. When Erick looked at Ben and the other Rangers, they seemed unfazed. He saw only game faces and men focused and ready for combat.

As the squad approached the landing zone, no one had any idea that some of them were now wearing Innis's vomit. The Rangers exited the Black Hawk for their predawn operation. The raid went off without a hitch. They captured the guys they were looking for without a shot being fired. The sun was now up, and the Rangers began making their way home.

As they got into the chopper, there was no mistaking the streak of vomit down the side of the aircraft. Ben then looked down at his plate carrier and uniform. There were chunks on him that were starting to reek. The other Rangers noticed the same thing on their uniforms. They had all been puked on by Private Innis. Led by Ben, they razzed Erick the whole way back.

Ben and his squad in Iraq. Ben was relieved to get his feet wet on his first deployment as a Ranger. On the flight home, he asked if he could stay with the next platoon.

For Rangers, it's critical to ensure they're going after the right individual on a mission. They would often carry a picture of their target for positive identification. Sometimes they know exactly where their target lives. Other times they only have a general idea. They might have to get to an area and talk to the residents of a neighborhood about where a target might be. For the Rangers, tracking a high-value target, or HVT, can turn into police work, piecing together clues to identify an individual and their location.

One night, the Ranger assault force was lined up outside the wall of a compound. Ben and Erick were at the back of the formation. From there, they could see other Rangers ahead moving toward the compound's gate. There were also snipers set up on buildings on the fringes of the area, covering their movements. Suddenly, Ben heard a blast of gunfire about thirty yards ahead. He could see his fellow Rangers firing through an opening in the compound wall, but he couldn't see what they were firing at.

Just as quickly as the gunfire erupted, there was silence. Ben and Erick, still together, followed the column of Rangers into the compound. Inside, in front of a small home, two men lay dead on the ground. Near each was an AK-47. One man had part of his skull missing. Ben and Erick walked up to the two dead fighters. They were the first bodies either had seen in combat. They were overcome by a powerful smell and realized it was the stench of human brains. Ben and Erick decided it was about the worst thing they'd ever smelled. The Rangers left, taking into custody some of the other men who had not returned fire.

As they left the compound, they heard wailing coming from the families of the two men. Several Iraqi women screamed and howled in grief at the top of their lungs.

The neophyte Rangers had never heard anything like this before. Everything had happened so quickly. The enemy—armed with automatic weapons—hadn't fired a single shot. As Ben would soon learn, that was generally how things played out for them in Iraq. The people they were targeting weren't trained and hardened fighters. They were instigators, usually plotting to get materials to construct and deploy IEDs.

Third Platoon stayed very busy, which allowed Ben to pick up valuable experience and win his platoon's acceptance. Night after night they conducted raids, and night after night they captured or killed their targets. Being a Ranger was all Ben thought it would be and more. He wrote to Desirae Nelson about it:

December 1, 2007

In a little over a month we will be heading back. It's going to feel really good to be on US soil again and to have all the comforts of living back home. I wish everyone (who was capable) could come over here and fight this war and see how these people live, they would appreciate everything in their life A LOT more. But all I have to do is see pictures from 9/11 or hear the "Star-Spangled Banner" and I get the chills, and all that bullshit about not seeing anyone or not being able to do shit or have the freedoms everyone else has goes right out the window. Oh yeah, and getting put into a combat zone works too, ha ha.

Ben

By the end of the deployment in early January 2008, Ben's confidence was at an all-time high. He was good at his job, confident in his skills, and had a full Ranger deployment under his belt. Getting ready to take off for home, Ben sat on the floor of the C-17 with a sense of satisfaction—they'd successfully completed dozens of operations with no major casualties. He couldn't believe his first deployment had passed so quickly.

Most of Charlie Company was aboard the aircraft, waiting to fly to Germany and eventually Fort Benning. Ben asked no one in particular, "Is there any way I can stay and just continue with the next platoon?"

Steven Shipe, who was part of Ben's squad, was sitting next to him. "Shut up, Kopp," he said. "You can't stay. We're going home."

Auburn University – Auburn, Alabama

It's about a forty-five-minute drive from the Ranger barracks at Fort Benning in Columbus, Georgia to the campus of Auburn University in Alabama. To young Rangers, Auburn represents Southern college girls, SEC football, and campus parties where the beer flows freely—all the trappings of college life they passed up to serve their country.

It's common for a squad of Rangers to jump in vehicles and make the trek west, crossing the Chattahoochee River into Alabama. Despite their college age, enlisted Rangers stand out at Auburn with their fit frames, high-and-tight haircuts, and visible tats. Ben and his Ranger pals would show up in jeans, their Army-issued boots, and t-shirts that showed off their rigorous training. They were a stark contrast to the SEC college boys with moppy, Bieberesque haircuts swirling and spilling into their eyes, khaki shorts, preppy shirts, and moc loafers. While the Rangers trained many hours a day, the college boys were already growing soft on weeklong beer binges and weekend tailgating. On foreign turf, the Rangers would hang together and were often loud and invasive party crashers that could sometimes put their hosts on edge.

One night, Ben and Ryan Lundeby were hanging out at an Auburn party. Lundeby happened to be wearing a Kona Brewery sweatshirt, and a pretty Southern girl approached him, using his shirt as an opening. She asked if he had been to Hawaii; Lundeby replied he had. The young lady said she and her family took vacations there as well. Lundeby was intrigued. What he didn't realize was that her jealous boyfriend had noticed their conversation and was growing redder by the second.

Ben was standing on the other side of the room, taking in the scene and watching his friend enjoy the company of the pretty co-ed. As Ben's eyes drifted across the room, he caught the irate gaze of the boyfriend and realized his Ranger brother might soon find himself in a fight. Lundeby could handle himself, but they were on foreign turf, and if anything shook out they were outnumbered. Ben looked calmly around, then moved toward a table and grabbed an empty beer bottle. He shoved it in his back pocket, hoping he wouldn't have to use it. Ben then casually walked up to the smiling Lundeby, who was completely lost in the white teeth, pretty eyes, and flowing hair of the young lady in front of him.

Kopp grabbed his friend by the arm and pulled him away. "Hey dude, come check this out outside real quick," Ben suggested.

Lundeby wasn't happy about the extraction. Ben led him out the door and onto the lawn.

Lundeby spun around so the Rangers were face to face. "Hey, what's up?" he asked, annoyed.

"Dude, that boyfriend was about to punch you upside the head."

They didn't go back inside, deciding to leave campus instead. Lundeby quickly realized that Ben was a very good wingman and may have saved him from a sucker punch or worse. Lundeby had become one of Ben's best friends in Third Platoon. They would soon head to Ranger School together, and Lundeby realized his friend—the same one he'd once saved from falling over a cliff—always had his best interests at heart.

Ranger School

In March 2008, Ben and Ryan started Ranger School. During the two months of grueling tests in the mountains of Georgia and swamps of Florida, they would forge an even closer bond.

While the Ranger Indoctrination Program weeds out those not strong enough in body and mind to become Rangers, Ranger School serves as follow-up training. It's a sixty-one-day physically and mentally grueling course that begins with a series of tests at Fort Benning. Ranger School isn't just for Rangers. Soldiers from other Army units may also attend, and there are slots open to other branches of the military as well. Ranger School pushes soldiers to the limit—in the year Ben and Ryan entered, only 49 percent of those who attempted the training went on to graduate.

For much of their time in the course, soldiers are sleep deprived and survive on just two MREs per day, a small, sealed, and well-preserved collection of rations. It's not much considering they're burning significant calories. The "Crawl Phase" of Ranger School starts at Fort Benning. The training then moves to "Mountain Phase" or "Walk Phase," which is conducted at Camp Merrill in the remote mountains near Dahlonega, Georgia. During Mountain Phase, soldiers conduct long night-time marches and exercises on the steep precipices at the southern end of the Appalachian range. And finally there's "Swamp Phase," also known as "Florida Phase" or "Run Phase." It's carried out at various locations near Camp Rudder at Eglin Air Force Base in Florida. Much of that phase is conducted in the swampy jungles of that region.

Crawl Phase went just fine for Ben and Ryan. Things got a bit more challenging when they moved to Camp Merrill for Mountain Phase.

By early April, Ben's Ranger School class was out in the field for four or five days at a time. Eating just two MREs per day, his weight crashed from his usual lean 175 to about 155 pounds. The training consisted of long marches, moving five to ten hours a day with sixty-five-pound rucksacks over hilly terrain. Ben struggled with the restrictiveness of the training, comparing it to prison in a letter home.

Ben was also craving a dip. He loved chewing tobacco, especially Copenhagen. The deprivation was killing him. Always the schemer, he devised a plan. He called Erick Innis at Fort Benning, about three hours south, and asked him to buy a few tins and drive them up. Erick agreed, though he knew he might get in trouble. They agreed on a rendezvous point and time, but there was one big problem: Erick didn't have clearance or any good reason to be at Camp Merrill. After driving from Fort Benning, he could be turned away at the gate.

Erick jumped in his Ford Sport Trac and made the drive north to Dahlonega. Along the way, he stopped at a gas station and picked up a roll of chew canisters. Erick was nervous. *What am I gonna say if they ask why I'm there?* As he pulled up at the Camp Merrill gate, he flashed his military ID and acted confidently, like he had business there. The guard waved him right in.

Now the plan got more complicated, especially in the dark.

Ben had told Erick he would be hiding in the woods along the base's airstrip. Erick meandered through the base in his truck, looking for the runway. He finally found it, but it was hard to make out anything in darkness. There were also many wooded areas around the airstrip; Ben could be anywhere.

Erick scanned the tree lines. He could see the shadows of the mountains rising in the distance. He parked alongside the road, cut his engine, and shut off the headlights, letting his eyes adjust. As he sat there thinking about what a ridiculous idea this was, he saw a flashing light in the distance. He knew it had to be Ben. He fired up the truck and closed in on the location. As he approached, Ben ran from the woods and jumped in the back of the truck before Erick could stop. The two friends exchanged greetings and chatted for a few minutes, then Erick handed over the roll of tobacco tins. Ben jumped out and headed back to his quarters without incident.

Ben and Ryan ended up getting recycled from Mountain Phase. "Recycled" is a military term for having to repeat a segment of a course. A soldier can be recycled for a variety of reasons, anything from disciplinary action, an injury, or an entire team failing to complete certain goals. Why Ben and Ryan were recycled was not disclosed. The setback slowed their progress by a matter of weeks.

Recycling in any aspect of Army life, whether it's basic training or Ranger School, can become a challenge in fighting boredom. Ben and Ryan busied themselves pulling weeds and completing other menial landscaping tasks around Camp Merrill. Ben also took to reading. He completed two Harry Potter books; his buddy teased him for it but later ended up reading the books himself. Ben also picked up *A More Elite Soldier* by Chuck Holton, a former Ranger. Holton's book details his life as a Ranger in the eighties, his combat deployment (by parachute) into Panama, and his growing Christian faith. It would prove to be an influential book to Ben, both in terms of his life as a Ranger and his walk down a spiritual path.

The break from training also allowed Ben to take care of a few personal matters, like ordering flowers for his mom for Mother's Day. The downtime also gave him time to reflect on his life. He thought about his mom and how much she'd sacrificed to raise him on her own. He sent her a letter:

May 2008

You raised me from day one as a single parent, and I can't thank you enough for that. You were always there for me every day of my life. I can't say you gave me everything, but I'm a better man for it now. If I had the money I would buy you a house, a car, and everything else.

Ben

Jill was so touched she wrote him right back:

It's real nice to hear you thank me for raising you alone and for being there for you. And also for saying you'd buy me a house and a car. Honestly, Ben, I have already reaped the rewards of raising you by having you be more of a man by age twenty than many men will ever become.

The sparse training diet gave way to eating anything Ben and Ryan wanted while they were recycled. They dined on blueberry pancakes every morning at the Camp Merrill dining facility. They also had access to rejected care packages from Fort Benning. To that Ben added ice cream every day at lunch and dinner, including Ryan's portion, which he surrendered daily. Several weeks later, Ben had packed an unthinkable thirty pounds back onto his frame. And because they were recycled, they weren't even allowed to work out.

"You've gotten really fat," Ryan pointed out.

Ben didn't need to be told. He was suddenly in the worst shape of his adult life.

After some of his food binges, Ben would lay on the ground, feeling sick. But after the emaciation of the initial Ranger School phases, he didn't care. He shared his new binge diet with his mom over the phone.

"You must've gotten sick," Jill said.

"Yep, we did. But it was so worth it," Ben replied.

Ben was also exploring his faith, an interest that grew while he and Ryan were recycled. Desirae Nelson had always challenged Ben to walk that path. Now that he was starting to do so, he wrote to her about his experiences:

May 5, 2008

I've been going to church every Sunday. We sing songs to the tune of an old rickety piano and they never forget to thank "US Rangers" for being able to jump out of airplanes and conduct combat operations in a mountainous environment, etc. The preacher always yells and gets teary eyed every time he talks, LOL. They are good people, though. I always leave thankful that I went and with a good feeling inside.

Ben

Ben also couldn't get his mind off Brittney. He would call and they would chat. She wrote him a letter during Ranger School that put her feelings out in the open:

May 14, 2008

I have been thinking about you a lot. I just don't know what it is about you that I love and miss so much. I feel like you are my soulmate and that I can't fall in love or be with anyone else because you are the one that still has my heart. . . . So when are we getting married? I love you. Be good!

Always,
Pretty Girl

Ben and Ryan got back on track to finish Ranger School. Mountain Phase had been a bear. *God didn't put me here to fail*, Ben told himself before buckling down for a second attempt at the grueling training in North Georgia. The duo ended up spending twelve weeks at Camp Merrill to complete Mountain Phase. Ben's last day there was Friday, June 13.

The next day, Ben and Ryan arose at 3:00 a.m. to head for Florida and Swamp Phase. Those in the Ranger School class who were airborne-qualified, Ben and Ryan among them, climbed onto an aircraft for the short flight and parachuted onto Eglin Air Force Base.

Ben had written home during this time at Camp Merrill to tell Jill about encounters with scorpions, oversized wolf spiders, and a four-inch millipede. But during Swamp Phase, a bunch of the guys were sitting around outside when Ben saw a snake slithering toward one of them.

"Don't move!" he told them. He grabbed a shovel and killed the snake with a single quick blow. It was a timber rattlesnake, about four feet long. The guy in its sights hadn't realized it was right behind him.

Ryan and Ben completed Swamp Phase and were finally ready to graduate from Ranger School. Ben again had Brittney on his mind. Without access to a phone or computer during Ranger School, he wrote to his mom repeatedly asking her to invite Brittney to his Ranger School graduation. But Jill wrote back to say Brittney couldn't take the time off from work. The news left Ben heartbroken. The accomplishment of finishing Ranger School had just the opposite effect. Ben was thrilled to be done and to have solidified his place in the battalion.

07/03/2

Ranger School graduation, July 2008. Jill was struck by the pomp and circumstance on this Fourth of July weekend at Fort Benning. Note the freshly pinned Ranger tab on Ben's left shoulder.

Ben and Ryan graduated from Ranger School on July 3, 2008. Ben's mom and grandfather, Jon Burud, came down from Minnesota. It was the day before Independence Day, and Fort Benning was ready to celebrate in patriotic fashion. Jill and her dad enjoyed the pomp and circumstance. She felt there was nowhere she'd rather be to ring in the nation's birthday than watching her son get his Ranger tab.

As the small black-and-yellow patch reading "RANGER" was pinned on his shoulder, Ben and Jill both beamed with pride. "I'm so proud of you, Ben," Jill told him later. "Thanks for making me look so good."

Jill and her dad planned to hang out in Columbus and take Ben out to eat for a few days, but Ben learned soon after the graduation ceremony that he would be deploying in six days to Iraq again.

"Mom, since we deploy in a few days, can we go down to Panama City?"

"Yep, sure, let's go," Jill said.

Ben also wanted to let his buddies know he had his tab. He logged on to Facebook and found Shane Harris's page. Shane was already on his second deployment with Charlie Company. Ben posted "tab check" on Shane's page, a cryptic message only Shane or another Ranger would understand. It was Ben's way of saying, *I'm out. I graduated. I did it. I have a Ranger tab and you don't!* Ben was now what Rangers called a tabbed specialist—an E-4 with a Ranger tab.

Panama City, Florida

The caravan rolled into the Gulf Coast party town in Ben's reasonably new 2003 Chevy 1500 pickup, which he'd nicknamed the Black Stallion. They were just in time for the Fourth of July weekend. Jill and her dad got hotel rooms on the water. By that night, Ben and his Ranger pals Nathan Bell and Ron Kubik were chilling on the beach.

The Rangers now had a confidence they didn't have when they visited Panama City the first time. They were proud of what they'd become and didn't mind letting others know. They shed their Ranger uniforms for board shorts and lay on the white sandy beach, soaking up the Florida sunshine and gazing at the rolling blue-green surface of the Gulf of Mexico. Ben reached over from his beach chair and stuck his hand into an Igloo cooler filled with iced-down cans of Miller Lite. They drank and recalled the close calls of the previous year. They also made it their duty to patrol the beach for other Army guys who might be out of line, especially dog tag offenders. "Hey! Don't wear your dog tags on the beach in public like that!" Ben warned one violator.

While Ben was hanging out with Kubik and Bell, Erick Innis had also arrived at the beach to join them. Erick was splitting time with his friends after coming down with his wife, Christina. The newlyweds had found their own quiet spot on the beach. Christina and Erick were lying in the sun when they heard screaming and hollering. Someone was acting obnoxiously about thirty yards down the beach.

Christina was in the middle of a mid-summer nap, the sun's rays baking her, and she didn't want to lift her head to see who it was causing the racket. "I wish that guy would quiet down," she mumbled to Erick.

But whoever it was wouldn't shut up, and it was now agitating her. She finally looked up from her nap and saw the culprit. "Hey, you know that guy I've been complaining about? Well, look who it is."

Erick looked up to see Ben carrying on loudly, flailing his arms around as he yelled. He was the center of attention and seemed to be enjoying it.

"Look at his tattoo, that's his calling card right there," Christina said, gesturing to the "KOPP" that ran across Ben's back. Erick looked up briefly and put his head back down.

"Why would anyone get a tattoo with their last name?" she asked. "You know who you are. I don't get that."

"I'm not sure, but it doesn't help his case if he runs from the cops shirtless," Erick joked.

"Yeah," Christina said, chuckling. "Now they know exactly who you are."

Night fell, and the Rangers, Jill, and Grandpa Jon watched fireworks up and down the Gulf Coast. Suddenly, there was a flash of pyrotechnics on the beach just ahead of them. Something didn't seem right about the way it ignited. There were screams, and someone cried out in pain. Ben and Erick rushed over, their training kicking in as they went into medic mode. A young man had burned his inner thighs with a firework and was in extreme pain. The Rangers helped calm him, assessed his wounds, and treated him until help arrived. They didn't leave the young man's side until EMTs had arrived.

People who'd gathered around were amazed by the quick reaction of these two young men. "Who are those guys?" someone asked. The answer was simple: they were Rangers doing their job.

From left to right: Nathan Bell, Ron Kubik, and Ben Kopp. Less than two years after this picture was taken, two of these three Rangers would make the ultimate sacrifice for their country. Kubik was killed April 23, 2010, while serving in Afghanistan.

This incident aside, the Rangers had a lot of fun on their beach getaway. But the fast approach of another Iraq deployment was weighing on Ben. He'd been to Baghdad before and things had gone well. Ben was looking forward to joining his platoon in a matter of days. As they spent a last day on the beach, they decided to take a few pictures. Innis pulled out a digital camera. Bell and Kopp got on either side of Kubik, who crossed his arms to show off his muscles and full-sleeve tats. All three gripped their beers. Erick knelt and looked through the lens, framing his friends against the pale blue sky. Nathan, Ron, and Ben may've been smiling on the inside. It was too beautiful a place, and they were having too good a time not to be. But they were Rangers and didn't generally smile for pictures. With the press of Erick's finger, the trio's image was captured. None of them could know that within two years, two of these three young Rangers in the picture would be dead.

Fort Benning, Georgia

As Ben prepared to leave for Baghdad on July 12, he stepped into the office of Sergeant Jeramy Smith, one of the Charlie Company members who had smoked him over the conflict with Morgan Garrett. Sergeant Smith wanted to talk with Kopp before he left for Iraq.

"Ben, first off, I want to say I'm sorry for how I treated you when you first came here. I told you once upon a time that you better live up to the Ranger you took away, and you have."

"Thank you, Sergeant."

"I'm so proud of you and the things you've done here. You've lived up to it and more. You'll be a great team leader, and I hope I'll be your platoon sergeant someday."

Ben looked at Smith and smiled. He felt a sense of satisfaction in completely turning this person around, from hazing him to now respecting him.

"Sergeant, I would love to work for you," he said.

Smith helped get Ben and his gear into a truck, drove him to the airfield, and said good-bye. Smith stood on the side of the field long enough to watch the C-17 and Ben Kopp take off for Iraq.

Baghdad International Airport

About twenty-four hours later, Specialist Kopp arrived in Baghdad and joined the rest of his platoon. The Rangers were at BIAP again but in a different compound. They were on the other side of the airport, and instead of tents, they had rooms built by Navy Seabees inside sheet metal hangars. They also had their own helicopter landing zone nearby and were now part of two special operations task forces housed in adjacent compounds. In the sprawling expanse of BIAP, the Rangers were beginning their deployment with what they considered good facilities. They had a nicely appointed large gym, where many of them worked out together. They could hit the dining facility anytime, which was about a football field away from their barracks. Security was so tight that even inside the base they had to show their badges to reenter their own special operations compound.

With Ranger School behind him, Ben's days of being hazed were over. Many of his fellow Rangers were now close friends. A newer private, Chase Vanderhule, hailed from South Dakota. He and Ben had become friends, hanging out in sports bars back in Columbus watching MMA fights and football games while gorging on wings and beer. Ben and Chase had a lot in common besides their Midwest roots. They shared an interest in pickup trucks, and both drove "lifted" 2003 Chevy 1500s. They were also both workout warriors and assigned to Third Platoon's Third Squad. Ben took Chase under his wing, telling him, "I was in your shoes not too long ago. I know what you're dealing with." Ben, however, would miss his closest friend, Erick, on this deployment. As Ben was leaving for Iraq, Innis was heading to Ranger School.

Once Ben got his Ranger tab, he became a bit of a disciplinarian. He hardly had his bags unpacked and Chase was already getting smoked. Ben was never really mad at Chase, of course. During these "smoke sessions," he always wore his familiar smirk.

Privates on their first deployment don't necessarily get on the assault team. Instead, they're assigned to other tasks, like CSAR or driving or manning the machine gun on a Stryker, a large armored vehicle. Private Vanderhule started his deployment as a gunner on the Stryker. In a matter of weeks, he'd advanced to the assault team. When Ben arrived, he took Chase's spot on the assault force, and Chase went back to manning the gun. A short time later, however, leadership switched them again. Ben was pissed—he had more time and experience than Chase, he outranked his friend and had his Ranger tab. Even though he and Chase were friends, Chase was going to pay.

Inside the room they shared they were friends. Outside, Ben was all business, smoking Chase whenever he could with push-ups, running, and "the electric chair." The electric chair was a torturous test of will where soldiers squatted with their backs against a wall and on tiptoes, hands straight out, for about five minutes. It was so named because after a few minutes, soldiers would start to shake like an executioner had just flipped the switch.

The platoon had a new officer on this deployment. First Lieutenant Dan Krueger was tall, maybe just over six foot two, and lanky. He was a 2006 West Point graduate and the son of an Army Corps of Engineers colonel. Like many of those who grow up in military families, Krueger didn't really claim a hometown, though he'd graduated from high school in Collierville, Tennessee. His arched upper lip on his young ruddy face quickly revealed an easy smile and dimples. The enlisted guys sometimes gave him flak for what they claimed was a baby face. Lieutenant Krueger was also well spoken.

Perhaps more than the rest of the Army, Ranger platoons depend on strong leadership from the NCOs. Krueger understood this, and that, coupled with his good nature, helped him get along with the guys and become an effective officer. The guys in the platoon generally liked Dan Krueger, which isn't always the case when young lieutenants are assigned to a Ranger company.

The NCO everyone in Charlie Company looked up to was First Sergeant Greg Knight. Knight commanded as much respect as any NCO in the regiment, and the men who served under him would never want to lose that respect.

Knight was solid and stoic on the surface, his deliberate Southern drawl nearly always calm and reasonable. He was also a model Ranger—tough and smart, yet deeply caring about his guys. He could be hard on his guys, but there was a method to the madness. Knight did things by the book and led from the front; Rangers always knew where they stood with him.

Ben (right) with two Ranger squad mates after raiding a house in Iraq. The Rangers were extremely busy on this deployment, sometimes completing more than one operation in a 24-hour period.

On this deployment, First Sergeant Knight was splitting time between two of his platoons in Afghanistan and one in Iraq. As first sergeant of the company, his responsibilities ranged from daily operations and personnel issues, to training while deployed and leading missions. It was an all-encompassing job best suited for a jack-of-all-trades, which he was.

Once again, Ben and his fellow Rangers were incredibly busy on this deployment. They referred to it as a "high op tempo." They were sometimes completing multiple missions per night. By one estimate, the platoon completed 117 operations in just over one hundred days. The type and focus of their missions had changed, though. During Ben's first trip to Iraq, they were going after Sunni extremists. Now, in the summer of 2008, they were focused on the influx of Al Qaeda. They were going out at night either by Stryker or by Chinook helicopter. Their plan was to catch their targets by surprise and capture them, a task they often pulled off without shots fired.

Rangers might be gritty fighters doing America's dirty work, but they have a lot of technology at their fingertips. That technology allowed them to home in on Al Qaeda operatives and other IED fabricators. Ranger operations were directly connected to the intelligence-gathering community. Once intelligence was developed on a target, the Rangers would go to work.

The Rangers of Charlie Company's Third Platoon developed a pace to their operations, getting better each night they went out. They'd hit one target, interrogate the individual or others in the building, and learn new information about other Al Qaeda associates or IED makers. Rangers and some of their enablers were trained in law enforcement protocol and would take photographs, fingerprints, and retina scans of the captured, the dead, and anyone else they suspected of running with terrorists or plotting against American troops. They would get back on the radio with the TOC (tactical operations center), where commanding officers and support staff stood by to help make decisions on what to do next. Rangers could quickly get orders while the intel was hot to go after a new target they'd just learned of, though their operations rarely lasted past sunrise. Night vision goggles allowed them good sight in the darkness. Darkness gave Rangers natural protection and allowed them to operate when the streets of Baghdad were less busy, letting them strike while most of their targets slept.

The enemy didn't always surrender peacefully, though. The platoon also got into engagements and killed or captured their targets or those protecting them. But overall, the success on this deployment kept morale high. The 2008 Iraq deployment was so efficient that no one from Ben's platoon was killed or even seriously wounded. Ben and the rest of the guys liked the busy pace. It made the time go faster. No Ranger wanted to deploy to Iraq or Afghanistan only to sit around and watch TV or play video games.

Ben's friends started to notice that he was on a spiritual journey and seeking opportunities to grow in his Christian faith. Battalion Chaplain Mike Shellman would periodically lead Bible studies and worship services at BIAP when he came through on a "battlefield circulation." Shellman would stay a few days, then move on to other companies. Like First Sergeant Knight, he was splitting time between Iraq and Afghanistan.

If Shellman wasn't there, Charlie Company's fire support officer, Captain Lane Sandifer, would take the spiritual lead. Captain Sandifer tried to make an effort to connect with the guys and encouraged them to attend Bible study. Sandifer led a team of seven guys called "forward observers" trained to provide fire support to Rangers on the ground. That could mean artillery, mortars, attack helicopters, AC-130s, fighter jets, or other close air support.

Bible studies would come at a tough time, generally mornings after nighttime operations. They were conducted weekly in a back room at the dining facility. Despite his fatigue, Ben attended frequently with Lundeby, Marcus Engebretsen, and others from their platoon. They would get about a dozen guys per meeting ranging from officers to privates.

Captain Sandifer liked to share passages from the New Testament. The soldiers would then talk about Scripture and spend time praying for each other. Ben was normally outgoing, vocal, and even boisterous. However, during Bible study, he became a listener. New to his faith, Ben seemed to be taking it all in. He hadn't grown up going to church, but he was discovering something that felt powerful to him, and each week he was drawn back to it.

It was also common for the Rangers to say a prayer in the "ready room" before an operation. The ready room is the football locker room of a special operator's life, where Rangers would put on gear and double check equipment before an operation. Chaplain Shellman was visiting and entered the ready room to check on the guys. Shellman was from Ben's hometown of Rosemount, Minnesota, but was about twenty-five years Ben's senior, so they didn't have any common friends. Shellman had left Rosemount when he was sixteen, moving to Texas. But Ben liked Shellman and appreciated that he was from Rosemount.

Shellman was always aware that the Rangers he ministered to felt like they were invincible. That could be a double-edged sword. That feeling gave them the confidence to do their very dangerous job, but it also meant they might be overlooking some of the spiritual realities that could come in handy during a tragedy or time of crisis. On this day, Shellman looked around the room and saw the faces of warriors. They were charged up. Shellman had been doing this for a long time and was conscious that during a mission someone might have fears and hesitations under their tough exterior. Chaplain Shellman today wanted to deliver an energized prayer, touch hearts, and make them realize that what they were doing was the right thing. He called the Rangers to prayer.

"We are working as God's instrument of his holy righteousness," the chaplain started. "These orders are coming from higher up. And this is a mission that we need to execute, and we're gonna do it. And so we, therefore, can go boldly and with courage knowing that we're doing great things. And I also pray, Lord, that in that moment that our faith might become weak that you give us strength. I pray on your behalf the Lord's protection on you and the Lord's strength upon you.

And I pray for mission success and for your safety."

The faces in the room were steady and somber, helmets on. Plate carriers in place, weapons ready, MH-47 chopper standing by. Heads lifted. Mission time.

Ben was clearly discovering his faith. But his reverence could quickly give way to a devilish mischievousness. After one all-night operation, the platoon came back exhausted. Ben and Ryan removed the bunk flaps from a bed frame that supported another Ranger's mattress, then gently placed the mattress back on the frame. The unsuspecting Ranger walked in and plunked down on his bunk only to crash to the floor. Ben and Ryan were doubled over in laughter. Unfortunately, the victim outranked them both, and they were soon on the floor doing push-ups. They continued laughing hysterically through exercises. To them, the punishment was worth the crime.

Winnetka, Illinois September, 2008

The Green Bay Trail extends for miles through the affluent suburbs of Chicago's North Shore. It's a paved trail for bikers, joggers, and walkers, paralleling the tracks of commuter trains that each day transport the Windy City's elite and powerful to the corporate suites, law firms, and trading floors of Chicago's downtown Loop. For hundreds of years, Native Americans, traders, and trappers used the same corridor to travel between Chicago and Milwaukee, even as far as Green Bay.

Fifty-six-year-old Judy Meikle was walking the trail with her tan-and-white cocker spaniel, Ginger, and her friend Liz Nesler and her dog. At a lanky five foot eleven, Judy normally ate up ground with her long strides. But today she was struggling. She'd been battling what felt like a cold. Walking along the trail, she was short of breath, and she felt a stabbing pain at the top of her rib cage that made her stumble.

"Give me a second," Judy gasped. She spoke with a deliberate

Chicago accent filed down by a lifetime in the suburbs. Judy paused, put her hands on her knees, coughed a couple of times, and caught her breath. When she recovered, the group continued their walk, but Judy was still laboring.

Judy Meikle and her beloved dog Ginger. Judy discovered during long walks with Ginger and her friend Liz Nesler that something was wrong with her health. She would soon learn that she needed a heart transplant.

Judy's cropped blond hair was graying now. She was quirky, perpetually single, and lived in the house she'd grown up in. It was a modest home by Winnetka standards, just a few blocks from New

Trier High School, where she'd graduated in 1970. She still handed out the same phone number for the occasional date as she had when she was a student at New Trier. But Judy's strong personality, unwavering opinions, and general intensity were often too much for most men. She was bright, sarcastic, witty, and driven—she worked in the wholesale subprime mortgage industry, where she clocked fifty to sixty hours a week.

Judy and Liz made their way back to Judy's house, where she promised her friend she'd do something for her cold. But in the days that followed, nothing seemed to work. Judy and Liz continued their walks, but Judy felt the same sensation every time. It didn't matter if she was on the Green Bay Trail or walking along Sheridan Road past Winnetka's collection of Lake Michigan mansions; the shortness of breath and the pain at the top of her rib cage continued. Her friends offered advice and suggested remedies, to no benefit. But Judy wasn't too concerned. She wasn't a worrier by nature. She went to the doctor, who told her she likely had pneumonia. She picked up a prescription but still didn't get any better. What Judy didn't realize was that her condition was much more serious. Her clock was ticking, and she was running out of time.

Tigris River, Baghdad

One of the more spectacular operations Third Platoon rolled out on during this deployment involved a rendezvous with a small fleet of SOC-R boats courtesy of the US Navy.

Ben and about forty of his fellow Rangers and their enablers left their quarters at Baghdad International after nightfall and loaded onto a couple of Chinooks. After a short flight, the Rangers rendezvoused with some vehicles that took them to the Tigris River, where they hooked up with the Navy. The Rangers were going after an HVT they believed was involved in the manufacture of IEDs and roadside bombs. They had intel their target was sourcing the components used to build the devices, which were killing American service members in Iraq in increasing numbers.

For a variety of logistical reasons, Ranger leadership decided the best way to get to their target was by boat ride on the Tigris. Climbing aboard the SOC-R boats, the Rangers marveled at their firepower. The thirty-three-foot vessels were heavily armed with five gun mounts that included dual M240B machine guns, a .50-caliber machine gun, and a mini gun (a Gatling gun that sprays 7.62 rounds). The boats were also equipped with mounted grenade launchers. They were essentially floating death machines.

The platoon crowded onto four of these boats and glided down the river for about twenty minutes. The temperature had dropped significantly, and it was surprisingly cold and windy on the unprotected river. A number of the guys grumbled about the chill. Ben smirked; his Minnesota roots wouldn't let him give into cold. He'd been a lot colder than this out duck hunting with Kyle Hildreth in high school, when they had to break through the ice just to give the ducks a place to land. Even if he did feel cold, Ben would never let anyone know it.

The location where the Rangers needed to disembark was just ahead. The Navy crewmembers slowed the boats and pulled up along the bank. Rangers in full battle gear—helmets, headsets, night vision goggles, plate carriers, ammo, and weapons—readied themselves to jump. But as they started to exit, enemy machine gun fire erupted, the rounds screaming overhead and tearing into the riverbank just beyond their position.

Squad leaders thought it sounded like a .50 cal coming from the far side of the river. Navy boats that hadn't landed yet spun and countered with a massive show of firepower. Thousands of rounds ripped from the small fleet in the direction of the enemy fire, the tracers from the machine guns lighting up the river. Under the cover of the Navy guns, Rangers jumped onto the bank, ran up through the brush to a small berm, and flattened out on the other side of the rise. Squad leaders yelled at everyone to get down. The machine gun fire was still coming from across the river. There might've been as many as two or three enemy guns firing.

The platoon was spread out behind the earthen rise in the darkness, adequate protection if they kept their heads down. Ben peeked out across the river through tall brush, snaps of machine gun rounds whipping above his head and into the bank behind him.

After an initial barrage from the US Navy, all guns went quiet. Rangers listened for any sign of follow-up fire. There was nothing. Ben was convinced the Navy guns had taken care of the enemy. But after about a minute of silence, the insurgent machine guns started again.

If the Navy couldn't get it done, the Rangers would have to go to another service branch: the US Air Force. Pinned down behind the rise and unable to get up the side to their objective, the Rangers decided to call in an air strike.

An unmanned aerial vehicle (UAV), more commonly known as a drone, flew overhead, keeping watch on the Rangers and giving those at the TOC back at BIAP eyes on the enemy. Captain Sandifer was in the TOC tracking the firefight through the eyes of that UAV. "Hey, you still have some guys up there waiting for you," he warned. He could see the enemy position on the far side of the Tigris.

They called in an AC-130 gunship. The converted cargo aircraft has two main guns, a small cannon that launches 105mm howitzer artillery shells, and a 40mm machine gun. The fire support sergeant attached to the Rangers was on the ground with the platoon. He talked directly with the crew of the AC-130, making sure that, through their targeting device, they were looking at the same thing he was. The aircraft soon circled overhead at just above eight thousand feet. The crew on the AC-130 used an infrared camera and watched TV screens on the plane to identify the target. The technology was so good they could see people and even weapons and could fire accurately from that altitude. The big aircraft orbited the target counterclockwise, the guns on the left side of the plane so they were never off target.

"Going hot!" came the warning from the aircraft to both the TOC and the fire support team on the ground to clear airspace below in preparation to fire.

"Clear to fire!" came the command back from the forward observer on the ground.

The big propeller aircraft started dropping 105mm rounds, and the Rangers readied themselves for impact. Company Medic Michael Melvin had his head pressed against the sand. His presence in a battle like this one brought comfort to the Rangers he served with. Melvin was highly respected for his knowledge and practice of battlefield medicine. Each platoon had its own medic, and Melvin was responsible for training them all. Melvin was African American, a big guy for a Ranger at six one, 215 pounds. The guys he took care of adored him. They saw him as a levelheaded, deeply caring guy who often tried to act like he wasn't. Melvin had been through a lot. On Charlie Company's 2006–2007 deployment to Iraq he was with Jimmy Regan, who was killed in February 2007 when an IED detonated near his vehicle. Rangers who were there that day watched as Melvin and another medic did everything they could. When Regan was declared dead, Melvin took it very hard and held himself accountable, though no one else in the company did.

Ben was next to Melvin, flattened out behind the berm. Other Rangers prepared for the concussion from the AC-130 rounds. *Boom, boom, boom, boom*—the artillery shells exploded one after the other across the river. The night lit up, and the ground shook. Twenty minutes after the Rangers landed on the banks of the Tigris, the enemy machine gun sites had been wiped out. For many of the younger guys, this was their first real taste of combat and the first time they had come under enemy fire.

Once the all clear was given, the Rangers moved inland toward their target house. When they reached it, they surrounded the small dwelling. A team then broke down the door, surprising everyone inside. Not a shot was fired. They took several men into custody and left as quickly as they had arrived. This time they avoided another chilly boat ride; they walked several kilometers with their prisoners to a rendezvous point, where the MH-47s picked them up.

When they got back to BIAP, they put away their gear and gathered for a debriefing. One squad leader chastised Private Vanderhule, noting he'd repeatedly popped his head up to look for the source of the machine gun fire. "Hey, I don't want to have to call your mom and dad and tell them that you're gone," he said.

"Yes, Sergeant," Vanderhule replied.

Ben found this funny and for the next few days referred to his friend as "Jon Cena" and "the Marine," after an action movie that had just come out. As the meeting broke up, the guys talked about the intensity of the operation they'd just been through.

"The pucker factor was high," said Sergeant Melvin, who had been around gunfire many times before.

"That was a sweet mission," said another Ranger.

That Tigris River mission earned several of the new guys their Combat Infantryman Badges (CIB). The CIB is awarded to infantrymen below the rank of colonel with an infantry or Special Forces unit after the unit is involved in ground combat. It's a beautiful award, a silver and light blue rectangular badge with an infantry musket over an elliptical oak wreath.

Ben's platoon returned from the Iraq deployment in mid-October of 2008. There was already talk that their next deployment would be very different. They would likely be going to Afghanistan, and their challenges would be even greater and more dangerous than what they'd faced in their last two deployments to Iraq.

Chicago, Illinois

Judy Meikle had been so healthy all her life that she didn't even have anyone she considered her regular doctor. With her lingering cold, her mother's former caregiver drove Judy to *her* doctor. Judy's shortness of breath was getting worse. Not even rolling down the window of the car for some cool October air seemed to help. The doctor, on seeing Judy, told her to go straight to the nearest hospital, which was Swedish Covenant on Chicago's Northwest Side.

After a battery of tests and an interview with the emergency room doctor, Judy was told she was being admitted. But doctors still couldn't say exactly what was wrong with her. After four days at Swedish Covenant, Judy got a vague but stunning diagnosis. "We know it's your heart," the cardiologist told her. "But you're going to need to seek help at another hospital."

That was both disturbing and confusing. Swedish Covenant was considered a good hospital, but they couldn't help her. Judy was moved to Northwestern Memorial Hospital in downtown Chicago, which was a tremendous inconvenience. Judy couldn't even go home to see her beloved dog. The only thing she could think to do was call her neighbor, Lynne Goodreau. Lynne, a nurse with a master's in cardiology, specialized in cardiothoracic nursing and worked with cardiologists in the transplant unit at Northwestern. Because Lynne would sometimes get stuck at work, she would often call on Judy to pick up her kids from school or drive them to hockey practice. When Judy's medical tests were transferred from Swedish to Northwestern, Lynne promised she would take the results to one of the cardiologists she worked with, Dr. William Cotts.

"I'm not taking any new patients," he told Goodreau.

"Would you just look at her chart?" she pleaded. Goodreau tried a new tack. "You know when you keep me late at work, and I make a call to someone who takes care of my kids?" she pressed.

Dr. Cotts nodded.

"Well, this is her."

Cotts smiled, understanding, and agreed to take a look at Judy's chart.

Rosemount, Minnesota

Ben Kopp returned to his hometown after his second Ranger deployment. He was now a veteran special operator who'd been in the Army for more than two years. He was thrilled to see his mom and to let off a little steam with his high school friends.

It was now October, the season had changed in Minnesota, and that was refreshing to Ben after four months in Baghdad. One of his high school buddies, Eric Pittlekow, had promised to throw him a kegger to celebrate Ben's return from deployment. The party crew included Tyler Nelson, and they met at Shenanigans, an Irish pub in Rosemount. They drank beer and shared stories until past midnight, then rambled over to Eric's house to continue the party. By the time they finally tapped the keg, it was about one in the morning.

Ben and his friends were enormously competitive, and standing in the attached garage, Ben challenged Tyler to a pull-up contest using the rafters. Tyler agreed, and the young men quickly showed off their beer-fueled strength, rising and dipping above the garage floor. Despite his Army training, Ben lost to Tyler by one pull-up. Ben, ever the competitor, wouldn't let it go, following Tyler around the party criticizing his "lame" pull-up technique and offering a few other excuses.

Eric, Ben, and Tyler now turned their competitive spirit to another target. There was a good-looking young lady at the party, and the three young men jockeyed to see who could hook up with her. There were plenty of girls present, but for some reason they all felt the need to vie for this particular girl's attention.

The night was mild for Minnesota in October, and the party

eventually moved to Eric's backyard. As the beer flowed, someone started a chant. "USA! USA! USA!"

It was past two in the morning in a neighborhood where the homes were packed closely together. The chant grew louder until everyone in the yard was bellowing at the top of their lungs. Despite their good-natured fun, someone must've complained to the police. About two minutes later, a couple of squad cars rolled up. Police officers came to the edge of the yard and told the group they needed to break it up. But one of the guests recognized an officer, pulled him aside, and explained they were celebrating Ben's return from deployment and that they would be quiet. The officer agreed to let the party continue on that condition.

The officer strolled back to his squad car, got in, and slowly rolled away. He was about two blocks away when Ben, like an orchestra conductor, started the patriotic chant again. "USA! USA! USA!"

Everyone at the party joined in once more. This time the noise was even louder. "USA! USA! USA!"

The squad car roared back. By the way he slammed on the brakes, Ben and Eric could tell the officer wasn't happy. This time his strides bore more authority. "You guys are done!" he started, clearly pissed. "I got three blocks away and I heard you guys chanting again. Time to break this shit up!"

The party was over and everyone left, including the young lady Eric, Tyler, and Ben had chatted up. She left with Ben. *I don't know how he does it. Women love him,* Eric thought as he watched the two leave his yard.

Chicago, Illinois

At Northwestern Memorial, Judy had an appointment with Dr. William Cotts. She had mixed feelings about it. *What will he tell me? Will I need major heart surgery?* She'd been wondering and worrying for a few days and was about to find out.

Dr. Cotts entered the room. After a brief chat, he said, "Judy, we have some good news and some bad news."

"Okay, what's the good news?" Judy asked.

"We know exactly what's wrong with you." Dr. Cotts explained that the top of her heart was webby and had never closed up. Judy listened intently, already having an idea of where he was going.

"The bad news is that we can't fix it. You need a heart transplant."

His words punched her in the gut. Judy felt a surge of emotion flow through her at once. She felt disbelief. She hadn't spent a night in the hospital since she was released as a baby. She was stunned, fearful, and overwhelmed. She remembered hearing the news of the first heart transplants in her lifetime and recalled that most of those early patients had died.

Columbus, Georgia

After a break at home, Ben returned to Georgia. But for the first time he wouldn't have to live in the Ranger barracks at Fort Benning. He had moved off base to an apartment in Columbus, where he roomed with Rangers Stephen Shipe and Jim Robinson.

One night Ben and Jim, who went by Robo, came home from the bars to find the gates of the apartment complex closed. Ben's scan card didn't work at the security gate. Part of their training as Rangers was getting into places where they weren't welcome. Ben wasn't going to let a security gate stand in the way of getting to his apartment. Ben and Robo analyzed the gate, applied force to just the right spot, and within a few seconds were strolling to their room.

The next morning, Ben found an envelope hanging on his apartment door. Inside was a note explaining that he would be fined $1,000 for breaking the security gate. Ben was livid and a bit panicked at the hefty fine. That was a lot of money on an Army specialist's pay. He and

Robo went down to the front desk.

"Hey, what's going on?" Ben said.

The manager at the desk explained that they were being fined for breaking the gate the night before.

"We didn't do that," Ben said, playing dumb. "What are you talking about?"

The manager took them in the back and showed them the surveillance video. On the camera, you could see Ben examining the lock, then forcing the gate open. "Yeah, yeah, I'll pay." Ben could offer no further defense. He and Robinson agreed to split the cost.

Chicago, Illinois

Judy Meikle started to let her friends know about her failing heart, explaining that she needed a transplant. Judy's friends were everything to her. Both of her parents had died, and she was estranged from her sister. Her friends and her dog were all she had.

Ruthie Marion was shocked to learn the news. She knew if they couldn't find a match, Judy would die. Ruthie was scared and let Judy know she would never give up, and that they would fight to the very end to find her a heart. "I will go through everything with you," she said. "You don't have to do anything alone."

Judy also adored her friend PD Weatherhead. Paul David Weatherhead was, in the eyes of those who knew him, a unique and wonderful man. PD was Judy's first boyfriend when she was a freshman and he a junior at New Trier High School. He had even given her his class ring. The romance ended, but they remained close friends.

Now, more than forty years later, PD had a family of his own. He was an attorney, a CPA, and had an engineering degree. PD looked like an average guy but had the gift of being able to talk to anyone, including cardiologists. This skill was invaluable to Judy, because it was time for another meeting with Dr. Cotts.

PD, Ruthie, and Judy went to Northwestern together. Dr. Cotts spoke frankly about Judy's options. The medical team talked about putting in a device to keep her alive if a donor couldn't be found in time. Ruthie marveled that, despite looking at the possibility of death, Judy seemed optimistic.

Judy put on a good face, but privately, she had her own struggles. The word *transplant* kept ringing in her head. The statistics hit her too. Nationwide, eighteen people die every day waiting for a transplant. As Judy thought about her diagnosis, it hit her that someone else would have to die for her to get the heart she needed to live. She would be the beneficiary of their tragedy. The thought was overwhelming and led to feelings of guilt. *If you're praying for a heart transplant, are you praying for somebody to die?*

Columbus, Georgia

While Ben was living off base, he thought a lot about his life and the people who mattered to him. He especially thought about Brittney, whom he missed a lot. Their relationship had always been rocky, but they'd shared so much since they were fourteen years old. Despite their drama, Ben felt deeply that Brittney "got him," that she understood who he was and what he was about. When he was home on leave, he always called Brittney to get together, and she did the same. Anytime he was in town, she would dump whomever she was seeing and take right back up again with Ben.

Lying on his bed one night, Ben felt lonely and missed Brittney. He called her and told her he wanted to fly her down at his expense. Brittney readily accepted and said she was excited to see him, and to see what his life was like in Georgia. Her plan was to stay with Ben a few days.

Ben picked Brittney up at the Atlanta airport and brought her to his apartment in Columbus. She was impressed; Ben really had his life together, and he seemed more independent than she remembered. She was even more touched when she looked in his bedroom closet and found the inside was covered with pictures of her and the two of them together. Brittney felt like she was finally where she belonged, with Ben. Their visit was off to a great start.

A couple of days into the trip, Brittney was watching Ben napping in bed. Seeing him lying there looking so peaceful filled her with good feelings. She felt as if she was reconnecting with her soulmate. But she started wondering what Ben's life in Columbus was really like. *Who are his friends? Does he see other girls?* Brittney decided to look at his phone to find out.

Without waking him, she quietly grabbed his cell off the nightstand and started browsing. She went to his texts, and what she found made her stomach turn. It wasn't sexting or a lewd picture, but a simple invitation from Ben to another woman to go out sometime. It was innocent enough, especially considering that she was seeing someone else back in Minnesota. But Brittney's blood started to boil. She woke Ben up and screamed, "Why am I here when you're talking to other girls?"

Ben, groggy from being startled awake, wasn't sure what she was talking about. When he realized she'd been looking through his phone, he too got upset. "What the fuck?" he asked.

"What's going on here, Ben?" Brittney pressed. She stormed into the closet and ripped down all the pictures, tearing them into pieces. He rushed in and grabbed her and told her to stop. There was pushing and shoving and screaming, and things got out of hand. Brittney now wanted nothing to do with Ben Kopp, but she was trapped. Her ticket home wasn't until the next day. The next twenty-four hours were torture for them both.

When the time came to leave for the airport, Brittney was still furious. The ninety-minute drive from Columbus to Atlanta rolled along in painful silence. When she grabbed her bag at the curb at Hartsfield International, she had one last thing to say to Ben: "Don't call me ever again. Let me live my life."

Brittney Doran, the love of Ben's life, marched off. He would never see her again.

Chicago, Illinois

Judy had been stuck at Northwestern Memorial for weeks, and there didn't seem to be any hope of going home. Her frustration over the situation, combined with her strong personality, led to Judy being a handful for some of the nurses.

She had a run-in with one nurse after she complained about her care. After hearing Judy's comments, the nursing supervisor went to the bullpen and called in their ace, Cary Tyler. He had built a reputation on the floor as a guy who could win over even the most challenging patients.

Cary and Judy talked about family and their love of food. Judy talked about her dog Ginger and how much joy the little cocker spaniel brought her. Cary was a good listener, part of his talent as a nurse. He made it clear to his patients that their voices were being heard. He also had a great sense of humor and could always get Judy to laugh, no matter what her condition.

For his part, Cary appreciated that Judy didn't have a victim's mentality. In the entire time he knew her, he never once heard her complain about her condition.

It was now early November 2008, and Judy desperately wanted to vote in the presidential election. Illinois Senator Barack Obama was up against Arizona Senator John McCain, and in Senator Obama's adopted home of Chicago there was a lot of excitement surrounding his candidacy. Judy also felt voting was sacred, something she never missed an opportunity to do. As she liked to tell her friends, "Men have died on the battlefield defending that right" and "You get what you elect, and if you don't vote, shut up. You have no say."

Judy was supposed to get an absentee ballot, but it hadn't arrived. On the morning of the election, she got on the phone with the Cook County Clerk's Office. "I never got my ballot," she said.

The woman on the phone said they needed proof from her doctor that she was unable to get to the polls. Dr. Cotts faxed a letter saying Judy was hooked up to machines and was not going anywhere.

Still, her ballot quest went down to the wire. Her friend PD picked up the ballot on Election Day and brought it to her. She marked up the ballot then PD delivered it back to the clerk. Judy's vote counted that day, and her streak of never missing an election was preserved. That night, as she lay in her hospital bed, she could hear the crowds just a few blocks away in Millennium Park in downtown Chicago celebrating Barack Obama's victory.

Weeks passed. Visitors came and went. Judy had no idea when her transplant might take place, or if it would happen at all. As Thanksgiving approached, she begged Dr. Cotts to let her go home. He told her it wasn't possible, so Judy spent Thanksgiving in the hospital. At lunchtime that day, Cary visited, and together they ate the hospital's version of a Thanksgiving dinner. Judy ate the turkey, but rejected the green beans. She found them repulsive and had since she was a little girl. No one could make her eat them.

The next day, she got some news to be thankful for: after weeks in the hospital, she would be going home on Saturday.

The National Training Center – Fort Irwin, California

In the late winter of 2009, at the same time President Obama announced the surge of troops in Afghanistan, 3/75's Charlie Company got a new commanding officer, Captain Don Kingston. Captain Kingston and First Sergeant Knight now had to ready the company for an upcoming deployment to Afghanistan.

Charlie Company arrived at Fort Irwin and the National Training

Center (NTC) in California, a massive base about the size of Rhode Island nestled in the Mojave Desert. They intended to spend a couple of weeks of intense training for their May deployment to Helmand Province. NTC was ideal because it provided similar conditions to what the Rangers would face in Afghanistan.

Ben (right) and his buddy Erick Innis take a break from training at Fort Irwin and the National Training Center. The training at NTC in the spring of 2009 would prepare the Rangers for harsh conditions in Southern Afghanistan.

Their training was harder and more intense than previous training had been. During one long hike, Ben and Erick Innis talked about what they would do in the future. Afghanistan would be Ben's last deployment, unless he decided to reenlist.

"What are you gonna do when you get out?" asked Erick.

"I *should* be a porn star," joked Ben.

The friends cackled at the idea. Ben said he would probably go to college when he got back to Minnesota. He would have the option of leaving the Ranger regiment after his upcoming Afghan deployment. Ben was leaning toward getting out but keeping his options open.

Third Platoon had done four deployments in a row to Iraq, so it had been some time since any of these Rangers had been in Afghanistan. For most of Ben's platoon, this would be their first time there. Team leaders were getting on them about their mindset, warning that this was going to be different from Iraq. In Baghdad it was urban fighting, but in Afghanistan they would be at the mercy of more challenging terrain. Leaders also cautioned that this time they would be going up against battle-hardened Taliban fighters. "Hey, this is gonna be different," warned First Sergeant Knight. "You can't approach this the same way we approached targets in Iraq."

During training, they did a twenty-nine-kilometer trek in full gear, brutal in the high desert environment. Ben kept ordering one of the new guys, Private Sean Scappaticci, to his knees. He would then drink from Scap's Camelbak and tell him to carry on. It was Ranger hazing, but Ben himself had had more than his share when he was a private.

The Rangers took advantage of several mock villages to train for their deployment. The villages at NTC mimic real communities in Iraq and Afghanistan. They have a variety of buildings, such as mosques and compounds, and actors playing villagers, street vendors, and insurgents. The actors even speak Pashto, the language soldiers would encounter in Helmand Province. The Rangers trained under live-fire conditions, a practice that builds confidence and gets guys used to working and thinking around live fire.

But despite the preparation, Ben felt a growing worry about the upcoming deployment, a feeling he'd not encountered with his two previous deployments.

Chicago, Illinois

On the Northwest Side, Maria Burud was just getting the news about her old friend Judy Meikle. Maria and Judy had worked together for a few years in the mid-eighties at ADP in Arlington Heights, Illinois. It was Maria's first job out of college.

Judy was about thirteen years Maria's senior, and she took the younger woman under her wing. They would often go to lunch together, and they discovered that they had the same favorite lunch meal: a grilled cheese sandwich and tomato soup. Judy also occasionally talked Maria into donating blood on their lunch hour, a practice Judy felt strongly about and did monthly at the Red Cross.

A few years later, Judy left ADP, but she and Maria kept in contact, getting together every couple of years to catch up. In 1988, Judy and her mother went on a trip to Singapore and Hong Kong. Judy asked Maria to house-sit for her, which she did. But after that, time passed, Maria had three kids, and life got busy for both.

But Maria had just heard Judy needed a heart transplant and told herself she needed to call her old friend. That phone call and their rekindled friendship would prove to be life changing.

Prior Lake, Minnesota

Jenny Boll had hit rock bottom. One evening, after leaving a casino, she got dropped off on the side of the road. She was alone, walking along the busy roadway with no place to go. Her walk turned into a crawl, and when her crawl stopped, she started to pray.

Suddenly, her phone rang. It was Ben. He told her he sensed something was wrong and that he wanted to check in. Jenny confirmed that his suspicion was correct.

"Jenny, you're done. You need to go to treatment," Ben said. "I can't listen to you go through this anymore."

"I know, Benny. You're right."

"I'm buying a house here in Columbus. After that you'll always have a place to call home."

Jenny was crying, but she agreed that it sounded like a good plan.

"Get cleaned up and I'll buy you a one-way ticket down here," Ben promised. "You can just start over."

Jenny could barely speak. But she knew Ben was right.

"You need a fresh start," he said. "I think you just need to get out of there and get away from all those people."

"Okay."

Jenny hung up, immediately called her dad, and—inspired by Ben—asked him to help her get into treatment.

Rosemount, Minnesota

In April 2009, Ben got leave from Fort Benning and came home for a visit. In addition to visiting friends and family, he decided to check in on his old assistant principal from Rosemount Middle, Mary Thompson. She was the one who'd sentenced him to community service and awarded him the last credit he needed to graduate from high school. He walked into her office to say hello and apologized for all his shenanigans in school. Mrs. Thompson was happy to see him. She was impressed with how he looked and wondered how a boy with such a mischievous streak had turned his life into something so positive and noble.

While he was home, Ben got a call from Jenny's parents. She'd entered treatment just like she promised she would. The Bolls thought it would lift Jenny's spirits if Ben went with them to see her at the Hazelden Addiction Treatment Center. The only roadblock was that no one outside of immediate family was allowed to see patients there. They agreed Ben would pose as Jenny's brother, Dan.

It was Easter Sunday. When they walked into the room where Jenny was waiting, her face lit up at the sight of Ben. Her dad quickly coached her up on the scheme. "Hey, we brought your *brother*."

Jenny looked confused for a few seconds, but then caught on. "Ooooh, okay," she said, playing along.

Jenny didn't know Ben was home from Fort Benning, and seeing him here now, she started crying. They decided to take a walk outside.

It was so inspiring to her to look at him as they walked in the cool spring air. When it was time for Ben to leave, the two hugged.

Ben's visit, short though it was, meant the world to her. Jenny felt most of her friends had turned their backs on her, but Ben never did. He also never enabled her or accepted her addiction. *What a good heart Ben has,* she thought. She knew he would do anything for her. She also knew he wasn't afraid to die. She didn't think he was afraid of anything.

Jenny sensed something in Ben during their visit, something serene and knowing. He seemed different. He never mentioned it, but she had a feeling he knew he might not be coming back.

One night during that same spring leave, Ben came home late after drinking with his Rosemount friends. Earlier that night, he'd voiced his worries over the dangers of his upcoming deployment. A friend of Jill's quickly assured him everything would be just fine, but the gesture had the opposite effect. It seemed insincere to Ben, as if they were brushing off the reality of what he faced on his pending deployment.

Ben was so stirred up he sought out his mother in her bedroom late that night. "Mom? Are you awake?"

Jill was asleep, but hearing her son, she rolled out of bed and turned the light on. She squinted at him, her sleepy eyes still trying to adjust to the light.

Tears welled up in Ben's eyes and started to flow down his cheeks. He told her he was extremely worried about his upcoming deployment, and that he didn't have a good feeling about it. He said he knew what they would be doing would be much more dangerous than in Iraq. He also told his mom that her friend that afternoon had told him not to worry, and that everything would be okay. The comment had been bugging him all night. "How the fuck do they know everything will be okay?" he asked.

Jill got out of bed. Ben, sobbing, turned and fled from her room. She followed him to his ground-floor bedroom. He was inconsolable, and it was clear now to Jill that he'd been drinking.

"Do you have any idea what it's like to be the last guy off the boat?" Ben started. "The youngest guy? And dodging bullets around your head?"

Jill didn't fully understand what he was talking about, but she nodded in that knowing way only moms can. Her heart ached for him. He was barely twenty-one years old and he'd already seen and done so much. Now, he sat before her facing his own mortality. She thought of Ben's connection to his great-grandfather and his affinity and respect for World War II veterans. This was hard for Jill too. She had not seen him sob like that since he was a little boy. Unsure what to do, Jill stood up. "I'm gonna leave now," she said, moving toward the door.

"Fine! Get out of here," Ben shouted, tears still streaming down his face. But as Jill turned to leave, he cried out, "Mom! Come back."

She complied and comforted her son until he drifted off to sleep. It reminded her of when he was just a little boy, her little Benny.

Ben had expressed his concerns about his upcoming deployment to just a few others. He told his grandmother Mimi he had reservations. In response, she offered to take him to Canada. She'd lost her son, Jill's eleven-year-old brother, to a tragic traffic accident decades earlier. She knew the pain she'd dealt with as a young mother and didn't want her daughter to suffer the same hurt. Mary never mentioned a word of her offer to Jill. Ben had immediately turned her down anyway, saying he would never turn his back on his country or his Ranger brothers. That week, Ben returned to Fort Benning to face his destiny.

Winnetka, Illinois

By April 2009, things weren't looking good for Judy. She was having a serious reaction to Heparin, a blood thinner critical to the heart transplant operation. If Judy didn't respond to treatment to tolerate Heparin, she might never get on the heart transplant list.

Judy went to the hospital every week, undergoing tests to see if she'd become Heparin tolerant. Once she hit a certain number, she could get on the transplant list.

Judy had lost a lot of weight. At five foot eleven, her frame easily supported 150 pounds. She had now dropped to a frail 118. Her hair was also graying at a faster pace, and even friends told her she looked terrible. She was homebound and couldn't travel or even visit friends who lived in the area.

Then Judy suffered another blow: Ginger was diagnosed with canine leukemia at four and a half years old, and under the strangest of circumstances. Because of Judy's health issues and her extended hospital stay, her friend Ruthie Marion had been taking care of Ginger. It was during that time that Ginger was diagnosed. Ruthie's black Lab had just died from leukemia, and Ruthie's husband was also battling the disease. "I think you have a leukemia hot zone at your house," Judy told her friend.

Ginger had been Judy's daily companion. She'd also brought her endless comfort during a difficult time. But Ginger was clearly declining and had to be put down. Judy was devastated by the loss.

Rosemount, Minnesota

Jill Stephenson looked at her ringing phone. It was Ben calling from Fort Benning.

"Mom, I've got good news," he said. "Maybe I can come home for Mother's Day, and we can surprise Mimi."

Ben's voice crackled with excitement, and Jill was equally thrilled he might be home in a matter of days. Even though it was a short leave—Friday through Monday of Mother's Day weekend—Ben wanted to spend it at home.

Ben and his grandmother, Mary Barnes, during his surprise trip home for Mother's Day in 2009. This was Ben's last visit home before returning to Fort Benning and deploying to Afghanistan.

They spent much of Friday and Saturday going out to eat with Mimi. The next day, Mother's Day, Jill found flowers and a card waiting for her in the kitchen. Ben would normally pick out nice cards and sign them "Love, Ben" without writing anything else. But this card was very simple. On the front was a retro picture of a mother and a little boy. Inside, Ben had written the following:

Mom,

I can't thank you enough for everything you have done for me over the years. Especially the last three since I've been in the Army. You have stood behind me through every decision I have made and supported me. Since day one you always let me be who I wanted to be and never judged me for it like most other people would. I know we sometimes disagree, but sometimes I'm just a punk twenty-one-year-old with not enough freedom and a mad-at-the-world attitude. So you know I don't mean the shit I say and do. You are probably the best mom a guy could ask for, and I love you to death for being the mom that you are. Have a great Mother's Day!

Love, Ben

On the back of the card Ben had written, "The world needs more mothers like you."

Winnetka, Illinois

With Ginger gone, Judy's house felt empty and lonely. She dialed her friends, PD and Ruthie, on a conference call. "The house is too quiet. I need another dog."

"We know," they replied almost simultaneously. They had anticipated her call.

"I kind of found something on the internet . . . ," Judy said, her voice testing their willingness to cooperate.

Ruthie and PD laughed. Judy told them about a rescue event at a big pet store in Lake Geneva, Wisconsin. It was a bit out of Judy's travel radius, but Ruthie agreed to go with her on Saturday.

When they arrived, Judy saw the collection of dogs and puppies. Before she could scan the room and observe which dog might be a good fit, a milk chocolate cocker spaniel—the same breed as Ginger—walked up and sat down between her legs. It didn't move.

"Oh my God, she's picked you," Ruthie said.

The cocker spaniel didn't look around, and it didn't want to get up. Judy quickly fell in love and spent about forty-five minutes petting and talking to the pooch.

"Let's go for lunch and then we'll come back," Ruthie suggested.

When they returned an hour later, Judy again scanned all the dogs to see what was available. But that same cocker spaniel walked up and plunked down between her legs again.

"Judy, you can't go home without her," said Ruthie. "This little girl has picked you for a reason. She needs you."

"I know it," Judy said, vibrating with excitement.

However, the event required anyone adopting an animal to have a home inspection. Judy set up an appointment, but she had to leave that cute little cocker spaniel behind and hope no one else picked her.

On the way home, they stopped at a Dairy Queen in Fox Lake. Judy was as giddy as a child over the cocker spaniel, telling everyone in line that she was getting a new dog. "If you tell one more person, I'm going to have to put you back in the car," Ruthie warned.

Later that night, a woman from the rescue came to Judy's house. Judy passed with flying colors, and the little dog was hers. Her name was Lacey, and Judy spent the next week parading around her neighborhood bragging about her new companion.

The following weekend, Judy finally got the news she'd been waiting for. She'd hit her numbers for Heparin, and on the first Monday in May she was placed on the heart transplant list. It was thrilling news. She made the list as what was labeled a 1B, meaning she wasn't in the hospital but was on medication. In Judy's case, she could be home, but she was hooked up to a portable device that distributed her meds twenty-four hours a day. The highest priority for transplant was 1A, meaning hospitalized and on medication. The system is set up so sicker people get the first shot at an organ.

Her medical team was vague about the timing of the transplant. The availability of a matching donor, they warned, was hard to predict. "It could be a month, or it could be a year or more," they told her. The transplant team at Northwestern told Judy not to travel farther than an hour from the hospital. Judy already lived thirty minutes north, so her radius of travel was quite restricted. Once the call came in, she would need to be at the hospital as quickly as possible.

The United Network of Organ Sharing (UNOS) is the nonprofit that connects those waiting on organs with incoming donors. If

UNOS let Northwestern know there was a matching heart available for Judy, an entire transplant team would jump into action. But there were protocols to follow. The hospital wouldn't send the organ procurement team until all key players were at the hospital. Judy's health would also have to be checked to make sure there were no infections or complications. Northwestern's procurement team would then travel to the donor's hospital. The heart would have a four-hour window from extraction to transplant, so speed was crucial.

Rosemount, Minnesota

On the Monday after Mother's Day, Ben had a flight to catch back to Georgia. After spending much of the weekend with his mom and grandmother, he wanted to use the morning to catch up with friends. The plan was to meet his old high school pals, Richard Rivera and Josh Maldonado, at Josh's house. Ben kept his truck in Columbus, so he borrowed his mom's car to drive over. The trio stood about halfway up the driveway. They reminisced about their Bigfoot adventure and all the crazy parties and good times they'd shared.

After a lot of laughter and recounting teenage pranks, girlfriends, and other gags, the conversation got serious. Rivera was in the Army Reserve. Josh, who didn't know much about the military, turned to Ben with a question. "So, what exactly do you do, Ben?"

"I'm an Army Ranger."

"Well, what's an Army Ranger?"

Ben started to explain what he did as a Ranger, but he cautioned that there were things he couldn't talk about, like where he had been or where he was going.

"Whatever, dude. You're not that hardcore," Josh replied.

"I jump out of planes," Ben countered.

"No, you haven't. They only do that in the Air Force," Josh replied. "You're not as hardcore as Navy SEALs."

Ben smirked, confident in his status as a special operator and not wanting to argue with his friend any longer. What Josh sensed was that Ben loved his job and loved what he did. But Josh had the growing sense that Ben's job was dangerous. Josh was a very sensitive and very caring friend. The tone of their conversation changed, then Josh's face grew somber. "Seriously though, Ben, you shouldn't do that. You might die."

"I know my risks," Ben said.

Richard jumped into the conversation. He had been to Army basic training and had a full understanding of what Ben did. Yet he took sides with Maldonado.

"He's right, Ben," Richard said. "It's too dangerous. Do a different job in the Army. You should do something that'll get you ready for a career when you get out, like me."

"Fuck that. I want to serve our country," Ben replied. "I'm a real patriot. If you're not in combat, you're not a real patriot."

"Dude, it'll probably mean your life someday," said Richard.

"Maybe," conceded Ben.

"You need to change your job and get the fuck out, because I know the way you think," Richard warned. "You're gonna put your life in some kind of crazy danger. You're not gonna think about yourself. You're gonna think about others."

Ben just stared at Richard with his arms crossed and shook his head, not in disagreement, but because he was bull-headed. Deep in his heart, Ben knew Richard was right, but he would never admit it. Besides, what could he possibly say?

"Dude, you live this crazy life," Richard continued. "You do all these crazy things, but you're gonna fucking die."

"If I fucking die, I don't give a damn. That's what I'm going to do," Ben replied stubbornly.

"You're not gonna make it back if you don't change your job," Richard warned.

"Whatever, dude. Yeah, I don't have a good feeling about this deployment, but I've gotta do what I've gotta do. This is my life."

The conversation wound down. Ben had a flight to catch. The three friends exchanged hugs. "I wish you the best," said Richard.

Ben hopped in his mom's car and headed home. After Ben and Richard left, Josh went inside, got on his computer, and Googled "Army Ranger." He was convinced he was right—Army Rangers couldn't be all that. But as he read about what Rangers *really* did, Josh realized his friend was indeed hardcore. *Oh my God, I'm so stupid,* Josh thought.

When Ben returned home, Jill was a bit peeved. He'd come home later than he said he would. Jill needed to stop by the bank on the way to drop her son at the airport, and now she didn't have time. "You write me this nice card and tell me how much you care," she said, "but you don't care enough to be home at the right time!"

"I'm sorry, Mom."

There was silence in the car as they drove north on Cedar Avenue toward Minneapolis–St. Paul International. But along the way, Jill's anger faded. "I'm sorry I yelled at you," she offered.

"It's okay, Mom."

Jill exited Interstate 494. Her path to Terminal 2 took them north on 34th Avenue past the main entrance to Fort Snelling National Cemetery. Ben looked at the white marble tombstones, thousands of them, like soldiers standing at eternal attention. Ay-Yi was buried there. For a moment, Ben thought about him and all the other service members buried just below, some who had fallen in combat and others who had served and then died in old age. It also reminded Ben that he had considered Fort Snelling before checking Arlington National Cemetery in his blue book.

A couple of blocks later, as they pulled up to the Humphrey Terminal, Jill realized she was saying good-bye to her son for what could be at least four months.

"You look good. You're handsome," she assured him.

Ben smiled, appreciating the compliment. He was wearing a white t-shirt, jeans, and an older pair of khaki Army-issued boots.

They each got out of the car. Ben grabbed his duffel bag from the trunk, and for a moment they stood facing each other in silence. Jill wanted to say something that would resonate with her son, something he would remember. "I'm proud of you," she said.

"Thanks, Mom," Ben said. He set down the duffel and wrapped his arms around her.

"Call me when you can," she said.

"I will."

Jill got back in her car and watched as Ben headed toward the terminal's sliding glass doors. She never took her eyes off him. She was comforted by his familiar gait, which was just the same as when he was little. Every time she dropped him off like this, she would follow him with her eyes for as long as she could. She would even watch him through the glass after he was inside the airport. But on this day, the glare from the sun was too bright; the moment Ben walked through the glass doors, he disappeared in a flash of light. Jill craned her neck to catch a glimpse of him, but she couldn't find him. Ben was gone.

Normally, Jill might wait a few weeks until Ben called home, but he phoned the next day with heart-wrenching news. His close friend Ryan McGhee had been killed in Iraq. Any hesitation or concern over his deployment was gone from his voice. "This is a game changer, Mom. It's game on, motherfuckers."

Ryan's death got a lot of Rangers fired up. He was killed on May 13, 2009, while on a mission targeting a weapons facilitator in central Iraq. A bullet found its way between his armored plates and into his abdomen. He was on his fourth deployment, with three before to Afghanistan, where Ben and Charlie Company were now heading. Ben would leave with a heavy heart at the loss of his friend.

Fort Benning, Georgia

Charlie Company's First, Second, and Third Platoons were getting ready to deploy. The First and Second were going to Kandahar Air Base, while Ben's Third Platoon would be assigned to Camp Leatherneck.

Everyone, including Ben, was plunking down their gear and hanging around the terminal, anticipating what would be a long C-17 flight to Germany and on to Afghanistan. There were a limited number of seats. Most of the Rangers were scattered across the floor, propping themselves up on their bags. Ben dropped his gear, walked away, and returned to find Sergeant Morgan Garrett sitting next to his stuff.

"Look, man," Garrett offered, "I'm sorry again about what happened back in RIP."

"Hey, don't worry about it," Ben replied, waving him off. It had been more than two years since their falling out during Ranger Indoctrination, and Ben was over it.

"No, I mean it," Garrett persisted. "I know you caught a lot of shit. I know the sergeant really laid into you pretty hard."

"Yeah, he did," Ben recalled, that familiar smirk coming across his face.

"Well, I want you to know I never said anything to anybody. I never told anybody it was you."

"I know," said Ben, nodding and smiling.

Garrett returned his grin. "I appreciate that," he said.

Charlie Company left Fort Benning on C-17s, stopping over in Germany before their final destination. Their focus would be on Helmand Province, a dangerous place still very much controlled by the Taliban. War in Afghanistan was about to escalate, and Ben and his fellow Rangers would soon find themselves right in the middle of it.

PART

III

Camp Leatherneck

In May 2009, Charlie Company's Third Platoon arrived in Helmand Province in Southern Afghanistan. The platoon's base of operation, Camp Leatherneck, was the US Marine name for what the Brits had originally established as Camp Bastion. Leatherneck was still under construction in spring 2009 as troop levels were increasing in support of NATO's International Security Assistance Force. As part of that buildup, the First Marine Expeditionary Force had already taken over the base. The move was part of a change in strategy from counterterrorism to counterinsurgency. The idea was to place troops near civilians to protect residents from the Taliban and build their trust. The alternative had been chasing the Taliban and Al-Qaeda through deserts, mountains, and remote valleys.

20/05/2009

Ben smiles while sitting in the back of a Humvee shortly after arriving at Camp Leatherneck in Afghanistan. Early on in the deployment, Rangers were still setting up their quarters and getting used to the harsh conditions.

Ben and his fellow Rangers had grown used to better-than-expected living quarters on their most recent deployments. Leatherneck was a step down. The section of the base where Third Platoon was assigned was being built for American special operations use. They were the first Rangers to arrive under the buildup and would serve under a joint special operations group dubbed Task Force South. They lived in what they referred to as Alaskan tents, inflatable yet rigid canvas and plastic structures. The tents were big enough to sleep a squad—roughly ten to fifteen guys—under one roof. Squad leaders, team leaders, and specialists like Ben got their own beds. The privates got bunk beds. The beds were brand new, which was a small consolation in otherwise challenging conditions.

They had air-conditioning, but it failed if they cranked it up too high (a common occurrence in the heat, which often hit 120 degrees). Army Rangers are a clever and resourceful bunch, so a few of the guys MacGyvered a system using plastic water bottles. After cutting the bottoms and tops out and taping the tubes end to end, they positioned the homemade ducts over their bunks so cool air would blow directly on their faces.

There were some commodities at Leatherneck that were easy to come by. Rangers had access to big flat-screen TVs, enough to have one per tent. Some of the guys had fifty- and even sixty-inch plasmas. They brought their own Xboxes and PlayStations and spent the first few days rigging up their AV entertainment. It was strange what was abundant and what wasn't. Most guys only had two pairs of pants for the entire deployment, but huge flat-screen TVs and energy drinks were in virtually endless supply.

The energy drink, known as Rip It, came in short cans about half the size of a twelve-ounce soda. They became quickly popular with the Rangers—it was too hot to drink coffee—but sometimes the caffeine-laced freebies became too much of a good thing. Before a briefing, one of the squad leaders had consumed too many Rip Its. His hand—and the laser pointer he held—shook uncontrollably as he tried to describe a target on a map, drawing snickers from his audience.

While the Rangers were missing a few creature comforts, Third Platoon had everything needed to operate militarily. Previous deployments to Baghdad had them nestled into neighborhoods. But Leatherneck was a massive base in the middle of the desert with nothing around for miles. That was good for security because soldiers would see any attack coming from a great distance.

A few weeks into the deployment, there was a huge dust storm that knocked over the portable toilets next to the operations center. This being the middle of the desert, there were no hoses to wash them off. When they were set back up, they reeked. The feces-covered plastic huts baked in the sun. Days passed, yet the smell from the porta-potties did not diminish. Local Afghans came about once a week to service them, but it was never enough. The smell would find the Rangers and crawl into their nostrils.

All the water they drank was bottled and delivered on countless pallets. There was no potable running water on base. Local Afghans were paid to truck in water and fill up tanks that fed the showers. There was also a trough sink Rangers could shave in. The shower tent had a metal frame and vinyl shower curtains that separated the stalls. The shower knob was on and off only; there was no temperature control. Whatever temperature the water was that day, was what the Rangers got. In the early days, when the logistics guys were leery of letting the Afghans onto the base to fill up the tanks, they sometimes ran out of shower water entirely. Ben once walked to the shower and found that nothing came out from the tap. Improvising, he poured a couple of bottles of water over his head, soaped up, and shampooed. He used another few bottles to rinse off.

The sand there, which the soldiers called moon dust, was every-where and got into everything. It was unlike sand found anywhere on US beaches. The sand in Helmand Province was a fine, chalky dust. It got inside their boots and clothes and covered their vehicles, which would get stuck in the dust. It could be humorous or annoying, depending on the day a soldier was having.

Ben, along with Private Sean Scappaticci and Specialist Roy Suarez, was now part of a three-man machine gun team assigned to the platoon's weapons squad. They carried the Mark 48 or Mk 48 machine gun, which fires a 7.62 x 51mm NATO cartridge. While it's considered a lightweight weapon, it weighs more than eighteen pounds, a heavy load on long treks in one-hundred-degree heat. Being part of the team meant knowing the gun inside and out. An NCO who'd once been on the machine gun team told men, "Treat it like a lady, and she'll be good to you."

Machine gun team members carried six hundred rounds of ammunition on average. Ben was generally the ammo bearer. Suarez, the team leader, was a pit bull—loyal and determined. Scappaticci, a schemer from Colorado, was the gunner.

Even with six hundred rounds, the ammo can go fast. The Mk 48 is capable of firing more than seven hundred rounds per minute, with an effective range of just over eight hundred meters. In the wide-open spaces of the Helmand River Valley, that would prove critical.

Compared to their last two deployments to Iraq, this one wasn't as busy. For a variety of reasons, their mission rate was much lower. The original plan for the deployment had Third Platoon set up at Leatherneck as a ground assault force. They were supposed to take Stryker vehicles outside the base to hit targets within driving distance. Charlie Company's First and Second Platoons, which were based at Kandahar, would be more of a helicopter assault force. But gaining access to targets by ground wasn't as easy as task force leaders thought it would be. And with a growing concern over IEDs and roadside bombs in Helmand Province, the ground force plan was soon scrapped.

The 160th SOAR, known as the Night Stalkers, flew the MH-47 Chinooks that carried Rangers and other special operators on their missions. They were based at Kandahar; there were no helicopters for the Rangers at Leatherneck. Charlie Company's focus shifted to Kandahar so completely that company commander Captain Don

Kingston moved his quarters from Leatherneck to Kandahar, because that's where the action was. That left Ben and the rest of Third Platoon in a pickle. Why should leadership send helicopters to Leatherneck when there were already two Ranger platoons at Kandahar ready to go? What it meant for Ben and Third Platoon was a much slower deployment.

Ben was given the job of whipping the privates into better physical shape. Some of the younger guys had grown a bit lazy and were even struggling to pass the PT test necessary to go to Ranger School. Over a few weeks, Ben helped get most of them into better shape, a big task considering a gym hadn't yet been set up at the base. They had to make do with two barbells and some extra weights. They bench-pressed lying on MRE boxes. It was challenging—they'd push the bar up and the MRE boxes would crumple and sink. By June better equipment arrived, and Ben found himself working out daily, getting pumped up, then tanning himself under the Afghan sun. He wrote to his mom:

> My jacked and tan program is in full swing, and I'm definitely getting results. I don't know how much the girls can love me any more than they already do lol, but I guess I'll find out when I come back home again.

To maximize his fitness program, Ben needed quality protein, but he didn't like what they served at the DFAC. He wrote home asking his mom for oatmeal, tuna and chicken foil packets, peanuts, cashews, peanut butter, beef jerky, and Chex mix.

One of the things Ben missed most was chew or dip. His brand of choice at the time was Copenhagen whiskey blend, but on deployment he'd take whatever he could get. Tobacco was extremely hard to come by in Afghanistan. He and many of the others were stunned when Company Commander Captain Don Kingston walked in with eight hundred dollars' worth of Copenhagen and started handing it out.

Kingston's in-laws and their church friends in Springfield, Virginia, were not only very supportive of Kingston but also all the men who served under him in Charlie Company. They took up a collection with the intention of sending some care packages of snacks or toiletries. But when Kingston's mother-in-law asked what he needed, he told her the guys were really craving dip.

After he'd explained what dip was and where to find it, a group of church ladies, most in their seventies, headed to a warehouse retailer to buy as much Copenhagen as they could for seven hundred dollars. As they stood in the checkout line, another shopper overheard them chatting and asked what all the chewing tobacco was for. When he heard it was going to soldiers stationed overseas, the eavesdropper chipped in another hundred dollars for even more Copenhagen. The church ladies packed up the rolls of the hockey puck–shaped canisters and shipped them to Afghanistan. Ben grinned ear to ear when the delivery arrived.

With extra time on their hands, the guys talked about what they would do when they got out. Ben was eligible to leave the Army in the fall, and he was leaning in that direction. He thought Afghanistan, and especially Leatherneck, "was a shit hole." But he told his mom he was "going one day at a time, keeping his eyes on the horizon, knowing this is my last one."

Ben was thinking about college, or maybe doing some defense contract or security contract work. He'd heard stories of other special operators making six-figure salaries. He'd also been talking with Jenny Boll's dad, Dave, about getting a job as a police officer in the Twin Cities or Florida. Ben had also plotted with his friend platoon medic Ryan Walker to buy a house in the Tampa area together, get college degrees, then open a gym. Ben was also making travel plans. He and Ryan Lundeby had bought tickets to Australia. They were going in September, after they returned home.

When Third Platoon did get an operation, nearly everything they rolled out on involved helicopters. They were generally dropped a few kilometers from their target, allowing them to quietly approach on foot in darkness. In Afghanistan they always had the feeling they were being watched. There were sometimes what looked like farmers in the fields in the middle of the night. Rangers quickly realized these weren't farmers at all; they were lookouts. They nicknamed this the "neighborhood watch program."

Third Platoon/Charlie Company Rangers run for the back door of a Chinook during their summer 2009 deployment to Helmand Province. For logistical reasons, Ben's Third Platoon was not as busy as they had been in Iraq.

The terrain in Helmand Province, coupled with the experience of the Taliban fighters, didn't allow for the element of surprise they enjoyed in Iraq. The land was more open and more rural, and required them to spend more time on foot engaging the enemy. But things remained slow. By early July, Third Platoon had completed just a handful of missions.

It was hard enough to sleep at night in the heat. And when they were operating, Rangers usually slept during the day, when it was even hotter. Whether it was day or night, Ben's sleep was increasingly filled with dreams about Brittney. He couldn't get her off his mind. He told his mom about his dreams in a letter and urged her to get Brittney to write to him, though he also shared his concern that doing so might disrupt her life.

Around this time, Ben also started reading a book. *The Road to Unafraid* was by another Ranger, Jeff Struecker, one of the key figures in the mission that inspired the movie *Black Hawk Down*. Struecker was a sergeant sent in a Humvee with a team to rescue and relieve the first special operators involved in the 1993 raid in Mogadishu, Somalia. He later became a chaplain in the Ranger Regiment. Ben ate up every page of the book, especially the parts that intertwined Struecker's Ranger service and his maturing walk with Jesus Christ. The memoir quickly found a special place in Ben's heart.

Highland Park, Illinois

By late May, Chicago had blossomed into a beautiful early summer. Everything outside was lush, and Judy was finally getting out more after a winter and spring that left her feeling as if she were under house arrest.

Now on the waiting list for a heart transplant, Judy was limited to traveling within a sixty-minute radius of Northwestern Memorial. On a visit to friends in Highland Park, about a fifteen-minute drive north, she said, "I've always got my bag packed and ready to go. I feel like a pregnant lady—I'm ready to pop any day!"

Just then, her phone went off. It was Northwestern calling to tell her she was the backup recipient for an inbound heart. The primary recipient—who had a higher ranking on the list and was a better match than Judy—was also on the way to the hospital. Because hearts are so rare and valuable, the logistics always include a backup recipient. It suddenly hit Judy that she was getting very close. Being the backup tonight meant she was on their radar. Judy hopped into her car and started heading toward Winnetka to pick up her bag. But before she could get there, the hospital called again to say the primary recipient was already at the hospital, and that Judy should stay home but keep her phone close.

After several hours, Judy called the hospital to follow up. Because of HIPPA laws, they could tell her very little, other than that the operation had been a success. That was a bit of comfort to Judy. She was now one person closer to getting a heart.

St. Louis Park, Minnesota

On July 1, Jill Stephenson drove from Rosemount to her hometown of St. Louis Park to attend a wake for one of her former teachers. With all the noise in the crowded funeral home, Jill didn't hear her phone ringing. When she finally looked down to check it, she felt sick to her stomach. She could tell by the line of zeros in the caller ID she'd just missed Ben's call from Afghanistan. She made sure she had her phone in her hand and that the ringer was on its loudest setting, even in a wake, so she wouldn't miss him again. She stared at the phone, willing it to ring. *Come on! Call me back, Ben. Call me back.* The mother-son telepathy must've worked, because minutes later, Ben called back. Jill moved away from the crowded room to answer the phone. They talked for about thirty minutes. Ben sounded somber, stressed, and down. He couldn't give his mom any details, but he said things were as difficult and challenging as they thought they were going to be. He told her how hot it was and how little sleep he was getting. He said the air-conditioning wasn't quite good enough, and their only means of cooling off was to pour lukewarm bottles of water over their heads. Jill struggled to find words to comfort her son, having no idea what he was really facing.

Ben's voice rose with enthusiasm when he told his mom he was reading a new book. The book, he told her, was *The Road to Unafraid* by Jeff Struecker, and he liked it as much as Chuck Holton's *A More Elite Soldier.* Jill saw this as a way to connect with Ben, and she agreed to get a copy and read it herself so they could discuss it.

When Ben suddenly had to go, Jill said, "I love you, Ben. I'm here anytime you can reach out. People are praying for you. I'm proud of you. Hang in there."

"I love you too, Mom."

Camp Leatherneck

"You're going to change the world this summer, and it starts this morning. The United States and the world are watching," Lieutenant Colonel Christian Cabaniss, Commander of the 2nd Battalion, 8th Marines, told his warriors.

The summer of 2009 in Afghanistan earned the nickname "Summer of Decision." A Marine campaign was sweeping across the country, a last-ditch effort to control the country village to village. The philosophy was different now, changing from counterterrorism to counterinsurgency. Instead of just fighting and killing terrorists, military leaders were moving to "clear, hold, build, and transfer" the country back to what they hoped would be a stable government.

On July 2, about four thousand Marines began what was dubbed Operation Khanjar. British troops had been fighting in Helmand Province since 2006 and were at a standstill. The Marines began their push by helicopter and Humvee south from Leatherneck, rolling into three Taliban strongholds: Nawa-I-Barakzayi, Garmser, and Khanashin farther south. The Brits were assigned to take Lashkar Gah. The fighting was intense. The Afghan presidential election was slated for August 20, little more than a month away. In that small window of time, Marines were trying to secure Helmand Province, a place that for years had been a Taliban stronghold.

Rosemount, Minnesota

The next day, Jill reflected on the events from exactly one year before. She and her dad had traveled to Columbus, Georgia, for Ben's Ranger School graduation. She was so incredibly proud of him that day. Before going to bed that night, she e-mailed Ben to wish him a happy Independence Day. Reflecting on that Ranger School graduation ceremony, she wrote:

> That was far and away one of the coolest, best, patriotic, most proud times of my entire life. Thank you so much for that experience, Ben. YOU ROCK! It gave me goosebumps as it happened, and it did again when I was thinking about it today. Be proud of yourself. You make your momma so proud! Happy 4th of July! Love you lots!
>
> Mother

Winnetka, Illinois

Judy Meikle went to Winnetka's Independence Day parade and celebration as she had every one of her now fifty-seven years. The parade—a colorful small-town collection of Boy Scouts, local civic organizations, politicians, and others—marched east on Elm Street. They stepped past the quaint shops of downtown Winnetka, across Green Bay Road, over the Metra railroad tracks, and finally to the Village Green. The marchers came to rest before a white stone war memorial rising from the west side of the park. Judy stood on the big front porch of a friend's home just across the street at the corner of Maple and Elm, taking in the Sousa music and announcements over the not-so-distant loudspeakers. After the reading of the Declaration of Independence, Judy crossed Maple Street to watch the running races. Determined suburban kids sprinted across the green for bragging rights in this village of about thirteen thousand people.

Judy's favorite race was the three-year-old-and-under category— moms at one end, dads at the other. The air horn blows, signaling the start, and panicked toddlers run in every direction. Some crash to their bottoms, some fall on their faces, some stand frozen, and some cry. Fewer still make it to the finish line. Legends are born.

Kandahar Air Base

Just before sunset each night, Ranger leadership—split between Kandahar and Leatherneck—held video conferences to discuss what was going on across southern Afghanistan. The teleconference from the Joint Operations Center (JOC), often included intelligence officers and Ranger leadership like 3rd Ranger Battalion Commander Lieutenant Colonel Dan Walrath and Charlie Company Commander Captain Don Kingston.

Most of the Ranger ops were planned from Kandahar. Lieutenant Colonel Walrath and his staff would meet with a variety of contributors, including members of the intelligence community, to determine targets or opportunities that could lead to a mission. They would then decide who would handle the job and start taking steps to make it happen.

Charlie Company's First and Second Platoons, which were based at Kandahar, had been getting the lion's share of operations. Back at Leatherneck, Third Platoon was collectively feeling a little left out. But in early July 2009, that changed. An intelligence officer reported they were again watching the movements of a high-value Taliban leadership target, key in the group's architecture. His code name was YETI. Task Force South special operators had tried to capture him three times before, but now intelligence believed he was in Garmser District, specifically the Laki area. When operators try but fail to capture or kill a target, they roll another number after his code name for the next mission. This would be their fourth attempt going after him, so the upcoming operation was dubbed YETI 4.

Electronic surveillance in Helmand Province was extremely difficult, especially in rural Garmser District, where there was little or no cell phone service. Instead, intelligence personnel focused on "pattern of life" intelligence, tracking a target's movements from a variety of sources, including people on the ground and aircraft overhead, both manned and unmanned. By early July, they had as good an intelligence picture as they could hope to gather on YETI. They stayed on top of the Taliban leader nearly daily. On July 8, a manned intelligence, surveillance, and reconnaissance (ISR) aircraft flew above the target and confirmed the Taliban leader had been in the area for the last few days.

The operation plan required the Rangers to head south from Leatherneck to Garmser District. Their target was about sixty-six miles north of the Pakistani border, an entry point for weapons smuggling for the Taliban. Where they were headed was well south of where Americans had been operating, and there were many risks involved in going there. Over the last week, Marines had set up an outpost at a schoolhouse about ten kilometers north of their target. Leaders felt that would be the best location to stage the mission from.

The plan was also a little more passive than the Rangers were used to. They intended to establish blocking positions around a one-square-kilometer area where they believed the Taliban leader was hiding out. When he surfaced, they would move in and capture him. They weren't going to raid a specific compound. They were going out to stage, wait, and act on their target, if and when they identified him.

Although there was no disagreement that YETI needed to be

captured, Captain Kingston wasn't convinced the conditions were right. But in the end, despite his reservations, he was overruled. The determination was made that this was as good an opportunity as they might get. Knowing the mission was moving forward and the time was now, Captain Kingston told First Sergeant Greg Knight he wanted him to go along. Knight's experience, leadership, and battle hardiness would come in handy. He'd been bouncing back and forth between Leatherneck and Kandahar and would now head back to Leatherneck to join Ben's Third Platoon. Getting aboard the MH-47s with him at Kandahar was battalion surgeon Captain Jay McKenna. Meanwhile, three Rangers from the Regimental Reconnaissance Company, along with a tandem of Ranger snipers—Sergeants Mark Pendleton and Nick Irving—had already been sent ahead to the staging area.

Camp Leatherneck

In the predawn darkness of July 9, Charlie Company's Third Platoon walked out of the ready room at Leatherneck and climbed aboard a fleet of Stryker vehicles for a short ride to the landing zone. Two Chinooks that had flown from Kandahar were waiting. Ben climbed onto the Stryker and took a spot on top, balancing himself on the surface of the armored vehicle. Normally in a combat situation, soldiers ride inside the Stryker. But because they were traveling just a short distance to the landing pad inside the base, several of the Rangers rode on top.

What they didn't know was that the driver of the Stryker was brand new, a private who was admittedly "conducting a task above his abilities." Because of a miscalculation, the Stryker Ben was riding on went off the road, hit a ditch, and nearly rolled over. Rangers were thrown about, and the guys riding up top hung on for dear life. Curses flew like grenades, and pulses skyrocketed. Fortunately, the driver got the vehicle under control. Had the Stryker rolled, the massive armored vehicle could've killed or seriously injured those on top, including

Ben. When they arrived at the airfield and the waiting choppers, Ben was livid. He grabbed the private responsible, pulling him face to face, and read him the riot act.

The Rangers started to climb aboard the big double-rotor choppers. It was a tight fit getting everyone aboard with weapons and packs. Not knowing how long they might be gone, the Rangers brought several days of MREs and other food items with them.

The assault force was a complex mesh of specialists: two federal law enforcement agents; at least five soldiers from the Afghan National Army, now under Ranger tutelage; Air Force J-TACS; snipers; medics; a K9 and his handler; and a combat photographer. The manifest contained sixty-nine names in total.

Just as they were about to take off, one of the Rangers got word he wouldn't be going. Fire support officer Captain Lane Sandifer was in full battle gear, prepared to go, but a phone call from the JOC in Kandahar changed that: "Sandifer, get on the helicopter, but when the platoon gets dropped off, stay on the chopper. We're bringing you back to Kandahar to work the day Fire Desk." There weren't enough fire support officers at the JOC to cover the day shift the next day. The battalion fire support officer worked at night and knew YETI 4 could take the Rangers into the daylight hours. He needed someone to relieve him, so Sandifer was a scratch. His role would still be important, but he wouldn't be on the ground.

When the full complement was aboard, the Chinooks took off into the darkness, flying south to their drop-off point, a small agrarian area in Garmser District called Mian Poshteh. The choppers flew between the cities of Lashkar Gah to the east and Marjah to the west, heading to a place in Helmand Province few Americans had ever been.

Ben hung tight on the wall of the 47. The double giant rotors washed out any sounds inside the chopper. His best friends were right here with him—Lundeby, Innis, Walker, Vanderhule. His machine gun team of Suarez and Scappaticci were there as well. He looked around at all the guys, studying their faces—they were his brothers. They were family.

Mian Poshteh, Helmand Province

In the still black of early morning, the choppers descended onto what looked like a lunar landscape. Their landing zone was the edge of the Helmand Desert, just east of the more fertile Helmand River Valley. The powdery sand blown up by the landing 47s snowed down on the Rangers as they exited the rear ramp. Marines nearby had been involved in fierce fighting on the agricultural plain that made up the Helmand River Valley. That fertile plain was about a mile wide and fed by a series of canals that diverted off the main river channel and through the valley. The canal system, built by Americans in the 1950s, allowed precious water to flow into and around the patchwork of farm fields. There was a main canal and many sub-canals that hydrated what would otherwise be an inhospitable landscape. Those canals then gave way to a series of drainage ditches that allowed the excess water to flow back into the Helmand River.

One week earlier, on July 2, the men of the 2nd Marine Expeditionary Brigade RCT 2nd Battalion 8th Marines Echo Company had stepped off their helicopters at Mian Poshteh. They found a small market town on the main canal, the shops little more than mud-walled storage rooms with shaded fronts. The Marines were immediately met by Taliban fire from the nearby schoolhouse. They took cover in the bazaar and behind canal embankments and mounted their own assault. The next day, they captured the schoolhouse and made it their outpost. But despite this foothold, they were virtually surrounded. The Taliban still had strongholds just a few miles away, to the north and south. These two fronts were the source of intense daily firefights.

The primitive schoolhouse with whitewashed mud walls had a long, narrow hallway down the middle. On either side of the hallway were small classrooms. Marines had sandbagged the large windows of those classrooms for protection. The dark green sandbags were stacked high in the crude windows, leaving little view out of the building but offering protection from the small arms fire and rocket-propelled grenades (RPGs) that hit them daily. The Marines would later name this place Combat Outpost Sharp or COP Sharp, after a young Marine who had died days before. On July 2, Lance Corporal Charles "Seth" Sharp, a twenty-year-old from Adairsville, Georgia, was killed after getting shot in the neck during a firefight.

When Ben and the other Rangers walked in, they found battle-weary Marines sleeping on dirt floors. The place smelled terrible. Rangers from Third Platoon also found some familiar faces. Sergeants Nick Irving and Mark Pendleton, both snipers from Headquarters Company, and three recon (RECCE) Rangers had arrived the day before to join them for their operation. Most of Third Platoon had seen the recon guys around before, but they didn't normally operate with them. Irving and Pendleton said they'd already seen action that morning, each of them scoring a kill as they helped the Marines defend their outpost. Irving was African American, had grown up in the Washington, DC, area, and had added a lot of extra muscle to his five-six frame. Pendleton had earned the nickname P-Murder.

The Marines had been under fire nearly every morning since taking over the schoolhouse. They still didn't have complete control of the area. Marines told the Rangers that it had taken them three days to advance eight hundred meters here under intense fighting. The Rangers got a taste of this during their short visit when a group of them standing outside the schoolhouse had to move inside when they started taking small arms and RPG fire.

Some of the Rangers took notice of the difficult conditions the Marines were living in. "When do you guys get out of here?" asked one Ranger.

"October."

"No, not your deployment. When do you get out of this place here?"

"October."

"All the respect in the world for you guys," the Ranger said, and others nodded in agreement.

Ben and other Rangers get some rest outside the Marines' schoolhouse at Mian Poshteh before heading out later that night on a complicated mission dubbed YETI 4.

As the sun in Mian Poshteh climbed nearly straight overhead, the heat became unbearable. Ben tried to get some rest before what they all knew could be one of the biggest and most dangerous operations of their careers. That weighed on Ben's mind, and he remembered the conversations back home he'd had with both his mom and his friends, Richard Rivera and Josh Maldonado. This was the kind of op he had been talking about with them. Ben was also drinking water to make sure he was fully hydrated. Other Rangers slept outside under Marine vehicles in the sand, finding any sort of shade they could. There were a few trees and some thorny bushes but little else to provide protection from the blazing sun.

The Rangers knew this wasn't their turf, and that bringing in more than sixty guys was something of an intrusion. But the 160th had just air dropped a few things for the Rangers, including MREs, Gatorade, Pop-Tarts, and Famous Amos cookies. Marines there had been living on a steady diet of MREs for more than a week. The Rangers were gathered by themselves eating their food when a few of the jarheads approached them. "Would you guys mind if we maybe had a Gatorade?" one Marine shyly inquired.

"Oh, hell no! Go right ahead," a Ranger offered. "All that stuff is for all of us. Help yourself."

The Rangers wouldn't even be there a full day, so their conversations quickly turned to business. Leadership discussed the operation, spending hours looking at maps of the Laki area, where they were headed. In the planning stages days before, they had discussed splitting up the assault force. It wasn't the way they normally operated, but given that the HVT could only be contained to a general area, they decided to separate into four squads.

One discussion centered on snipers in the area. The Marines were having a hell of a time with them. Someone mentioned the possibility of a Chechen sniper working for the Taliban in the area. There were various theories as to who it might be. One suggested it was a veteran of the war with the Soviets in the eighties who had never gone home. A Marine shared that they had heard the guy had somewhere in the neighborhood of three hundred kills. Ben shook his head in disbelief. Ranger sniper Nick Irving, himself red hot on this deployment, found the claim far-fetched. Marines also heard reports that suggested the "Chechen" was an incredibly unlikely persona—a sixteen-year-old girl who was a crack shot. That too caused heads to shake. No matter who it was, snipers could create major problems for Marines and Rangers alike.

Heading South

The sun finally retreated over the Helmand River, bringing relief. The falling darkness also gave the Rangers the window of cover they needed to operate.

At about 10:15 p.m., the Ranger assault force filed out of the schoolhouse. The Marines had agreed to drive them farther south, about ten kilometers to their objective. Because of a concern about IEDs along the canal road through the center of Garmser District, the Marines refused to travel that way. The Rangers also wanted to avoid any populated areas on their way to the Laki area so as not to alert Taliban lookouts. The plan was to head to the east into the desert, turn to the south, then leave the Rangers to walk a few kilometers to their target. One Marine driver shook his head in disbelief about where they were headed. "*We* won't even go in that area yet," he shared.

The Rangers had one immediate logistical problem: the armored vehicles that were available to take them to Laki would only hold about half of the assault force. Marines had advised mission planners back at Kandahar that they could do the trip in one leg, and that it wouldn't take long. In the end, both of those estimates were incorrect and ended up costing the Rangers hours of precious time and darkness.

The Marine vehicles would have to make two trips. That would leave half the assault force waiting in the darkness of the desert for the second wave to arrive. This time of year in southern Afghanistan, darkness fell a few minutes before 8:00 p.m. First twilight was remarkably early, about 4:45 a.m., with a sunrise at 5:15 a.m. That meant a fighting force that did its work under the cover of darkness would likely be running out of it by the time they were ready to operate.

The first half of the assault force rambled away from the schoolhouse. Once in the desert, the armored vehicles turned to the south. They kept lights out for security, so the drivers had to go very slowly to avoid hazards. From the elevation of the desert, the Rangers could see sporadic lights from the farming communities of the Helmand River Valley below and to their right. A lot of the guys used the drive down to sleep, knowing a long day was ahead of them. From the schoolhouse to the drop-off point, it took about an hour. Once the first group got dropped near a dune, it seemed like an eternity until the next group arrived. They waited for about two hours. Even at night it was hot and dry, and the Rangers were already draining their Camelbaks. The assault force still had a long walk to get into position.

South of Mian Poshteh, Garmser District grows more arid. Deciduous trees struggle to survive. Laki, the Rangers' destination, is one of the oldest communities in the district. It's also the last place south along the Helmand River where the soil is productively fertile.

By the time the assault force was reunited, they were more than seventy strong. They were still covered by darkness, but their watches told them that wouldn't last long. They had extraordinary challenges in front of them, and they were running out of time.

Laki, Helmand Province

Before they walked in, assault force leaders—including First Sergeant Knight; the company's executive officer, Justin Johanson; platoon leader Dan Krueger; and Air Force JTAC Stan House—gathered in a "commanders' huddle" to discuss last-minute strategy. House, whose job it was to communicate with support aircraft, reported that he had no communication with any nearby aircraft. They were starting their operation with no air support.

Knight seemed undeterred. "It takes a hell of a lot to kick a Ranger platoon off target," Knight replied, saying they were going in anyway. House hoped some form of aircraft would come online soon.

The assault force began their walk west. About six dozen men moved almost silently, the only sounds the grinding of their boots under the fine sandy loam and the swing of their packs rhythmically bouncing against their bodies. They moved quickly and efficiently. They needed to cover about three kilometers to reach their objective. As they marched, a glowing band of blue and orange spread on the horizon behind them, signaling the fast-approaching sunrise.

In the now bluish early morning light, the Rangers started to see shapes of crude buildings in the distance—single-story homes, some with multiple outbuildings and walled-in courtyards. A handful of these mud-walled homes had been here for hundreds of years. Some compound walls stood more than eight feet high, providing security from generations of desert robbers and raiders and now protection from war.

The Rangers descended a gradual ridge from the desert down about fifty meters to a farming valley. The area was nearly completely agricultural, farm fields cut and divided by a lattice of canals and drainage ditches that got increasingly smaller. Those ditches would prove critical to the Rangers as they moved across a landscape that otherwise provided few places to hide. The most prominent summer crop here was corn, but farther to the west there were marijuana fields. Rumors of endless fields of opium poppies were true, but not now in July. Poppies along with wheat were a winter crop in the Helmand Valley.

As the sand and gravel gave way to cultivated fields, the assault force split into four squads. Their plan was to isolate a one-square-kilometer area around their target with four different Ranger elements in strategic "blocking" positions. The plan called for all the Ranger groups to be in place and set up under the cover of darkness, but it was now 5:38 a.m. Dawn was spreading over the vast valley.

Intelligence sources had given the Rangers a general area where the Taliban leader would be. It wasn't a specific building, and that made things more difficult. They also reported that their target was known to ride a white motorbike. The hope was that one of the teams would identify YETI, then other squads would move in to help capture him, preferably alive. It was a matter of being in the right place at the right time.

The squads, now diverging, disappeared from one another's sight. They were in the heart of this farming community now, walking up to various compounds and past homes built from the mud of the land. Early-rising Afghans looked at them with wide eyes. Rangers could see shock on their faces. *This can't be good,* company medic Michael Melvin thought. Some of these Afghans in remote Laki Village might never have seen a Westerner before.

Captain Johanson and First Sergeant Knight led Charlie Company's Third Squad, which was now on its own. The officer and NCO remained calm, even though they knew time had gotten away from them. Knight told his men to be ready for anything. But while he was calm, a growing sense of urgency and uneasiness blanketed the platoon. Charlie Company had operated in daylight before, but usually because one of their nighttime operations had gone into overtime. This time, they were beginning at dawn.

JTAC Stan House was too preoccupied trying to contact aircraft to be worried about that. The first asset he checked on was a B-1 bomber. That was somewhat unusual for a Ranger assault force, as it wasn't the ideal aircraft for close air support. An A-10, Apache, or Cobra would've been preferable, something that could fire in close proximity to friendly forces. Still, it was an aircraft nonetheless. House couldn't see it; the aircraft was offset from their location and circling at twenty-seven thousand feet. He reported to leadership that it was now available.

Ben, with his machine gun team of Roy Suarez and Sean Scappaticci, was today attached to Second Squad. Their assignment was to go to the southwest side of the objective and hold that side of the perimeter. They had a bit farther to walk than the other squads. Suarez was the gun team leader and Scap the gunner. As the junior member of the squad, Scap carried the hefty Mk 48. Ben was the ammo bearer and lugged about six hundred rounds of linked 7.62 ammo in his pack. Along with Ben was the squad leader, Staff Sergeant Carl Benson. In the same group were Captain Krueger, Staff Sergeant Derrick Ball, and Specialist Erick Innis, toting his slightly smaller Mk 46 machine gun. Innis, like Ben, also carried about six hundred rounds of ammunition. Company Medic Michael Melvin was also with them.

As they moved toward the target area, they crossed small drainage ditches and canals. They walked up and over dirt roads and tried to parallel tree lines for cover. The single-story crude farmhouses and compounds were nearby but spread out.

Heading to the northwest side of the objective in a different group were Ranger snipers Nick Irving and Mark Pendleton, three recon Rangers (including their medic, Andrew Fink), and a combat photographer. Meanwhile, First and Third Squads were setting up their positions on the east side of the objective, training eyes on the target area and blocking roads in and out of the perimeter. They were ready to stop vehicles to make sure their HVT wasn't getting away, even though doing so in this kind of terrain could be extremely dangerous. The roads were raised above the fields, and going up onto a roadway could easily expose a soldier to enemy fire. Any of the squads might be tasked to rush up on the road to stop a vehicle.

At the southwest corner, Ben's heart was pounding from the brisk march. Buildings, once spread out, were now getting closer together. Ben and Innis noticed something disturbing. In the growing light they could see a military-aged man in the middle of a crop field watching them. *What is he doing out here at this hour?* Innis wondered. He wasn't working; he was just watching. After a few minutes, the man turned around and started running away from the Rangers. He was either scared or a lookout and on his way to report their location to Taliban leaders. Rules of engagement prevented the Rangers from shooting the man because he had no visible weapon.

Ben settled in with his gun team. They set up the Mk 48 and started to scan buildings to the northeast for any movement. Most of the guys below the rank of sergeant hadn't been fully briefed on the objective. But they knew that what they were doing out here now was out of the ordinary, even for Rangers.

Captain Krueger was growing more concerned because the squads weren't set as he wanted them. *This is going to get rather sporty pretty quick,* the officer thought.

Suddenly, over their headsets came a warning: "Keep your eyes and head on a swivel. Pay attention. They know we're here."

All four elements reported they were in position at 5:40 a.m. Ben, Scap, and Suarez had set up their machine gun on a road bordering a compound. By now light illuminated the pale structures of the Afghan farming community. The quiet of the early morning was suddenly interrupted by wailing. The Muslim morning prayer echoed from near and distant compounds.

Innis settled in along a mud wall, setting up his machine gun behind a bush. Nearby, Ben looked through the scope of his M4. About two hundred meters ahead of them on a building rooftop was a family of about eight, a mix of children, women, and teenage boys, but no men. *Have they gone to farm? Or are they hiding nearby, ready to fight?* Innis saw them too and watched them through his scope. He then realized his position wasn't very hidden as members of the family started to wave at him. Even without cell phones, it wouldn't be long before everyone in Laki knew they were there.

Joint Operations Center, Kandahar

Ranger leadership inside the JOC was watching the operation begin. Lieutenant Colonel Dan Walrath could be intimidating. Walrath was a man of few words, and when he spoke, officers under his command made damn sure they listened closely. Colonel Walrath was not the kind of guy you wanted to ask to repeat something. Walrath was also quite willing to strap on his helmet and go into combat, even as a lieutenant colonel and battalion commander. That willingness to enter the fight earned immediate respect from those who served under him.

Captain Sandifer, scratched from the mission itself, had just arrived at the JOC and got a briefing from the major who had worked the desk through the night. The JOC at Kandahar was the brain and nerve center not just for Rangers but for any special operators working in southern Afghanistan. Only those with secret clearance or better could get inside. The center was a long rectangular room with two rows of desks and tables. The furniture was primitive but functional, much of it built on site of two-by-fours and plywood.

While the furniture was simple, the technology was anything but. There were dozens of computers, more than a half dozen big screen TVs on the walls, phones that connected to just about anyone in the Defense Department, and radios in contact with everything flying over Afghanistan and the special operators on the ground. There were no windows, but the room was well lit. Members of the intelligence community were also present. There were sensitive discussions going on about Taliban leaders and other targets, the intelligence guys describing how they had been tracking these various individuals.

On those big flat-screens were live video feeds from surveillance aircraft, or "surveillance assets" as they were called in the JOC. At least two of these were now circling over the Rangers in Garmser District, keeping watch. The drones, either Predators or Reapers, were stealthy, and normally operated higher than ten thousand feet. Even Rangers on the ground below usually didn't notice their presence.

Captain Sandifer had a variety of attack aircraft at his fingertips to support the Ranger operation. Marine helicopters were at the ready, as were Air Force fighter jets. Sandifer spoke directly with pilots supporting the Ranger assault force. He now had fighter jets "on station," meaning they were cruising in a wide circle outside the target area but only with about an hour of fuel. A software program called Falconview revealed imagery of the target area. Sandifer also opened a chatroom that allowed him to communicate directly with people flying the drones back in the United States. Other chatrooms gave him data on air space safety and coordination, while a headset allowed him to speak directly with the radio and telephone operators (RTOs) on the ground. RTOs shadowed the commanding officers on the battlefield, allowing immediate communication with the JOC.

Among the others in the JOC were medical personnel who might need to advise a Ranger medic on the ground if a soldier was severely wounded and intelligence guys who could provide insight into identifying the Taliban target the Rangers were after.

Laki, Helmand Province

Ben looked over the Helmand River Valley now glowing in the morning sun. He had an uneasy feeling. Innis, a few feet away, was still unhappy with his cover. *This is not gonna be good,* he thought. Innis was considering moving when a shrill buzz interrupted his thoughts. First one small motorcycle sped by, then another and another, some with three men riding on a single bike. There were suddenly so many motorbikes it sounded like a swarm of bees. Rangers knew the average Afghan in an area like this couldn't afford a motorcycle. This was surely a sign the Taliban was nearby. They were rallying the troops, but none of the men appeared to be armed. The motorcycles disappeared up ahead, and things again grew quiet.

Then, just after 6:20 a.m., it started. *Pop, pop, pop, pop.* The crack of enemy AK fire resonated from various compounds and tree lines. The gunshots seemed to be coming from everywhere. Within a minute or so, three out of four Ranger positions around the village were under attack.

"We're in contact!" crackled a voice over the radio. The RTO with Captain Johanson got on the satellite radio to get word back to the JOC. "Troops in contact! We're taking fire!"

Everybody was in their own fight except for Ben's squad. He, Scap, and Suarez were scanning for targets, trying to figure out where the Taliban fire was coming from. They wondered who in their platoon was under fire as they listened to a flurry of activity unfold around them.

Recon Group

The Ranger recon team was approaching the northwest side of the target area. As they moved across an open field, Sergeant Nick Irving noticed a depression in the ground about six feet wide by three feet deep. With little other cover nearby, he quietly pointed to the hole as they walked by, his eyes suggesting it was a spot they could jump into if they came under fire.

Their group included three recon Rangers—Davis Johnson, Raymond Harrison and their medic, and Andrew Fink, who like Ben was from Minnesota. With them were two snipers from Headquarters Company, Irving and Pendleton, and a combat photographer. The recon group had ventured about a thousand meters from the nearest Ranger squad and had taken up a position in the middle of the field. They were supposed to report back that they were in position, but they were having trouble with the radio. They did their best to conceal themselves and through their scopes started to watch a group of buildings about eight hundred meters ahead of them. Pendleton pointed out a meeting involving what appeared to be a gathering of local elders. They all watched the early morning conference in silence until one of the recon guys decided he didn't like what he was seeing. "I got a bad juju 'bout this."

His gut feeling was right. Moments later, the dirt was bursting around them. They were under attack from a combination of small arms fire. The whizzing bullets flew at them from three directions. Irving remembered the hole he'd noted minutes before, and they all made a break for it. They dove in, bodies pressed on top of bodies. They started to return fire. Irving was at the bottom and at one point felt a searing pain in his neck. At first he thought he'd been hit, but then realized it was just a hot shell casing from one of his own guys above him laying down fire. They could also hear other firefights nearby and knew their Ranger brothers were dealing with the same thing. Irving wriggled his way past two others in the hole to the top of the pile to get a look around. About five hundred meters ahead and slightly to their right were three men just arriving on top of a building and setting up a large automatic weapon. Irving felt rounds exploding right in front of them, spraying dirt and debris in their faces. It was now clear to him they were in a chess match with a fellow sniper, and at this point, the enemy sniper had the upper hand.

The Taliban sniper was hard to pinpoint. There was so much fire going on around them that it was difficult to get a read on his exact location. Instead, Irving and Pendleton focused on the three men on the roof setting up the machine gun. Irving adjusted his body for a shot, careful not to expose himself. He pressed his SR-25 sniper rifle forward until it inched out of the hole. Taking a look through the scope, he could now make out the trio fidgeting with what appeared to be a tripod. He focused the crosshairs on one of the men and smoothly squeezed the trigger. He watched as the vapor trail of his bullet flew high and right. He adjusted, refocused, and fired again. This time he was on the mark, and one enemy fighter went down. Incredibly, the other two men didn't take cover and continued to set up the machine gun. Irving was now dialed in. He fired again and struck the second fighter, taking him out. The remaining Taliban warrior, witnessing two of his comrades drop at his side, picked up the machine gun belts and took off running. Irving squeezed off several more rounds but missed the fleeing combatant.

Just then, another enemy bullet whizzed between Irving and one of the recon guys. Bullets continued to snap overhead and bite the ground around their hole. They were in a terrible spot. The Taliban sniper had them pinned down, and the Rangers still had no idea where he was firing from. Trying to break for cover across the open field would be suicide. Minutes of fear turned into a half hour. They were fighting just to survive. The firefight got so intense that one of the recon guys turned to the combat photographer and told him to stop shooting pictures and start shooting at the enemy.

Irving had a growing sense of fear, something he hadn't felt very often on this deployment, or indeed ever. He looked over and read the same thing on his partner's face. They were outnumbered and pinned down. The enemy knew the Rangers' predicament, and some of the Taliban fighters were getting closer. They smelled blood and were moving in for the kill.

After struggling with spotty radio reception, they finally got a reply to their calls for help, but it wasn't what they wanted to hear: "We're dealing with our own shit right now. You guys take care of it."

Third Squad

Third Squad on this operation included First Sergeant Knight, Captain Johanson, and Captain McKenna, the battalion surgeon. They stayed east of the target area and approached their blocking position on foot. They'd just crossed a road and gone up a berm on the edge of a canal when a guy on a motorcycle zipped past them. Their group also included sniper Christopher Watkins; his spotter, Lyons; team leader Sergeant Andrew Hooper; Specialist Chase Vanderhule; JTAC Stan House; and others. Staff Sergeant Stephen Shipe and Platoon Sergeant Bobby DeRose had broken off and moved about one hundred yards away.

A U-28 manned surveillance aircraft checked in with Sergeant House. They were keeping close watch overhead. The aircraft had a variety of sensors that could detect enemy activity. It could see individuals clearly, track their movements, and even make out specific weapons. The aircraft began probing the target area the Rangers were surrounding. House was relieved there were finally air assets backing them up.

They also had about a half dozen Afghan national troops with them. As the Third Squad Rangers took cover and got their weapons into position, they looked behind them and found the Afghan soldiers lying down, their helmets off. They were socializing, apparently missing the gravity of the moment. A squad leader went over and chewed them out, telling them to get their helmets on and shut their mouths. Many of the Rangers felt having the Afghan troops in tow was more of a liability than a benefit. The Afghans' job was to help fight and take control of their own country. However, in previous operations, when fighting broke out, the Rangers put the Afghans behind them so they wouldn't get hurt.

From their concealed positions, some of the guys heard the rumble of an approaching vehicle. About half the squad rose from their ditch and scrambled up onto the dirt road to flag it down. But in moving to higher ground, the Rangers exposed their position. As soon as they emerged on the road, enemy fire opened up, AK rounds whizzing past them from three different directions. One Taliban fighter popped up and fired at them from only thirty yards away. The Rangers hit the dirt and rolled. They low-crawled under fire, trying to get back to the drainage canal behind them. Grass and other foliage surrounded the canal, which was about six feet deep. Most of the guys made it back, but some of the Rangers were still out front, dropping in place to avoid the onslaught of enemy fire. First Sergeant Knight and Captain Johanson were back in the canal together trying to determine where the fire was coming from.

Sniper Christopher Watkins suddenly felt a sharp pain on the side of his foot. He wasn't sure what it was, but he quickly realized he'd been shot.

"I'm hit!"

Watkins was lying about seventy-five yards in front of the canal next to a small berm he and Lyons had been using for what now proved to be inadequate cover. A bullet had ripped right through his boot and was lodged in his left foot. Knight and a few others were within earshot of Watkins and could communicate with him, but they couldn't reach the sniper through all the enemy fire. Knight yelled to Watkins, who responded that he was okay and could probably run. At these words, Vanderhule began firing his Mk 46 at a tree line about three hundred yards away, providing cover fire. Watkins and Lyons used the burst to make a break for cover. They were met in the canal by medic Ryan Walker who removed the boot and tended to the wound.

The enemy fire expanded as the Rangers hunkered down in the brushy ditch. They now had enemy rounds flying in from their back as well. Knight concluded they were facing AK fire, a PKM Russian machine gun, and (after a couple of single-shot rounds impacted within inches of them) an enemy sniper. He also realized they had not just stumbled upon a couple of Taliban fighters. They were now right in the middle of a complex ambush.

The fighter who had popped up just thirty yards away at the beginning of the ambush was still causing problems. They couldn't quite pick him off with their M4s. Vanderhule and Hooper made their way up the side of the ditch toward the road again. When they peered over some brush, bullets careened over their heads. They concluded that someone was shooting at them down the length of the canal. Vanderhule swung his Mk 46 around and opened up with a burst of machine gun fire down the canal. He turned and looked at Hooper, their heads tilting to listen for any follow-up to their machine gun rounds. Nothing. The gunfire had stopped, at least from that direction. Their burst of machine gun fire had either hit the Taliban fighter or made him take off running. Climbing out of the ditch, they looked behind them and saw the muzzle of an AK-47 sticking up in the air just above the brush that lined the canal. It was bobbing along with the walking rhythm of the person holding it.

"He's on the other side of the road!"

Vanderhule fired his machine gun in multiple bursts in that direction. He had no idea whether he hit the enemy fighter. In front of them they could see another Taliban fighter just across the road. He was so close Knight thought he could take him out with a grenade. The guy was persistent. He would appear and disappear, popping off rounds in their direction as he went. Knight threw one grenade and then another. Someone handed him another grenade and he threw that one too. But they all missed their mark. Finally Hooper threw at least two grenades, and the last one took the Taliban fighter out. Getting rid of the last fighter in close range gave the Rangers a window to make a move.

"This ain't working. We need to get out of here," Vanderhule said to no one in particular.

Rangers were used to surprising the enemy. Now they were on the receiving end of the ambush. First Sergeant Knight's experience told him they needed to get to a place that was more defensible, and they needed to get there in a hurry.

Joint Operations Center, Kandahar

Company Commander Captain Don Kingston had joined Lt. Col. Walrath in making decisions. Kingston felt a sense of frustration watching the battle unfold on the video screens in front of him. He'd gone out on nearly every Ranger operation with the two Charlie Company platoons assigned to Kandahar, but in this case he'd left YETI 4 in the hands of Captain Johanson, Captain Krueger, and First Sergeant Knight.

One thing he was mindful of was to resist the temptation to over administrate from the JOC. As a leader in the field, he would sometimes get frustrated when orders started flying from the JOC while they were still working out critical situations on the ground. Kingston's experience told him it was better to let the troops on the ground deal with their situation and be there for them with whatever support or resources they might request. Walrath got on the radio and communicated with the assault force. They were trying to bring in attack helicopters from the Marines. Attack helicopters were the one thing that scared the hell out of the Afghans, even more so than low-flying fighter jets.

Second Squad

Ben Kopp and Second Squad were holding their initial position. Most of the guys were sitting on the backside of a berm. Ben and the machine gun team were taking a breather in what was already intense heat. "Stupid hot" was how Company Medic Michael Melvin described it. The average high temperature for Helmand Province in July is 107 degrees Fahrenheit. Melvin was already giving an IV to one of the federal agents who was dehydrated and exhausted, and they'd barely been out on the operation for two hours.

Captain Krueger and Sergeant Benson were listening to intermittent radio traffic even though most of the transmissions came in broken up. A series of shots cracked in the distance, followed by more broken radio traffic.

"What's going on?" Doc Melvin asked.

"We don't know," replied Benson, a look of concentration on his face as he strained to hear what was next. Then a transmission came over the radio:

"Sierra . . . (crackle, static, garbled)." A chilling message followed: "We've got an eagle down!"

This was code for an injured Ranger. All they could make out was that one of the snipers had been shot. Captain Krueger also gleaned from the broken transmissions that the recon group was in trouble.

The officer broke off from Third Squad with a small team of about five and moved north a couple of hundred yards to try to get a better radio signal. That's when they realized that Irving, Pendleton, and the recon guys were in a life-or-death firefight. As the excitement level over the radio climbed, Krueger talked things over with Benson. They decided they were closest, about six hundred meters south of the recon group. But they needed to cross some open fields, roads, and irrigation canals to get there.

"Hey, we're gonna move to the recon team's location," Captain Krueger announced to the rest of the squad, which had now caught up. "They're pinned down. We're going to help them break contact."

With that, Second Squad headed across an open field to the north and climbed a rise across a dirt roadway. There were a few more than a dozen members of the squad trying to find some form of cover in the cruel landscape that didn't provide much. Trees grow the only place they can in Garmser District, along ditches and canals, their roots reaching desperately for what never seems to be enough water.

They then had to cross another field, where they'd be exposed. Ben ran with the rest of the squad, his pack still full of several hundred rounds of machine gun ammo. Enemy rounds whizzed by, most of the fire coming from behind them. They could hear more fire ahead of them. Ben and his squad were now moving targets and on the defensive, not the way Rangers like to play ball.

Despite the gunfire erupting around Laki Village, there were still Afghan people out and about. Some were even standing with shovels in their hands, openly watching them. The Rangers were incensed; they knew their every move was being tracked and likely relayed back to those who were trying to kill them.

Another frustration was that unlike traditional military forces, Taliban fighters often didn't carry weapons. Instead, they hid weapons in various places. They know carrying a weapon could get them killed. Stashing weapons allows them to take up the fight only when they have to, then ditch the weapon and move on undetected. They clearly knew the American rules of engagement.

Ben, Suarez, and Scap stuck close together. They now moved with the rest of the squad single-file along a larger canal, thinking that if they did come under fire, they could at least jump in. *We are going to get shot*, Michael Melvin thought. Krueger and Benson led the way,

Krueger mapping where they were with a gridded reference graphic (GRG). Ben hustled along—he was tired, hot, and thirsty. They were all breathing heavily, hearts pounding in the heat. Melvin looked back and saw some young Afghan men moving behind them. He couldn't quite make out any weapons. *Are they lookouts? Are they following us?* he wondered. Combat experience dictated that if guns were going off, bullets were flying, and military-aged males were still out in the open, they were probably an enemy. They saw one guy running about fifty to one hundred meters behind them, close enough to see his clothes and face. He was unarmed. The Rangers kept their weapons ready and eyes fixed on the running Afghan, but he ran off and never offered a threat.

The crack of enemy fire was getting closer as Second Squad continued north. They branched off from the larger canal, which was about twenty feet wide, and headed along a smaller connected ditch. They crested a rise and then descended; Captain Krueger believed they were now close to the pinned-down recon element. They paused on the front side of the rise to get their bearings, Ben and most of the others taking a knee to catch their breath. Ahead of them was a large open field, now overgrown by grass, some dead and some still green. Krueger turned and told the squad he thought the recon element was pinned down somewhere out in that field.

Third Squad

Still under fire and pinned in the canal, Third Squad leaders knew they had to get inside a building, or at least find some walls. First Sergeant Knight also thought the Ranger force needed to consolidate and fight as a single group. He was frustrated they couldn't "influence" the enemy the way they wanted to as Rangers. They could swap shots all day, but he knew this enemy knew the terrain and knew his own village. The Rangers were fighting in his backyard, and they had to acknowledge that.

There was a walled compound with a home and some other buildings about fifty meters away. But they might have taken fire from the building earlier in the firefight. *Are there enemy fighters still inside?* Knight wondered. It was impossible to know for sure. He got on the radio with Captain Johanson, who was nearby and could see the same compound. They agreed that getting there and getting inside was their best option.

Meanwhile, JTAC Stan House was on the radio trying to get air cover for the sprint to the compound. The only thing circling now was a B-1 bomber. He called for a "show of force" and within a minute the huge supersonic bomber was roaring at them at about one thousand feet. As the B-1 screamed past, it dropped some flares, devices meant to protect the aircraft against surface-to-air missiles. House wasn't happy about that, fearing the falling flares could injure friendlies below. But the show of force by the big bomber worked, and the enemy guns halted for the moment.

At Knight's command, he, Lyons, Vanderhule, Hooper, and one other Ranger moved up the canal and broke into the open under sporadic fire while running to the compound. Most of the fire now came from just one direction, so once they reached the outer walls of the compound they were shielded. The Rangers stacked up just outside the main gate, their bodies pressed against the outer mud wall. They readied to clear the structure. Vanderhule was in the lead, holding an Mk 46 machine gun. While the weapon was critical to their squad, it wasn't the ideal weapon to clear a building as it was heavy and cumbersome. He considered using his side arm, a Beretta M9, but decided to go with the machine gun. The South Dakotan went in first, followed by Lyons and Hooper. They found eight or nine Afghan women and children huddled inside. The Afghans were terrified to see the Rangers bursting into their home, but they cooperated and moved into a corner of the courtyard. There were no men over the age of sixteen. The Rangers cleared the building without firing a shot.

The Rangers nicknamed the compound the Alamo. Inside, two

sets of steel double doors stood at opposite walls. The dried mud walls protecting them were thick and at least eight feet high. The steel doors were turquoise on one end of the compound and slightly darker blue at the other end. Inside the walls was a grouping of small buildings.

Charlie Company's First Sergeant organizes Rangers just arriving at the Alamo compound. Some of the Rangers (left) are climbing ladders and taking positions on the roof.

Looking over the high walls, the Rangers got a better view of the landscape. They were still at least four kilometers east of the Helmand River. The area around them, especially to the west, was farm fields cut by more canals and ditches. A sparse scattering of buildings and compounds dotted the landscape in the distance.

Other Rangers were now arriving at the Alamo compound. They brought in the injured sniper and used their first reprieve in several hours to reload and check their ammunition. Vanderhule switched the drum on his machine gun. When full, the drum held two hundred rounds. He realized he'd nearly emptied his first drum in the initial firefight.

Another team from Third Squad had gotten separated during the fight. That team, which included Stephen Shipe and Sergeant DeRose, had taken over a separate compound less than one hundred meters away. About a dozen Rangers defended that location. Leadership believed it was in their best interest to keep some guys separated but close by.

First Squad soon arrived at the Alamo. Two of four squads were now safely inside the complex, but complications were arising. The recon team and two Ranger snipers were still pinned down by fire. They were in radio contact and reported that Taliban fighters were moving on their position, with enemy sniper fire impacting all around them.

Second Squad

A French fighter jet circled, its engines screaming over the fields of Laki. The jet passed, in the distance, where Captain Krueger believed the recon team of six was holding on. When the jet disappeared, there was silence; once again a show of force made the shooting stop. But about ten seconds later, Taliban guns again started cracking.

Captain Krueger and Sergeant Benson tried to identify the sniper's exact location. They could see buildings several hundred meters in the distance beyond the field. Krueger also contacted the French pilot, hoping to get him to drop some ordnance. But without an exact fix on the enemy location, the English-speaking pilot couldn't do it. Meanwhile, the Rangers watched enemy fighters moving around in the distance, but the targets disappeared quickly behind walls and into tree lines.

As Ben scanned the farm field for any sign of the recon group, the squad set up on a tree line hoping to provide cover fire and help spring the group from their hole. But they needed visual confirmation of their location before they could safely open up with their weapons.

They got on the radio. "We can't see you. Flash your panel." The panel is a blaze orange and fuchsia piece of material troops use to identify their position to friendlies and aircraft.

"Roger. But I'm gonna do it quick," came the reply.

The rescue crew scanned the field, hoping for a sign of the trapped recon team. Seconds later, the blaze orange panel went up. But the enemy saw it too, and they took another burst of Taliban fire. Fortunately, the enemy fire also gave the rescuers an idea of where they were hiding. Ben and the rest of the squad were now ready for a rescue and ready to lay down cover fire.

Following orders, Scap pulled the trigger while Ben fed a belt of ammo. The blaze of machine gun fire roared toward the distant structures where Taliban fighters had just fired from. Tracers flashed over the field. A line of Rangers opened up with their M4s as well.

Out in the field, Irving and Pendleton popped a couple of smoke grenades to mask their movement back to their rescuers, but the wind quickly blew the smoke away. Irving, Pendleton, the three recon guys, and the combat photographer jumped up and made a dash for it anyway. Pendleton and Irving were the last two to go, hauling ass out of the hole. "Fuck yeah, we are finally outta here!" Irving uttered as he jumped and started the run to safety.

When he neared the end of the field, he locked eyes with Ben, who saw the fear in the sniper's eyes. But the look faded to relief when Irving and the others crossed the threshold to safety. Ben smiled at Irving, and Irving forced a smile back. All six of the guys were relieved and thankful to be rescued. As Ben rose to his feet, his pal Innis walked passed him. While they were both exhausted, they knew they'd kicked ass in rescuing the recon team, and they took a moment to bump fists.

The consolidated group now numbered just under twenty men. Any chance at nabbing their high-value target was now on hold. They got on the radio with the command element, who told them to get back to the Alamo and join the rest of their force.

They started back along the same canal they'd come in on, Sergeant Derrick Ball leading the way. Ben's machine gun team was now in the rear. Irving and Pendleton walked just ahead of Ben, who was last in line.

Suddenly the snipers stopped short, fixated on a building in the distance. Captain Krueger, seeing them standing still, made his way back down the line. "Hey, what's up? We gotta go," he ordered.

"We saw something, sir," Irving said, never taking his eyes off the building.

The captain turned to look at the building and spotted an enemy fighter with a weapon several hundred yards away. Irving stood and raised his rifle to his shoulder. He fired, and the enemy crumpled. Captain Krueger shook his head in amazement at the remarkable shot, which Irving had taken without bracing the gun on anything but his own body. Ben noticed this too and was impressed. The group then jogged to catch up to the rest of their platoon.

Exhausted, dehydrated, and exposed, Second Squad and the recon group needed to get back to the Alamo. Captain Krueger and Sergeant Benson checked their maps and confirmed over the radio that they were heading in the right direction. Getting back wouldn't be easy. There was so much open land and so little cover it was hard to move without being exposed. There were some tree lines, canals, and drainage ditches that were the only cover that allowed them to move, but the Rangers knew that scanning Taliban eyes would pick up their location sooner or later.

They moved back across an open field, heading toward the cover of an irrigation ditch about fifty meters in front of them. Within minutes the shrill pitch of a small engine drew closer—an Afghan motorcycle was driving directly at them. Ben and Scap got the machine gun into place on the side of the ditch and put the motorcycle in its sight. Innis had his Mk 46 ready on the other side.

The guy on the motorbike spotted them. He swung the bike

around, kicking up dirt and sending the rear wheel spinning. He drove off at high speed, seconds away from a life-or-death decision by Rangers poised to shoot.

"He's gonna tip off somebody," Innis muttered. *I wish I would've shot him,* he thought.

The Rangers continued along a larger irrigation ditch that intersected a smaller ditch, which was about four feet deep. They turned at nearly a right angle, following the path of the smaller ditch. The smell coming from the drainage was repulsive. The Rangers noticed feces and dead animals floating in about a foot of brackish water. Several small freshwater crabs scurried over the top, feasting on the decay. The Rangers might've been less exposed moving through the ditch, but with the calf-deep sludge below, it would've been tough going.

They believed they were now about 450 meters from the safe house. Even though it was just after 8:00 a.m., the heat was rising. After ten minutes, they took a "tactical pause," kneeling in a shady spot along the ditch. Captain Krueger didn't want to stop moving, but he needed to let the Rangers back at the Alamo know they would soon be approaching. With all the shooting going on and Rangers moving in different directions, Krueger knew they were at risk for a friendly fire incident.

Eventually as the squad waited, some of the Rangers were so dehydrated they asked the medics, Melvin and Fink, for an IV. The medics said they couldn't spare it.

Ben was ready to move and was one of the first to rise. When they all caught their breath, the rest of the group got up and fell into line again. The twenty or so men moved deliberately in a line about seventy yards long. Ben was at the back when Captain Krueger approached him.

"I'm glad you're back here," he started. "I need to trust you to make sure no one is lagging behind. Make sure no one gets behind you."

Ben smiled and chuckled at the command as if to say, "No shit, sir." Captain Krueger nodded appreciatively at Ben's willingness to take up the rear, then hurried forward along the line.

In front of Ben were his machine gun teammates. The ditch border was an oasis of lush growth, with small trees, bushes, and higher grasses. Ahead of the gun team were the federal agents, the recon guys, and the snipers. Many, including Innis, struggled to walk under the weight of sixty to eighty pounds of gear in the searing heat.

As Second Squad and the recon team advanced, they approached a harvested field dotted with haystacks and piles of agricultural brush. Ben had heard gunshots all morning. They'd been targeted by occasional fire but hadn't had any close calls. They learned over the radio they were the last Ranger element still outside the compound. It was a few minutes before 8:30 a.m.

Suddenly, automatic weapon fire exploded. Trees behind the Rangers shredded from impacting rounds. An ambush! Taliban fighters less than one hundred yards away opened on them. Bullets snapped over their heads, *pop, pop, pop, pop.* Enemy rounds whizzed by, some exploding in the dirt at their feet. The long line of Americans tumbled into the ditch, some jumping, others rolling. Everyone splashed into the safety of the nasty muck except Ben's machine gun team. When the gunfire broke out, they simply hit the deck. Ben, Scap, and Suarez were now face-down in the grass, not daring to move. To their right, as they faced the enemy fire, they could see other Rangers recovering from their dives to safety and readying weapons to return fire. Just a couple of guys ahead of Ben, Innis opened up with his Mk 46—*bap, bap, bap, bap*—sending a burst of rounds in the direction of the ambush. Other Rangers also fired back, most now aiming their M4s at the enemy.

Squad leader Carl Benson gave an order for the grenade launcher to fire. Innis, realizing the Ranger with the M203 couldn't hear the order, repeated the command. "Two oh three! One hundred meters on my tracers!" Innis called out.

Innis referenced the spot ahead and to their right where the ambush had come from. He used the burst from his machine gun fire to guide the grenade launcher. The first grenade fell short, about halfway to the target, followed by a chest-thumping concussion in front of the Rangers' position. Two or three more grenades screamed from the 203, finding their mark at about the spot the initial flurry of Taliban gunfire had come from.

A bit farther up the line from Ben, Sergeant Irving had splashed down hard. He was soaked in the filth of the trench, but he recovered and came up firing, popping off a series of rounds from his SR-25. He saw an enemy fighter pop up in his scope less than one hundred yards away. He fired and through his scope watched as the man's head split in half. The sniper then heard loud popping to his left. He thought it was one of his own machine guns. He looked over as bullets snapped and whipped above his head. Enemy gunfire was ripping apart the trees along the ditch. Dust and dirt flew up where enemy rounds smacked the earth around them.

Ben pressed his face into the grass as the rounds impacted nearby. Scap's position was slightly more protected; his feet at least were now in the trench. Ben, still on his belly, got his M4 up to his face, fingered the selector to automatic, and released a burst of fire in the direction of the ambush. Scap pulled the bigger Mk 48 into position, swinging it around to the same direction.

Ben turned toward Scap. "Ten-second burst!" he ordered.

Scap let the machine gun rip, and a flurry of 7.62 ammo roared from the gun toward the initial ambush ahead of them, about ten o'clock from their original direction of travel. At nearly the same time, they started taking sniper fire from their rear.

Ben was still belly down in the long grass at the rear of the line, and he needed a better view. He rose, swinging his left leg forward and planting his left boot in front of him, holding steady on his right knee. He again brought his M4 to his right cheek and fired another burst.

The end of Scap's ten-second machine gun blast may have been the enemy's cue to return fire. As soon as the burst ended, Taliban bullets started snapping again. And then, a sickening sound—*thwap!*

It was like the sound of someone punching a pillow. Ben screamed.

"I'm hit! I'm hit!"

Incredibly, he managed to fire off several more rounds at the enemy. His machine gun teammates rolled backward into the protective filth of the trench. Scap saw Ben lying a few feet in front of him. He was still exposed, stunned by the bullet that had just ripped through his lower left thigh. Ben started scooting toward the ditch, but he was struggling. Scap reached up, grabbed him, and pulled him to safety, cushioning his fall into the trench.

"I'm shot in the fucking leg," Ben said, grimacing and writhing in pain.

Scap looked down at Ben's left leg. A crimson stain was spreading just above the knee, saturating the multicam pattern on his pants. For a split second, the nineteen-year-old Scap just stared, too stunned to move.

"Well, put a fucking tourniquet on it, man!" Suarez hollered.

His command snapped Scap back to reality. In the heat of the moment, Scap made a small mistake. Soldiers are taught to use the medical kit of the soldier who's been injured so it doesn't leave them without a kit if they're injured later. But in the intensity of the moment, he grabbed his own, removed the tourniquet, and started wrapping it around Ben's left thigh. He cranked it down as tightly as he could while yelling, "Medic! Medic!"

Nick Irving heard the screams for help. He pulled his eye away from his rifle scope, looked to his left, and—even at thirty yards—saw it was Ben. *Oh fuck, this is bad*, he thought. While the call went out for a medic, there was none in sight. The two medics were up ahead, and the two federal agents were now protecting the area where Scap was working on Ben, bullets still flying over their heads. Ben grimaced in pain, baring his teeth as he rolled his head back and forth.

When Scap finished cinching the tourniquet, Ben looked up at him. "Fuck, man, I don't want to die. Not here. This is a fuckin' miserable place. I don't want to die out here."

About forty yards up the trench, after the last grenade launched and detonated, the Americans stopped firing their weapons for a moment. They had killed or at least neutralized the fighter or fighters who'd unleashed that initial flurry. But they were still taking fire from other directions and kept their heads down. The sniper fire continued, individual rounds sometimes missing by just inches.

Captain Krueger could hear the calls behind him for a medic and knew one of his guys had been hit. He learned moments later it was Ben. Krueger moved forward in the ditch, keeping his head down. His job was to make sure his guys understood enemy locations and where the fire was coming from. He told his forward observer to bring in whatever air support was available. He then turned around and saw Nick Irving, who was signaling him to come over. Krueger bent down in the ditch and made his way to the sniper's side. With the noise of the sporadic gunfire, Irving needed to get close to the captain so he could talk to him. He reached up and grabbed a piece of Krueger's uniform, pulling the officer down so he could speak into his ear. Krueger now had his back to the enemy, hunched over in the ditch and listening to Irving. "Sir, we've got to get the fuck out of here," Irving advised.

Wham! Before he could respond, Krueger felt a blow to his back. It was as if someone had hit him with a baseball bat. He slumped over, disoriented. Irving, still holding onto Krueger's shirt, felt the spray of warm liquid on his face. He assumed it was muck from the ditch, but after wiping it away, he looked down and saw blood on his hand. Irving was stunned—Captain Krueger had just been shot and the bullet had flown within inches of him.

Pendleton watched this play out in front of him. He sprang into action, grabbing Krueger and setting him down in the ditch. Blood now flowed out of the captain's upper chest. The bullet had hit him in the upper back, passing between his spine and right shoulder and exiting his chest just under the clavicle. The platoon leader was frozen in disbelief, but he told himself to keep his head together and get his squad out of there before someone else got shot.

Irving too was stunned. He leaned against the bank and took a moment to compose himself. Pendleton put pressure on Krueger's wound. The officer was wearing his plate carrier, but the bullet had found its way through a seam. Andrew Fink, the recon medic, showed up and went to work. He inspected the officer and found the entrance and exit wounds. He shoved gauze into the holes, trying to seal them up and prevent further bleeding. The young medic's first concern was internal damage—*Did the shot hit an artery? Was there internal bleeding? Did it pass through the upper part of the lung?*

Krueger recovered his composure enough to give an order. He turned to Irving.

"I want you to kill that son of a bitch."

"I'm trying, sir, I'm trying," Irving replied.

Irving moved back up on the front side of the ditch and pushed his weapon over the edge. He scanned for enemy targets in the distance.

"Get air support!" Krueger hollered to his forward observer.

The Rangers near Krueger tried to find the other medic, Michael Melvin. "Where's Doc at?" one of them yelled. "We need Doc!"

Melvin had been near the front of the line. Hearing the calls, he started moving back, crawling down the ditch on all fours. He soon reached Captain Krueger. The platoon leader was sitting with his back against the front side of the ditch with his shirt open. Fink continued to work on the wound. Krueger, his face white as a sheet, was surprised to see Melvin; he thought he was already working on Ben. He felt sudden concern when he realized Ben, shot several minutes before, wasn't yet with a medic. Melvin, looking back at Krueger, concluded that he was in good hands with Fink.

"There's another casualty, Doc. Keep going!" he ordered, pointing in Ben's direction. The last thing Krueger wanted was to slow Melvin from getting to Ben as quickly as he could.

Melvin kept crawling down the trench. The muddy filth now soaked his pants from his thighs down; Taliban rounds continued to snap over his head. Ahead of him he saw the federal agents. One was hunkered in the ditch taking cover, while the other was up over the edge firing his weapon. As Melvin made his way around them, Ben came into view.

Ben sat in the ditch, his teeth bared and his face taut. As Melvin crawled closer, he looked down and noticed a reddish hue in the water around the wounded Ranger. It was blood spreading on the surface. Melvin immediately suspected the first tourniquet might not have completely cut off the blood flow. For his own peace of mind, he quickly went to work applying a second tourniquet. He cut off Ben's pant leg at the upper thigh and closely examined Ben's left leg, finding two wounds just above the knee. One appeared to be an entrance wound on the outside of his thigh and the other an exit on the inside. Melvin cinched the second tourniquet strap above the wounds as tightly as he could.

"Dude, that hurts!" Ben protested. He reached down to loosen the tourniquet.

"Hey, man, don't do that," Melvin warned. "That thing is saving your life right now."

Melvin talked freely to Ben in a calm and reassuring voice. Suarez and Scap were dividing their attention between the enemy and watching Melvin at work, Scappaticci firing the machine gun periodically. Scap noticed he'd already shot two "nutsacks," so-called because of the way the case of ammo hangs beneath the weapon, about 125 rounds each. Scap and Suarez admired how cool Melvin was under pressure in what was now a life-or-death situation. Ben was in a lot of pain, but there was nothing Melvin could do to relieve that right now. Morphine cannot be given until a patient is stabilized. Melvin also started an IV for Ben. This was the first time Scappaticci had seen anyone severely wounded in combat. He wasn't sure what to do or what to think other than to keep manning the 48. Suarez turned to Scap out of earshot of Kopp.

"Talk to him, man."

Scap hesitated. He couldn't think of anything to say. *What do you say to a guy who's just been shot?* He eventually tried to lighten the mood.

"Hey, now you'll get free license plates, dude," referring to the fact that Ben would get a Purple Heart for his injury. There was no response. Scappaticci realized his joke had fallen flat. Squad leader Carl Benson arrived and Melvin updated him on Kopp's condition.

"Am I good? Am I good? Am I good?" Kopp called out, nervously testing Melvin and hoping for a positive response. Melvin assured him that he would be okay.

About thirty yards up the ditch, Captain Krueger sat with most of his shirt cut away. He was bandaged and now visibly pissed. He rose to his feet and began making his way back to Ben. The platoon leader tried to wrap his head around the situation. His training had taught him that if a soldier gets hurt, attention turns from fighting to helping them and getting them off the battlefield. Krueger's attention was now split between Ben's condition and the Taliban location. He got on the radio to leadership back at the Alamo. "We're dealing with a couple of casualties," he reported.

"Roger that. Who?" asked Sergeant DeRose.

"Kopp's hit," Krueger reported.

"Who else?"

"I'm hit, but ah, I'm doing all right."

Krueger also reported that the situation around them was deteriorating. He was concerned that with Kopp down, they'd be vulnerable if the Taliban moved on them. He wanted to get moving just as soon as Doc Melvin said Ben was ready. But moving Ben would prove to be an enormous challenge even for the Rangers, who trained for just about anything.

Joint Operations Center, Kandahar

"Friendlies on the ground injured."

Word spread in the JOC that three Rangers were down on the battlefield. Even in the operations center the news made everyone's heart beat a little faster. For security reasons, radio operators in the field do not use the names of the wounded during their transmissions, out of concern that information could be intercepted. Instead, each soldier has a "battle number," a predetermined code usually comprised of the first initial of their last name and the last four digits of their Social Security number. The RTO relayed the codes. Back at the JOC, the radio operator called out the battle numbers, which were then compared with names on the manifest.

"That's Krueger, Kopp, and Watkins."

Company Commander Don Kingston was standing in the JOC with Lieutenant Colonel Walrath. The news brought a look of concern to both of their faces as they listened to the radio operator. "What kind of injuries?"

"Gunshot wounds, one to the leg, one to the foot, the other to the back. That's about all we know."

The two officers now turned their attention to getting the wounded Rangers help as quickly as possible. They needed to get a medevac to them, but the timing was tricky. *Do we wake up our own helicopter pilots or call in a general theater medevac?* The theater medical choppers were spread around the country to help reduce response times.

They agreed that their ground forces had to first get the situation under control and get all casualties together before they could send in a medevac. The last thing they wanted to do was bring in a helicopter and endanger its crew if the guys on the ground weren't ready to go yet.

Captain Sandifer, meanwhile, communicated with aircraft in the area. As some of the planes ran low on fuel, he made sure there were more inbound. He also worked his channels, trying to get some Marine attack helicopters to back up the Rangers on the ground.

Second Squad

"How much time do you need? Is he stable? Are we able to move him?"

Captain Krueger wanted a report from Doc Melvin. He and Sergeant Benson were hunkered down in the ditch, watching the medic work on Ben. Sergeant Derrick Ball had also made his way back to Ben's location.

The Rangers had been pinned down and dealing with the injuries for about forty-five minutes. They were still taking fire. No one wanted to lift his head above the ditch, but they had to make sure Taliban fighters weren't running toward them in a sneak attack.

Melvin's medical kit was now floating in the water. Some gauze had escaped and was drifting in the slow current. The medic finally looked up. "He's good to go."

Relief washed over Krueger. It was time to move out and get Ben the help he needed.

Alamo Compound

"Who? Who? Who?" Specialist Vanderhule asked, hearing there were two casualties out in the field. He was listening to Sergeant Hooper communicate over his radio.

"The PL is hit?" Hooper repeated, trying to understand the crackling transmission.

"Jesus Christ," Vanderhule muttered. He knew that PL meant platoon leader, and that meant Captain Krueger.

More information came over the radio. Hooper's face turned somber, but he nodded in understanding. He turned to Vanderhule.

"It's Ben."

"Did you say Ben?" Vanderhule repeated, incredulous.

"Yeah, it was Ben."

Meantime, Captain Johanson and First Sergeant Knight conferred on what to do with the casualties and how to defend the compound. Knight ordered Lyons, Vanderhule, and several other Rangers to get on the roof of one of the compound buildings. He wanted machine guns and sniper rifles to provide cover for the returning squad bringing Ben and Krueger back to safety. Knight himself was up on a wall, using binoculars to locate the group, but through the heavy brush, tall grasses, and scrubby trees, they were hard to see. He asked them over the radio to periodically flash their panel so he could track their location. The first sergeant wanted the cover fire as close to their flank as possible.

Air Force JTAC Stan House also climbed the walls of the compound, trying to get eyes on Taliban fighters. He worked his radios, communicating with circling aircraft. He wanted aircraft to drop munitions in the field to the west to scare off the Taliban. But without an exact idea of where the friendlies were, leadership on the ground and the pilots above didn't feel comfortable doing that. Two Marine helicopters reported they were on their way, a Vietnam-era Huey with an old-school door gunner and a more sophisticated Cobra. House was relieved; *they* might be able to pinpoint the location of enemy fighters.

Meanwhile, Vanderhule scrambled up an aluminum ladder to the top of the flat roof. Rangers Tre Randall, Andrew Hooper, and Jason Harbaugh were already up there. There was no rise or lip on the edge to give them any cover. Vanderhule set up his Mk 46 machine gun. A few feet away, Harbaugh got the slightly larger Mk 48 ready to go. Hooper, meanwhile, was lying flat and getting ready to fire Christopher Watkins's sniper rifle. Watkins was on the ground getting treatment for the gunshot wound to his foot.

Most enemy fire was coming from a strip of trees and a compound about eight hundred meters to the west. Single rounds hit the face of the building they stood on top of. Hooper started firing, engaging targets in the distance. They were ready for Ben, Krueger, and the rest of the group to make a run for the compound. Now it was a waiting game.

Second Squad

Doc Melvin had done everything he could. Ben sat in the ditch, his left leg now wrapped in bandages and double tourniquets. He was stable and alert, though he was in a lot of pain, most of which seemed to be from the tourniquets.

Calmly at first, Ben asked Melvin to loosen them.

"Melvin, seriously, I'm good. I'm all right," he said. "I just really need you to loosen this fuckin' tourniquet!" His voice rose to a frustrated crescendo at the end of his demand.

"Hey, man, you gotta keep it on. You know that, Ben," Melvin replied in his soothing voice.

It was time to move. Taliban fighters knew the Americans' location and knew they were stationary. The longer they were pinned down, the more danger they faced. Most of Second Squad had disappeared around a bend in the ditch ahead. Staying behind to help move Ben were squad leader Carl Benson, Sergeant Derrick Ball, Roy Suarez, Sean Scappaticci, and Doc Melvin. Irving and Pendleton grabbed some of Ben's gear, including his rifle and his pack. They crawled forward, disappearing around the bend.

Benson and Ball were trying to determine the best way to get Ben through the ditch to the compound about four hundred meters away. They asked Ben to try walking on his wounded leg. Ben tried, but the leg wouldn't bear any weight. They talked about putting Ben in a flexible Skedco litter, a portable stretcher Rangers carry, but that seemed more trouble than it was worth. The "six-man carry" Rangers train for wasn't possible because Ben's body and their heads would rise above the protective level of the ditch, leaving them exposed to enemy fire.

"Can you bear crawl?" Ball asked.

Ben tried, but the wound and tourniquets had rendered his leg virtually useless. Finally, Ball crouched in the ditch behind Ben, who now was sitting on his rear end.

"Put your arms in the air," Ball suggested.

Ben, sitting down, reached back toward Ball, who was crouching behind him. Ball grabbed Ben's hands and gripped his curled fingers in his own. Ball gave Ben a pull backwards. It seemed to work. Suarez was on the other side of Ben, bear crawling and pushing the wounded Ranger forward. The team started inching Ben to safety. They had only moved about fifty feet when they realized they had ripped out Ben's IV. Melvin told Ball and Suarez not to worry about it.

After about fifty meters, Ben's hands and fingers got fatigued. Ball adjusted, shoving his hands under the shoulders of Ben's protective vest and dragging him by it. Meanwhile Scappaticci, the last Ranger in the line, was on his back, slithering backwards in the calf-deep muck. His machine gun rested on his belly, trained on the edges of the ditch behind them. Scap's job was to protect their rear against an ambush. As they moved forward, enemy fire flew over, impacting trees and the ground around them.

Moving Ben was grueling and took tremendous energy. But Ball and Suarez were strong and determined. Ben struggled with the pain and continued nagging Melvin to take off the tourniquet.

"Hey, man, you gotta keep it on," Melvin reminded him.

Ben groaned about how much his arms hurt. The blood was draining from holding them up in the air so Sergeant Ball could pull him. "I can't feel my arms," he said, his voice foggy with pain and fatigue.

They took a break to let Ben get his circulation back. He was understandably miserable. Other Rangers moved back through the ditch to check on them and offered to relieve Ball and Suarez. But the tandem felt they had worked out a good system and were making progress. Their goal was to get out of that ditch and back to the Alamo as fast as possible. But it wasn't fast going. Every crawl, every drag, every pull and push of Ben through the filthy grime was exhausting. The water was putrid. The ditch reeked. Their exertions sometimes sprayed slop in Ben's face. Ben's neck got tired, and his head fell into the hazardous stew. He got some of the filthy liquid in his mouth and at one point started coughing and gagging on it.

Suarez and Ball had more energy than Ben could handle. The Rangers stopped, rested, and reevaluated. Ball worried they weren't going fast enough. At one point, they heard voices and noises just behind them. They moved under heightened alert, weapons ready, thinking Taliban fighters were coming up to ambush them from the rear. But the enemy didn't show. They were all parched, teased by the flowing water in the ditch, but it was so disgusting no one dared wet his mouth.

Doc Melvin carried an aid pack. He'd converted it from a larger radio bag so he could carry more medical supplies. It normally weighed about forty pounds dry, but it was now waterlogged and very heavy. Even at a powerful 215 pounds, Melvin struggled crawling under its weight. Sergeant Benson kept a careful eye on the effort to bring Ben to safety. He coordinated by radio with Knight back at the Alamo. Even though Captain Krueger was nearby and outranked Benson, it was still Benson's squad, and the NCO felt responsible for his guys.

The effort of Ball and Suarez was Herculean, dragging a wounded fellow Ranger through a muck-laden ditch for more than an hour in oppressive heat. But the end was near. As Suarez looked over Ball's hunched shoulder, he could see the area where other Rangers were gathering. It was the end of the line, the closest possible point to the compound, where they would have to make a break across an open field, possibly under fire. Ball and Suarez were now at the point of total exhaustion.

The battle had been raging for hours, and now those Marine helicopters finally arrived. They circled overhead, trying to engage targets.

That gave the guys on the ground some relief.

Ahead of Kopp and his rescuers was the rest of Second Squad, as well as the recon Rangers, the snipers, and the federal agents. They had crawled under fire a quarter mile through water, mud, feces, and blood and now had reached the point where they couldn't go any farther. From the ditch, they looked at the walls of the safe compound and the steel turquoise double doors, their gateway to safety. What lay ahead was a dangerous fifty-meter dash across an open field to those gates. They radioed to Rangers inside the compound that the first small group was about to make a run for it.

Irving and Pendleton moved to the front of the line. In addition to their own gear and weapons, they also had Ben's rifle and kit. They climbed to the edge of the ditch, preparing to spring forward. Once out in the open, they would likely be targets for enemy fire. Together, the sniper team counted down, "Three . . . two . . . one . . . go!" They took off running, five meters, ten meters, twenty meters. Then Irving's worst fear: a hellacious burst of gunfire at close range. The ground shook. Irving fell, ducking the fire. Pendleton, turning as he ran, saw Irving go down. He retreated a few steps, reaching down to his partner to drag him to safety.

"You all right? You all right?" Pendleton screamed over the continuing fire.

"Dude, get down, we're engaged!" Irving warned.

"No! Those are our guys."

Pendleton pointed toward the roof of the house in the compound, about twenty-five meters in front of them. Irving looked up and saw a handful of Rangers with machine guns and sniper rifles laying down cover fire for the others, who were now running past them. Irving was waterlogged, but he popped up and galloped the rest of the way to the compound. As he neared the doors, he came upon a white cow just outside the entry. Irving felt fear course through him. The deadly sniper was afraid of large animals. He wasn't even sure if cows kicked or bit. He felt more afraid approaching the cow than he had facing the bullets that had been flying over his head the last few hours. Fortunately, the cow didn't attack, and Irving followed Pendleton safely into the compound. The first person they saw was First Sergeant Knight, who was coordinating the defense of the Alamo compound. Irving was exhausted and dehydrated. He had left earlier in the day with just one bottle of water.

Behind them, Fink was helping the wounded Krueger out of the ditch. Krueger jogged across the field and into the compound, his right arm dangling.

Those carrying Kopp would be most at risk as they would be moving the slowest. Ball, Suarez, and Scappaticci, completely spent from dragging Ben back, handed the wounded Ranger off to some of the others waiting to cross the field.

As Scappaticci struggled up the embankment, another Ranger in front of him thought Scap was handing him his weapon. He took the machine gun and took off. Scap ended up running across the field unarmed.

Back in the ditch, someone handed Sergeant Ball a bottle of water. It was the most precious gift anyone could have given him. Ball put the bottle of water to his lips. He was so desperate to get it down, he chugged it in seconds. He then climbed the embankment and took off running. But as soon as he crossed the threshold of the compound doors, Ball bent over and vomited everything he'd drunk a minute before.

Doc Melvin took off toward the gate. As he ran, he switched his M4 to auto. Swinging it to his right, he opened fire across the open field. Suddenly he looked around and realized he was making the mad dash by himself. As he crossed through the big steel doors, he nearly collapsed. He was completely gassed and needed a moment to recover. He had spent the last ninety minutes focused on Ben Kopp's care, but he would have to let that go for a minute. Ahead he saw platoon medic Ryan Walker and battalion surgeon Captain McKenna. They were ready for Ben.

Air support would give the last group bringing Ben to safety some extra protection. JTAC Stan House was communicating with two F-15s circling their perimeter several miles out. House asked the F-15s for a show of force as the remaining Rangers brought Ben to safety.

"Thirty seconds," he barked into his radio, asking the fighter jets to be over the target in that timeframe. The fighter jets peeled off and started a low approach.

The last group in the ditch readied Ben to carry him across the field. He was now wrapped in a Skedco litter, a flexible piece of rolled-up plastic. They grabbed the litter, emerged from the tree line, and dashed across the open field. The Ranger team on the roof opened fire, machine gun bursts coupled with sniper rifles cracking toward enemy buildings in the distance. But as the F-15s bore down on their location, House asked everyone to hold their fire for the aircraft's safety. There was a split second of silence, then the sudden roar of jet engines. As the final team of Rangers bounded to safety, the F-15s screamed in just five hundred feet off the ground, shaking everything in a sudden and small earthquake. To the guys on the ground, the jets looked like they were just above the tree tops. As fast as the Air Force fighters appeared, they shot out of view.

Rangers, concerned about Ben's condition, watched from the compound as the last group approached. For most of them, watching Ben get carried back to the compound seemed to take forever. Their hearts were with him, but they didn't really know much about his condition. They only knew the guys carrying him were busting their asses to get him to safety.

They jogged the fastest they could. The black plastic carrying Ben bounced and bobbed as the Rangers struggled over the field. The litter was starting to come undone and sag as they approached the turquoise doors. Specialist Innis, standing at the gates and watching, dropped his machine gun and ran outside the compound to help. He grabbed hold of the stretcher near Ben's legs as they carried him in through the doors. They were covered in the rancid muck of the ditch and the blood of a wounded Ranger, but the last group had finally entered the safe area. The steel doors shut behind them. It was 9:25 a.m.

Leadership quickly did a head count. After hours of vicious combat, firefights, ambushes, and casualties, every member of the Ranger assault force was present and accounted for. First Sergeant Knight then ordered some of the new arrivals to use ladders to climb up on the eight-foot surrounding walls, pull security, and take stock of the situation. Their priority was getting the three casualties the care they needed as quickly as possible. But they were still under fire, and bringing in a medevac helicopter might prove difficult, if not disastrous.

Ben arrives back to the safety of the Alamo compound after being dragged through a drainage ditch under fire. Those who pulled and pushed him were utterly exhausted. Ben was alert and conscious after arriving back.

Having nearly everyone together created new challenges. A handful of Rangers were holed up in a separate compound about one hundred yards away, but most were assembled here now. The Taliban knew exactly where the Rangers were. Would they try to attack the compound? Did they have access to mortars that could make them sitting ducks? No one knew for sure. Knight, Johanson, and Ranger leadership back at the JOC now started dealing with the pressing question of what to do next.

Joint Operations Center, Kandahar

Lt. Colonel Walrath, Captain Kingston, and Captain Sandifer were keeping a close eye on the battlefield, watching video feeds from overhead surveillance aircraft. They also put the word out for a medevac helicopter to deal with the casualties. They found one already in the air that was willing to divert to the Rangers' location. But the chopper might not be able to land nearby because the area was considered too "hot" with steady gunfire still raging.

Also at Kandahar, Rangers from Charlie Company's First and Second Platoons had gotten word of the intense firefight. Leaders from both platoons had now made their way into the JOC. They were lobbying Walrath and Kingston to let them get involved. The plan on the table was to have Second Platoon head south with water, ammunition, and other supplies and join Third Platoon to stay the night. Walrath and Kingston were also weighing sending their MH-47s directly to the Rangers' compound to pick them up. But they didn't want to do that in daylight. The other option would be to get the Marines at Mian Poshteh who had driven the Rangers down to Laki to come back and retrieve them.

Then one of the drones over Laki zoomed in on a troubling sight. At least two Taliban fighters were in the same ditch the Rangers had just used to transport Ben back to the Alamo. The fighters were armed and moving quietly through the ditch in the direction of the Rangers' compound.

Alamo Compound

Battalion Surgeon Jay McKenna had set up a triage area for the three casualties along a wall near the main building in the compound. Sniper Chris Watkins was sitting still. He had been treated about an hour before. Captain Krueger was now being checked out.

Captain McKenna was new to 3rd Ranger Battalion, joining them just in time for this deployment. McKenna's medical degree was in family medicine. He wasn't technically a surgeon, but he'd gained plenty of experience in the Army. McKenna had enlisted right out of high school, becoming a Special Forces medic. He completed medical school in 2005 and became the surgeon of the Rangers' Special Troops Battalion, then the 3rd Ranger Battalion.

Looking over Captain Krueger, McKenna was concerned that he might have a collapsed lung. He asked Krueger a few questions, and the platoon leader was able to talk clearly and say he felt fine. McKenna pulled out his stethoscope and listened to Krueger's lungs. They sounded clear. McKenna now lifted the dressing on the wound on Krueger's right shoulder. What he found was mostly white gauze in the bullet holes, a good sign. Normally, gauze stuffed in a bullet wound was all red. The clean gauze indicated to McKenna that no major blood vessels had been ruptured. Careful not to disturb the gauze, he put the dressing back over the wound.

The guys were just putting Ben down in a shady spot. He was screaming in pain. Unwrapping the black plastic litter revealed Ben's legs were covered in blood. His left leg was exposed as Melvin had cut the pant leg at the upper thigh. Ben was soaked with the water and the now-caked muck from the drainage ditch. He was conscious but dazed.

As Captain McKenna finished with Krueger, one of Ben's closest friends, medic Ryan Walker, looked over Ben's wounds, cleaning and bandaging them. McKenna also turned his attention to Ben, trying to comfort him. The screaming was actually a good sign to McKenna that Ben had a clean airway. McKenna was also pleased to see the double tourniquet. He'd preached over and over that getting tourniquets on soldiers quickly saved more lives in the field than medics or doctors. But in looking over Ben's wound, he was concerned that either a large vein or artery had been hit. He was worried about blood loss.

Ben was still screaming in pain. Dr. McKenna offered him comfort. "Hey, Ben you're going to be okay," he said. "I'm here. You're gonna be fine."

Ben knew his wound was serious. He gathered himself, looked up at Captain McKenna, and asked, "Am I going to die?"

"No, you're not. Not right here," McKenna assured him. "You're good."

Ben grimaced, grinding his teeth.

"I'm taking care of you. I'm gonna help you with your pain," said McKenna, continuing to reassure him. "You're gonna be okay. You're with the doc now."

McKenna noted that Ben had a high heart rate, but that was expected given the battlefield conditions, his pain, and his anxiety over his wound. His oxygen saturations were good. McKenna took Ben's left arm and gave him an IV.

Michael Melvin came over now and reported to McKenna and Walker that Ben's wound had been fairly simple to deal with. Despite some blood loss, and the fact that Ben was now likely in shock, they all agreed the wound wasn't immediately life threatening. Melvin gave Ben antibiotics because of his exposure to the tainted water in the ditch.

The pain in Ben's left leg was nearly unbearable, and he was getting upset and impatient. His eyes were closed, and his face was red and wrinkled from both the heat and from grimacing in pain. He was seated but bending forward, holding his left leg with both hands. He yelled out and brought the wounded leg closer to his chest. He looked up at Ryan Walker. "My knee's burning. Give me some morphine," Ben yelled. "Give me some fuckin' morphine!"

It hurt Walker to hear this. Walker administered the minimum dose, five milligrams of morphine. Within minutes it took effect. Ben became calm.

Ben was the most seriously wounded of the three casualties. Dr. McKenna assessed Ben as alert and in pain and called his condition "urgent surgical," meaning he needed surgical attention to save his leg as soon as possible. But, most important, he was stable.

Most of the other Rangers were too busy now defending the compound to get an update on Ben's condition. "Is he gonna die?" someone whispered.

Sergeant Ball overheard the question. "No, he'll be all right," Ball stated.

In fact, the sense in the compound was that Ben was going to be fine. It was a leg injury, and Melvin and McKenna seemed confident Ben was in good shape. Ben was in good hands. At least for now.

Casualties aside, the other Rangers were fighting to defend the compound. First Sergeant Knight was working to ensure everyone was doing something to defend their perimeter with the biggest enemy threat to the west.

As he directed the soldiers, Knight felt some discomfort under his left arm. When he finally had a free second to check it, he discovered something shocking: a bullet hole in his shirt. The projectile had penetrated his uniform, grazed his skin, and exited. He had come within millimeters of a major injury. Knight realized this must have happened during the initial firefight when Watkins was hit. Captain McKenna also found at least two grazes on his arm and bullet holes in his uniform from the initial firefight. Watkins would later find bullet holes in his gear.

Knight turned to the snipers, who seemed at least partially recovered from their brush with death earlier in the day. "I need you up high," he ordered. Pendleton and Irving jumped on the ladder and climbed to the rooftop, joining a machine gun team. The guys had their helmets off. Raymond Harrison, one of the recon guys, had a sniper rifle and was scanning for targets in the distance.

"Dude, we're killing everybody," Irving said to Pendleton as he climbed onto the roof. Hooper was up there too. He was using Watkins's SR-25 rifle. Lyons was also dialing in long-range targets.

"What's the distance?" Irving hollered, trying to get locked in. His rangefinder was ruined from the crawl through the sludge of the drainage ditch.

"Eight hundred meters."

Snipers Lyons and Nick Irving take aim from atop a building within the Alamo compound. Their targets were up to 800 meters away. Ranger snipers were likely the difference in keeping the Taliban at a distance during the day's operation.

Small buildings and compounds dotted the landscape in the distance, providing enemy cover. The snipers also focused on a tree line at about the same range. The elevation from the Rangers' compound to the enemy location was flat. Irving adjusted his scope accordingly. He could see activity inside the distant compound. The sniper deliberately aimed at a spot on the distant wall and fired, following the vapor trail through the glass to see where it impacted. The round fell short of the wall, exploding in the dirt. Irving was confident that if he came up two mils, he would be dead on. He could now see several Taliban fighters moving around the compound.

On the other side of the Taliban complex, a white van pulled up and a handful of armed men got out. Irving motioned to Pendleton, knowing his partner's .300 Win Mag would be more effective against the vehicle than his 7.62mm rounds. The enemy fighters were moving around hurriedly, rarely stopping to give the Rangers a chance to take them out. Irving picked one fighter out and led him by three mils. He missed. He upped his lead and watched the man drop. Pendleton focused on the area around the white van. He connected with a target eleven hundred meters away. Irving tracked his partner's bullet and saw the man's chest pop. Looking through his sight again, Sergeant Irving knew he was dialed in, and he dropped another Taliban fighter. Irving felt something stirring inside himself. After being pinned down and facing death, then seeing two of his own guys get wounded, he had shut off all emotion. He was a killing machine.

First Sergeant Knight took stock of their remaining supplies, especially water and ammo. Irving and Pendleton told Knight they were out of water and running low on ammo. Irving had even been bumming ammunition from one of the machine gunners, whose linked 7.62 ammo worked in his SR-25 rifle. Lyons reported that all of Watkins' ammo had been used up. A well in the compound teased them with what looked like clean water, but most of the Rangers steered clear, preferring to battle their thirst with willpower.

As secure as they seemed in the compound, there were some

strategic concerns. First, they were outnumbered. By some estimates, their force of just over seventy was facing a Taliban militia of well over one hundred. The Rangers could end up surrounded, or worse. If the Taliban came up with some mortars, the Rangers could be shelled; in that regard, they were sitting ducks. They were also getting intel from the JOC that some of the Taliban fighters were moving on them, using the canals and ditches to make their approach. At least two Taliban fighters were getting uncomfortably close.

Hearing this, Knight decided he'd had enough. "Fuck this!" he announced. "I'm gonna go take care of it."

Knight was sick and tired of his guys taking fire all day. He thought of the three casualties they were already dealing with, and he didn't want any more. This was now personal. Knight grabbed an M4 and walked out of the gate by himself. Remembering his Army training—never go anywhere without a buddy—Knight turned and looked back up at a machine gunner on the wall. "You got me?" he said.

"Roger," the gunner replied.

Knight crept toward the ditch, looking for any signs of the fighters. Moments later he saw movement in the brush. He made out the figure of at least one enemy fighter moving toward the compound. Knight emptied his entire magazine, exterminating the threat. He then returned unscathed to the compound.

Ryan Lundeby and Erick Innis were switching spots on a ladder against the compound wall. They could hear Taliban rounds hitting the wall just below them; some snapped as they passed overhead. Innis's Mk 46 was planted on the top of the wall. He was looking through his sight, watching a compound where about thirty people moved about. He was so engrossed tracking movements that he was momentarily unaware of what was happening right in front of him. He looked down and was stunned to see an older Afghan man only about thirty feet away running parallel to the wall he was guarding. The man suddenly made a ninety-degree turn and headed straight for the Ranger compound. He looked up at Innis, and the pair locked eyes.

The Afghan then looked down and without losing stride continued running right at him. *Does he have a suicide vest?* Innis wondered. He trained his machine gun onto the loping man and fingered his selector lever to fire. Then he looked at the man's withered hands and saw he wasn't carrying anything.

"Hey, I got a guy running to the wall!" Innis hollered. He was trying to get an order or feedback. He also wanted to tell the guy to stop. As the man approached, Innis thought he would have to shoot him. The runner was now just below Innis's position when he suddenly cut around the side of the compound and disappeared. Innis let out a deep breath, his heart pounding. He now realized the man was likely a spotter for the Taliban and had just pointed out the Ranger location, as if to say, *I'm going to run to the building where the Americans are hiding, watch me.* Platoon leaders were listening over the radio to Taliban leaders giving orders. Translators told them the Taliban wanted to move closer.

From the roof, snipers were fighting not only the enemy but now the brutal heat. Irving's boots felt so hot he thought his soles were melting. He, Pendleton, and the others watched for anyone getting too close. Within a matter of minutes, four enemy fighters emerged within fifty meters. Irving, Lyons, Pendleton, and Harrison spotted them and agreed to hit them simultaneously. Each called out which target they would hit, Irving taking a fighter in a checkered shirt. Three of the four were carrying AK-47s. The fourth was cloaked in a belt of ammunition, his hand on his partner's shoulder. They disappeared behind a wall, but as they rounded a corner and came into view again, the snipers counted down, "Three, two, one!" Rifles cracked, and all four bodies dropped simultaneously about thirty-five meters away.

Getting Out

"Medevac ten minutes out . . . prepare for exfil."

Shortly after 10:00 a.m., word came over the radio that the medical helicopter was minutes away. That was a relief to Captain McKenna and the medics, but there was still more work to be done. Landing a chopper in a combat zone provides an exposed target, especially during the day and especially when you're still under fire.

Ben looked up. He could hear Captain Johanson, First Sergeant Knight, and the other leaders organizing a team to go outside the walls and provide security for the helicopter. Other Rangers volunteered to carry Ben to the incoming Black Hawk. Vanderhule wanted to be part of the team carrying Ben, but he knew with his light machine gun he'd be more valuable covering the exit. Without hearing an order, he climbed down from the roof and headed toward the turquoise doors. Vanderhule only had about one hundred 5.56 rounds left. For a machine gunner, that could go in a matter of seconds. Captain Johanson made his way over to check on Ben. He put his hand on the wounded Ranger's head.

"How you doing, Ben? You hanging in there?" Johanson asked.

"I'll be all right, sir," Ben replied.

Leadership warned anyone providing cover for the casualties to keep an eye out for Taliban teams bearing rocket-propelled grenades (RPGs). Among the biggest fears of helicopter pilots are RPGs. A single RPG proved especially deadly in Afghanistan in 2005 during operation Red Wings, screaming into the open rear door of a hovering MH-47 and killing eight crew and eight SEALS on detonation.

The Ranger platoon needed to show the incoming helicopter where to land. Stan House was already communicating over the radio with the pilots. House needed to move out to set up the landing zone. He didn't want to pop a smoke grenade because that would draw the enemy's attention. Instead he grabbed the brightly colored panel to signal to the pilots.

As the security team was being thrown together to cover the chopper's landing, one team leader turned to Innis and gave him an order. "Take your machine gun and go."

Innis felt crushing conflict. Ben Kopp was his best friend, his brother. He wanted to be a part of the team that carried Ben to the helicopter. He had never in his Army career disobeyed an order. Until now.

"Fuck that," Innis said calmly. "That's my best friend. I'm gonna carry him out."

The team leader said nothing, understanding Innis instantly. Innis moved quickly, trading his machine gun for a lighter M4, and made his way to where Ben was resting in the triage area.

Ben could hear the vibration from the incoming UH-60. Melvin and Ryan Walker now worked together to get Ben onto a litter. The rattle of the rotor blades grew louder, and the chopper suddenly roared right over the compound, where it hovered for a moment. Melvin looked up and caught the eyes of the crew chief standing in the open door, looking down at him. The helicopter then lifted and circled again, looking for the designated landing zone.

"You're going on the bird with them," Melvin told Walker. Walker was pleased to hear it. He wanted to be with Ben as long as he could. Melvin went to grab the litter to help carry Ben out.

"Hey Doc, you can't go out there, you don't have your helmet on," First Sergeant Knight warned. But there wasn't time to put it on now. Melvin looked down at Kopp. Ben was serene.

"I'll see you when we get back," Melvin said. Ben's eyes were open, but he didn't reply.

Innis, Ryan Walker, and a handful of others picked up the litter. Ben then rode out through the turquoise doors to the waiting Black Hawk. As the Rangers lugged their wounded friend toward the landing zone, Ben logged one more complaint about the tourniquet. "Aaaaah, this fuckin' thing is on tight."

The Black Hawk slowly descended to land about seventy meters from the compound doors. The crew carrying Ben was beating the Black Hawk to the LZ so they paused, lowered Ben to the ground, and waited on the chopper to land.

Vanderhule had moved to a protective position between the landing zone and the enemy compound in the distance. He and his machine gun were ready. Overhead the Marine Huey and Cobra circled, protecting the medevac. Vanderhule turned away from potential targets for a second and watched the crew carrying Ben. With them were the two other casualties, Captain Krueger and Sergeant Watkins. Vanderhule looked back at the helicopter and wished he had said something to Ben before he was carried away. Now it was too late.

Dust and dirt kicked up from the rotor wash. Walker leaned his chest over Ben, shielding him from the flying debris. Once the Black Hawk was down, they moved in under the rotating blades. They loaded Ben first, sliding him inside the open door. Walker looked up at the medic on the chopper. "I'm his medic. I'm coming," he said.

"Come on!"

Walker hopped aboard the helicopter. Watkins and Krueger also climbed in. Innis let go of the litter, and for the first time since Ben had been shot had a moment to pause and look at his friend. He looked Ben in the eye and reached out his right fist. Though he was sedated, Ben lifted his arm and bumped fists with Innis.

"Alright, dude. I'll see you when we get back," Innis shouted over the noise of the chopper.

The blades picked up speed, gathering momentum for liftoff. Those who had carried Ben turned and jogged back to the compound.

Inside, Dr. McKenna relayed by radio that he wanted Ben to go directly back to Camp Leatherneck. It was a little farther, but he believed Ben was stable enough to make the flight and would be in the best hands there. McKenna knew that at Leatherneck they could do the surgery necessary to repair whatever blood vessels had been damaged in Ben's leg. However, the decision was made to get the wounded Rangers to the closest medical location, Camp Dwyer.

The Black Hawk finally lifted off into the Afghan sky. With the wounded now airborne, Knight and Johanson turned their attention to what was next. They first needed to defend their position with a dwindling supply of ammunition and water. Questions swirled through their minds. Should they get resupplied and continue after their high-value target? Or with three casualties and a battle-weary assault force, was it best to simply cut their losses and get out?

Joint Operations Center, Kandahar

Lieutenant Colonel Walrath had to decide whether YETI 4 would continue or terminate. He got on the radio with First Sergeant Knight to weigh three options: One, stay overnight in the compound, get resupplied, then hit the HVT again tomorrow. That plan also included the possibility of sending another Ranger platoon to Laki. Two, stay until dark, when leadership could use their own Nightstalker pilots to bring in a couple of Chinooks and get the Rangers out. Or three, go out on the ground the same way they'd come in with the Marines.

Knight told the battalion commander he recommended against committing more Rangers to come in. He thought they ran the risk of more guys getting pinned down and suffering casualties.

They also quickly agreed that they didn't want to wait another nine or ten hours for darkness to bring in the Chinooks. The delay could give the Taliban the chance to reset, plan, and reattack their compound. If the pace of the fight picked up, the Rangers risked running out of ammo, and most guys had already run out of water. The enemy knew the Americans were stationary.

They finally agreed that bringing the Marine vehicles back was their best option. Knight requested that this time they bring more vehicles so they could all exit in one trip. Company Commander Don Kingston reached the Marines in Mian Poshteh and relayed to Knight that they were only willing to get as close as eight hundred to a thousand meters east of the compound. That would leave the Rangers to fend for themselves as they exited in daylight. *Could we be ambushed again?* Knight and Johanson had to consider the possibility.

Camp Dwyer

The medevac Black Hawk raced over the verdant squares and rectangles of the Helmand River Valley. To the east and west was desert wasteland. Medic Ryan Walker placed an oxygen mask over Ben's face and gave him an IV. The plan was to take Ben, Krueger, and Watkins to Camp Dwyer, where there was a small Navy surgical hospital. It was a relatively short flight northwest, about fifteen minutes.

Despite the dose of morphine, Ben was in a lot of pain again. Walker consoled him, holding his hand and telling him he was going to be all right. Captain Krueger also looked at Ben. His upper chest was burning. Bothering him just as badly was the hollow feeling of leaving his platoon behind.

Watkins locked eyes with Ben. He knew Kopp's condition was serious. Watkins could feel his emotions welling up. He'd always felt that he and his fellow Rangers were ten feet tall and bulletproof. But seeing Ben like this was more than he could take. The sniper broke down and started to sob. The flight medic noticed and grabbed Watkins hand, placing it in Ben's. Ben looked back at Watkins and without saying anything firmly squeezed the sniper's hand. Watkins gave Ben a thumbs-up and did his best to pull himself together. "Ten minutes out!" the announcement came over the chopper's communication system.

"We're ten minutes away," Walker repeated, his mouth close to Ben's right ear. "Hang in there."

Ben's blue eyes were open but glazed over. He looked drowsy, as if he was fighting sleep.

"Stay awake. Keep looking at me, Ben," Walker urged.

They flew on, and a general hush fell over the seven men on board. There wasn't much that could be said now. They knew what had to be done, but each minute passed like an hour.

"Five minutes out," the flight crew announced.

The chopper was now flying over desert. Camp Dwyer was in a desolate area without any inhabitants nearby. Some of the Marines based there referred to it as "Hell" because of sandstorms and temperatures that would often rise above 120 degrees.

As the Black Hawk descended, Ben started to lose consciousness. The relatively new medical camp below looked like the moon with a bunch of tents dotting the surface. The chopper set down at Camp Dwyer at about 10:40 a.m. Ben was barely awake as the chopper landed.

Some Marines met the helicopter in a Humvee. As the top priority, Ben was unloaded and raced about four hundred meters to the combat surgical hospital. Krueger and Watkins got into a separate vehicle, while Walker jumped into a waiting golf cart. When Walker caught up, he walked into a building and headed into the treatment area. A couple of Navy medical personnel interviewed Walker about Ben's wounds and the treatment he'd received so far.

When Ben was rolled into surgery, his heart was racing, 119 beats a minute peaking at 140, more than double his resting heart rate. Three Navy surgeons entered the operating room—a general surgeon, an orthopedic surgeon, and a trauma/critical care surgeon. After removing the two tourniquets, they examined his leg and found "brisk bleeding" from the popliteal artery. They first attempted to suture the severed artery. When that didn't work, they slowed the bleeding with vascular clamps. There was also bleeding from the popliteal vein, which they controlled with sutures. They reconnected Ben's popliteal artery with a shunt, and a pulse returned to his left foot. Ben remained stable through the entire operation. The blood loss during surgery was estimated at four hundred milliliters, a little more than a twelve-ounce soda.

Meanwhile, just outside the surgical area, Captain Krueger underwent his examination. The medical team was concerned about his wound because they still didn't know the extent of his internal injuries. They told the officer he would be sent back to Camp Leatherneck for MRIs and other tests. But Krueger was worried Ben might lose his left leg.

"What's going on with Ben?" he asked the nurse.

"They're done with surgery. They were able to save his leg. It looks like he's stabilizing," the nurse said.

That was the good news Krueger had been waiting to hear. It seemed Ben would be all right. For Krueger, it was now time to go. After an hour at Dwyer, he left the medical tent and headed for the helicopters. A Black Hawk was waiting to take him back to Camp Leatherneck where more thorough tests could be run on his wound.

As Krueger's helicopter lifted off, Ben emerged from surgery. The doctors explained to Ryan Walker what they'd done. Nearby, Christopher Watkins reclined on a medical cot, waiting to go into surgery, a bullet still lodged in his foot.

Walker looked at Ben. He looked peaceful, though he wasn't conscious. Ben faced more surgery to repair the damage inside his leg, but he seemed stable and out of the woods. Ben was recovering in the waiting area under the care of a nurse anesthetist and an RN.

A few minutes later, multiple alarms on the medical equipment monitoring Ben started beeping and buzzing—Ben was in cardiac arrest. Hearing the alarms, a naval doctor ran to Ben's side and started chest compressions. Walker heard the alarms too. He watched the doctor, but he didn't like what he was seeing. He thought she wasn't giving deep enough compressions to save his friend. He ran to Ben, pushed her aside, and started CPR himself.

The machines indicated more problems. Ben's oxygen saturations were falling. A short time later, one monitor didn't register any oxygen saturation. Ben's complexion darkened. He was taken off the ventilator and hooked to a portable bag ventilator instead. Ben's breathing was now faint.

The medical team grabbed a defibrillator, but it wasn't charged. It didn't power up by battery as it should have. The reading on the EKG showed no sign of a stable heartbeat. Ben was given epinephrine and rushed back to the operating room.

Walker followed as far as he could, then watched through a window. The anesthesiologist performed an ultrasound on Ben's heart and reported no heart activity. Surgeons then sliced open Ben's chest, exposing his heart. One of them grabbed Ben's heart and started squeezing it, a procedure called cardiac massage. They were literally pumping Ben's heart by hand.

Watching his friend was more than Walker could take. He walked back to the recovery area, where Watkins was still waiting for surgery.

"Who was that?" asked Watkins.

"It's Ben!" replied Walker, a look of disbelief on his face. Walker had been a big part of Ben's care in the field, and he sure as hell didn't want to lose his friend now. He could feel emotion welling up inside him. Up to that point, he'd been in training mode, unemotional and focused. But now that calm was leaving him, and filling the void was the realization his fellow Ranger could die. Walker walked outside into the heat.

He was just a few steps outside the tent when he started sobbing. Two Navy corpsmen spotted Walker and came to console him. "They're doing everything they can in there," one said. The other offered him some menthol cigarettes. Walker wasn't a smoker, but something made him grab the smokes. He lit one and then another and another. He was on the ground in a heap outside the Navy hospital chain-smoking.

A short time later, one of the corpsman came back out with the update. "They got him back! They've got a heartbeat back!"

Walker ran back inside the medical tent, where a nurse told him Ben was now stable. This was their opportunity to move him to a base where he could get more help. It was time to get Ben back to Camp

Leatherneck, about a thirty-minute chopper ride away.

As they rushed Ben down the hospital walkway, Walker kept pace alongside the rolling stretcher. The Ranger medic leaned over his friend and said a prayer. They put Ben into a Humvee ambulance. Walker had been at Ben's side for hours, but Ben was now leaving Dwyer, and Walker wasn't going with him. Walker said a quiet good-bye to his friend, not knowing when he'd catch up. The Humvee took Ben back to the airfield, where he was loaded onto a waiting Black Hawk.

Ben was now gone, and Walker was stuck at Dwyer. The medic wouldn't get an update on Ben's condition until he finally got a chopper ride out four days later.

Alamo Compound

First Sergeant Knight briefed the remaining assault force inside the compound that the Marines were on their way back to pick them up.

Initially, the Rangers had taken fire from different directions, but as the day wore on, the big open agricultural fields to their west became the battlefield. Like the Rangers, the Taliban had apparently also consolidated forces to their own compounds. This would allow the Rangers an opportunity to escape to the east, away from where most of the fire now came from.

As Knight reviewed the day's events, he concluded that the Taliban here had had a defensive plan in place. He believed the battle wasn't a chance encounter but a carefully planned ambush. Even at the early hour the Rangers arrived, the Taliban fighters were ready in multiple positions. Knight didn't think they'd planned on the Rangers coming that exact day, but because of the Marines' big push south in Helmand Province during the prior week, the Taliban had clearly anticipated they were going to see Americans at some point.

It was time for the Rangers to get out. Leadership from the JOC radioed to let the Rangers know the Marines were approaching Laki from the north. The Marine drivers also made it clear they didn't want to sit and wait any longer than they had to on the edge of a battlefield.

Ranger leadership weighed several options during YETI 4. They decided the best plan to exit the area was the same way they entered, by Marine vehicles. Rangers look out of the compound in the direction the Marines were supposed to arrive.

After six hours of intense fighting, the Rangers and the rest of their assault force were ready to call it a day. Knight gave them a quick speech as they lined up along the interior wall. They were getting ready to head through a gate on the opposite side of the compound from where most had come in.

When Knight finished talking, he approached Nick Irving.

"Hey, Irv, I want one sniper in front, one in the rear, and one in the middle," he said.

"Yes, Sergeant."

The Rangers also had the benefit of some recently arrived air cover to protect their exit. Two A-10 Thunderbolts patrolled overhead, ready to strike at a moment's notice if Sergeant House so directed.

Knight then got a break. The Muslim call to prayer began in near and distant compounds. The Rangers could hear the voices. Knight immediately recognized this as a tactical opportunity to move.

Specialist Innis and another machine gunner were first out the door, one looking left, the other right. They set their automatic weapons up along a road just outside the compound, machine guns facing opposite directions to cover their movement. The Rangers behind them looked out from the open doors and could see the Marine vehicles on a rise in the distance. There appeared to be five of them, MRAPs and some others about a half mile or so to the east. The Rangers realized their path to the vehicles would be across open fields, and they'd be exposed to fire. No buildings, no brush, no cover.

Those with sniper rifles fell into line—Irving near the front, Harrison near the middle, and Pendleton taking up the rear. As they flooded out of the compound, Irving braced himself for D-Day–level resistance.

Sure enough a burst of fire erupted nearby. "Troops in contact!" someone yelled. But they quickly realized it was a false alarm. An Afghan national soldier who was with them had fired his weapon as he went out the door, making the others think they were under fire.

Once things quieted, they filed between the machine gunners toward the Marine convoy. The Rangers moved quickly, some running. They took with them five Afghan prisoners they'd taken into custody during the fighting. The prisoners wore hoods; their hands were secured.

As Innis sat he scanned for any sort of trouble; he noticed some Afghans standing down a dry and dusty road. They appeared to be unarmed teenage boys. They watched the Rangers leave the compound in silence. Innis looked around and saw no adults were present. As the last member of the platoon passed behind him, Innis and the other machine gunner fell back into line. The Rangers crossed a footbridge over a canal that led to a field. Once they hit the field, they had about five hundred meters to the Marine vehicles on a ridge.

Ahead, Irving was in an all-out sprint. As he closed in on the convoy, he could see individual Marines casually sitting and leaning on the vehicles. There were about four guys per vehicle. Some were smoking cigarettes as they watched the Rangers run like hell. By the time Irving reached the vehicles he was breathing hard, his chest heaving as he tried to catch his breath. He approached a Marine leaning casually against the back of one of the armored trucks, legs crossed, a smoke dangling from his mouth.

The Marine removed the cigarette. "Well, you guys had a day," he said, his tone nonchalant.

Irving gritted his teeth.

"No shit," he replied.

The Marine vehicles were a beautiful sight to the weary Rangers. The jarheads had even brought water. The last of the guys arrived without being shot at. That seemed a first for the day. As the Rangers climbed aboard the trucks, there didn't appear to be enough room. They piled in, stacking bodies atop bodies, some sitting on others' laps. Including the handful of prisoners, they numbered about seventy-five. They filled every nook and cranny the trucks offered. As they got underway, limbs fell asleep under the pressure of crammed bodies, but they didn't care. They were relieved to be getting out.

Minds now turned to Ben, Krueger, and Watkins. Irving thought about Ben and how Ben had come to his rescue when he was facing death. He now regretted not checking on Ben while he was being treated in the compound.

In the daylight, the Marine drivers could move faster than on the way down, about thirty-five miles per hour. The Rangers were now busy dousing their mouths, throats, and heads with bottled water. They were completely exhausted.

Mian Poshteh, Helmand Province

When they got back to the Marine schoolhouse, the sun was falling beyond the Helmand River. Guys were exhausted, dehydrated, and preoccupied with concern over the three casualties. The Marines were quick to help them get food and water.

"What the hell just happened?" said one Ranger to no one in particular.

Michael Melvin, now on his fifth deployment, shared that in all his time in combat, this was the most vicious firefight he'd ever been in. Greg Knight, perhaps the most battle tested among them, told the platoon it was among the most intense battles he'd ever seen.

Leadership assessed the next move. Knight also tried to get a count of enemy casualties. Irving reported he had started the mission with 210 7.62 rounds and returned with seven. He had three confirmed kills that day, but he believed the real number was a lot higher. The official enemy death toll for the YETI 4 operation was twelve. However, many Rangers believed that too was actually much higher. Rangers later learned the Taliban had been stockpiling weapons in the Laki area, in preparation for a counterattack against the Marines.

After standing down at Mian Poshteh for a few hours, the Rangers got orders to come back to Leatherneck. They loaded onto a couple of MH-47s and headed back. They left their prisoners with the Marines. The prisoners were questioned and later released.

Downtown Minneapolis

Halfway around the world that same afternoon, the city's commuters were clearing out. On Fridays during Minnesota's brief summer, the state's cabin culture dictates that people do just about anything to get out of work early. They jump in their vehicles and head "up north" to the state's ten thousand–plus crystal-clear lakes—and the resorts, cabins, and pine forests that surround them.

At a few minutes before 3:00 p.m., Jill Stephenson was still at her desk at Wells Fargo. She was finishing some work before heading off with friends. They had plans to meet at the Basilica Block Party, a concert and fundraiser in front of the Basilica of Saint Mary, a massive Catholic church on the edge of downtown Minneapolis.

Jill was about to finish up when her cell phone rang. She looked down and saw a series of zeroes. *Ben.* She answered quickly, anticipating his voice.

"This is Jill."

"Jill, this is Don Kingston. I'm Ben's company commander." Captain Kingston was sitting in Lieutenant Colonel Walrath's office at Kandahar Airfield. He had taken a few minutes to work up the nerve to make the call.

"Yes?" Jill said nervously. This wasn't a name she recognized.

"Ben has been shot," Kingston said.

He explained that the wound was to Ben's left leg. He said that her son had undergone surgery, had not yet awakened, and they weren't sure when he would. They were monitoring him, and the next move would be to get him to Germany. Jill furiously scribbled his words onto yellow Post-it notes.

"He's unconscious," Kingston continued. "We'd like to get him to Walter Reed in Washington as soon as we can. We're just not sure what's going to happen."

"When? When will he be there?"

"I'm sorry, I don't know. We're hoping to get him there as soon as we can, and we'll make sure we get you wherever he's going to be."

"Is his leg okay? Is he going to lose his leg?" she asked.

"His leg will be fine," Kingston assured her. "Someone else will be calling you back from the Rear D at Fort Benning," Kingston said. "Rear D" referred to rear detachment, the element of their command that coordinates communications and logistics between soldiers and their families.

Jill thanked him and hung up. Her head was spinning, and she felt numb. After telling her boss, she called her mom and dad and broke the news to them, promising to keep them posted.

Her friends came by to pick her up, but Jill was now in no mood to attend the block party. She said she wanted to go home, but they convinced her to stay with them until she learned more about Ben's condition. They walked a few blocks to the Basilica, a structure that could easily sit alongside many of the great churches of Europe. Inside, the walls soared seventy feet from the floor. The cathedral was massive, its nave two feet higher than even that of St. Peter's Basilica in the Vatican.

As Jill walked inside she felt foggy, like she was in a bad dream she couldn't escape. She and her friends sat in one of the pews and prayed silently for a while. Jill felt powerless, but she was thankful to have friends with her. She realized that going home and sitting alone by the phone was the worst thing she could do right now.

They left the church and went outside to find a spot to sit in the grass. As soon as the music started, her phone rang. She rushed to a quieter place to take the call. It was the Rear D commander calling from 75th Ranger Regiment headquarters at Fort Benning. He had no new information on Ben, but said he would be her contact for whatever she needed.

After that her phone started ringing continually. Her parents had obviously spread the news, but Jill couldn't take the calls. She didn't want to hear herself say over and over that Ben had been shot. She let her phone ring and ring.

It started to rain. Jill grew weary of the concert scene and decided to go home. One of her girlfriends accompanied her to Rosemount and stayed with her that night. Now Jill was doing what she dreaded: sitting by the phone and waiting for any news about her son. This went on for three days.

Camp Leatherneck

Ben arrived back at Leatherneck at 6:00 p.m. on July 10. By the time the rest of his platoon got back, Ben was already at the base hospital. First Sergeant Knight, Captain Johanson, and Captain McKenna went directly from the landing helicopters to see Ben. Knight realized he was filthy after a day of intense combat, but he couldn't spare another minute without checking on Ben.

Walking into Ben's room, Knight, Johanson, and McKenna saw he was unconscious. He was hooked up to a variety of tubes, wires, and machines. Nurses told Knight they were waiting for him to wake up from surgery, but for some reason he wasn't. Knight had a gut feeling something wasn't right. He grew angry. When he and the medics had gotten Ben onto the helicopter, he'd been stable and conscious. Knight had assumed Ben would be okay, but now he seemed anything but. Standing at Ben's bedside, Knight turned to silent prayer. "God, please. Please intervene here."

Dr. McKenna went to talk to the other doctors who were treating Ben. They too were frustrated. They told McKenna they knew something was wrong but weren't sure exactly what it was. An initial CT scan indicated there might be some sort of brain injury, possibly from a lack of oxygen or blood getting to the brain. McKenna was in disbelief. He had treated Ben himself hours earlier and fully expected to see him in better shape.

The trio of Charlie Company leaders also asked about Captain Krueger's condition. They were told he was now in surgery after undergoing a series of MRIs and X-rays. Knight, Johanson, and McKenna then left the hospital and returned to their quarters.

Rosemount, Minnesota

When the next phone call came, Jill talked with Dr. McKenna, who had treated Ben in the field. McKenna told her they were sending Ben on to Landstuhl, Germany, where there was an American military hospital. McKenna expressed concern that Ben was having issues with brain pressure and brain activity. A medical team was going to further assess his condition at Landstuhl. Depending on what they found and how stable Ben was, they would decide whether they could send him to Walter Reed or not. The Ranger Regiment would then send Jill to either Germany or Washington, DC, depending on Ben's location. Jill cringed at the idea of having to fly eight hours to Germany while her son clung to life. She prayed he would be able to make it to Walter Reed instead.

Camp Leatherneck

The morning of July 11, Captain Krueger woke up. After a day of combat, a gunshot wound, surgery, and anesthesia, Krueger was groggy and straining to get his bearings. He soon realized Ben lay just across the room, unconscious and hooked to several machines.

A nurse entered the room.

"Hey, what's going on with Ben?" Krueger asked.

"He had surgery."

"Is he going to be okay?"

"We're not sure what's going on," the nurse replied. "We had him on sedatives. We've taken him off, but he's not waking up." The nurse walked over to Ben's bed and gently nudged his arm. "Ben . . . Ben . . . can you hear me?"

She turned back to Captain Krueger.

"He bit down on his breathing tube earlier, so that's encouraging. But it would really help if you could talk to him too."

Krueger immediately got up and walked over to Ben.

"Hey, bud, we're here," he said. "Hope you're all right."

Meanwhile, a doctor entered and gave Krueger the news on his own wound. The bullet had passed cleanly through his back, exiting his upper chest just under the clavicle and above his rib bone. Dan Krueger was remarkably lucky—the round had passed just a few inches right of his spinal cord and narrowly missed the top of his lung. It was a million-dollar wound. No bones had been hit or damaged, and no blood vessels had been ruptured. Krueger did suffer a bit of nerve damage. He concluded he'd been hit by an AK-74 round and not the larger AK-47.

Later that morning, a group of Rangers came to visit, including Knight, Captain Sandifer, Johanson, Sergeant DeRose, and Michael Melvin. Squad leader Carl Benson was there too. Krueger got up and walked around with them, conferring on the events of the last twenty-four hours.

"That's the luckiest shot you could ever get," McKenna told Krueger. Krueger nodded, his thoughts still on Ben.

"The doctor said Ben is just waiting to wake up," Krueger reported.

Knight was silent for a moment, realizing the medical staff hadn't given Krueger the full picture. "Hey, this isn't going as well as you think it's going," he replied quietly. "He's had some other complications."

It suddenly hit Krueger: Ben's situation was grave. He felt a wave of shock come over him. They had both been shot at nearly the same time in the same place. *How could things work out like this?*

Captain Sandifer, whom many of the Rangers looked to for spiritual leadership, went over to Ben. He had been leading prayers for Ben back at Ranger quarters in the overnight hours. Sandifer put his hand on Ben's arm, leaned toward his ear, and quietly talked with him and prayed. Sandifer reminded Ben that God was with him. Each of the Rangers who had come to visit spent some time alone with Ben.

For Michael Melvin, seeing Ben in this condition was more than he could take. The company medic was overcome with emotion and had to leave.

As the day wore on, other Rangers from Third Platoon visited, including Ryan Lundeby. Lundeby and Ben had done three combat deployments and gone through Ranger School together. His heart broke seeing Ben like this. They had plans for a trip to Australia together in the fall. Though Ben was unconscious, Lundeby talked to him about learning to surf and about the girls they were going to meet in Sydney. Lundeby hadn't slept the night before, thinking and worrying all night about his friend. He wouldn't sleep for days. Ben's friends and fellow Rangers prayed he'd pull through. There was nothing else they could do but pray and wait.

Pakistani Airspace

The same day, an Air Force C-17 cruised over Pakistan on its way to Camp Leatherneck. The big cargo aircraft had taken off a couple of hours before from an airfield in Qatar. In the cargo hold, Tech Sergeant Alicia Pratt and Master Sergeant Jim Welch of the New York Air National Guard were preparing for injured service members to be brought aboard. The flight was an "alert mission" for injured soldiers and Marines, many of them in serious to critical condition. This was the tenth mission on her first deployment for the twenty-four-year-old Pratt from Troy, New York. Pratt's team had been busy in recent weeks on flights around the region, providing medical evacuations from both Iraq and Afghanistan. She was still having a hard time adjusting to seeing America's best young men severely wounded from combat.

The military hospitals in Afghanistan were a collective system. The more remote they were, the fewer beds they had, and the less sophisticated the equipment was. The goal within the system was to get wounded service members back to the United States as soon as possible. Within the chain of care, Landstuhl in Germany was better than anything in Afghanistan, Bagram better than Leatherneck, and Leatherneck better than Dwyer. Medical teams were tasked with evaluating the severity of injuries and determining what kind of treatment was needed and what spots were available at hospitals and on outbound aircraft. Ben Kopp was a very high priority, even during what was a violent time in Afghanistan.

After crossing the Persian Gulf and passing through Pakistani airspace, the C-17 landed at Camp Leatherneck. The time had come to move Ben to the larger hospital at Camp Bagram. There were about twenty casualties being brought aboard the C-17, all with a variety of injuries. Captain Krueger walked aboard under his own power, as did Sergeant Watkins. Ben was last to come aboard. He remained unconscious and on a ventilator as he was wheeled aboard and locked into place. A Critical Care Air Transport Team (CCAT) came aboard. That team included a doctor, a critical care nurse, and a respiratory therapist. That team focused specifically on Ben, the most seriously wounded patient aboard the aircraft.

Sergeant Pratt's job on the flight was to assist the CCAT team. She asked his medical team about his condition. Pratt, Welch, the rest of the air med crew, and Ben's medical team gathered for a quick briefing. The aircraft took off at about 7:15 p.m.

Once they were airborne, Watkins and Krueger insisted that all medical attention be focused on Ben. Sergeant Pratt was struck by how much the Rangers were pulling for him. They also were appreciative of her care.

"We're taking care of the people who make sure we're safe," Pratt told them. "I want to make sure you guys get the best care you can because of what you all are doing for the rest of us."

She walked over to Ben. His eyes were closed. The only signs of life were the healthy color of his flesh and the movement of his chest, forced by the respirator. She looked into his face. *He's so young*, she thought, *younger than I am*. She looked at his chart and realized there wasn't anything she could do for him medically. All she could think to do was to hold his hand. Standing next to him, she gently squeezed it. As she did, she said a silent prayer—*God, please help him pull through.* After about a minute, she gently let go, feeling in her heart that he would pull through.

It was only a thirty-minute flight from Leatherneck to Bagram. As quickly as they'd reached altitude, the larger base approached, and she and Welch sat back down for landing. Once on the ground, the aircraft taxied to a stop. The rear ramp opened, revealing waiting sand-colored ambulances. Ben and his CCAT team were first off the plane. They loaded Ben aboard an ambulance. A small medical bus awaited the rest of the patients, and Krueger and Watkins climbed aboard. The rear bay door slowly closed, and the aircraft taxied back toward the runway. Inside, Sergeant Alicia Pratt couldn't stop thinking about that young Ranger, hoping and praying he would be all right.

Bagram Air Base

Krueger and Kopp spent a couple days at Bagram together. Ben was assigned to the intensive care unit. Krueger was nearby in a room with other guys who were less seriously injured. Krueger was on a lot of painkillers, his mind swimming with stress and a sense of loss. He kept thinking about his guys in Third Platoon at Camp Leatherneck. He knew they were all worried about Ben, and he wanted to be with them. Krueger went to Ben's room regularly to check on him. He sat on the edge of Ben's bed and prayed for his friend. He also asked the nurses who came by for updates. However, it was now becoming clear Ben's condition was not getting better.

On July 13, Ben left Bagram aboard a C-17 at about 3:40 a.m. headed for Landstuhl Regional Medical Center in Germany. It was the standard next stop for nearly all injured service members leaving Iraq and Afghanistan.

Captain Krueger flew to Germany about twelve hours after

Ben and was met by the unit liaison, a SOCOM (Special Operations Command) sergeant. "You're with Kopp, right?" the sergeant said.

"Yeah."

"He literally just left."

Krueger was disappointed; he had hoped to see Ben one more time. But at the same time, he was also relieved. Three days after being shot in combat, Ben was finally flying home to the United States.

Rosemount, Minnesota

The last three days had been agonizing for Jill. Every moment, every second dragged on. Things felt so dark, like being in a room with no windows or lights. She knew there was a way out, but she didn't know where or how. It was a test of her faith to trust Ben would be okay. It hurt so badly that she couldn't see him or talk with him. She was at the mercy of unknown forces—people whose phone calls she was waiting on and, most of all, God.

Jill finally got the call that Ben was on his way to Walter Reed Army Medical Center. The Ranger Regiment said they'd make airline and hotel reservations for her and her mother. Jill would leave the next day, July 14.

Before she left for Washington, Jill started a CaringBridge page for Ben. All she could say at this point was that Ben had been shot, he was unconscious, and he needed prayers. She posted:

> I believe in miracles and know that people overcome odds every minute of every day. Ben is tenacious as hell and has a strong will to survive. He would not have been where he was if he didn't. The best way to get Ben to accomplish anything is to make it a challenge. Obviously, this is not the kind of challenge any of us would wish for, but if anyone can do it, Ben can!

The word quickly spread to Ben's closest friends and family, including Jenny Boll's parents. Dave Boll called his daughter right away.

"Where are you? What are you doing?"

"I'm out with my girlfriends," Jenny said.

"Can you come home?"

"Why? What's going on?"

"Just come home," he said. "We need to talk about something."

Jenny sensed something big was wrong.

"Is it Ben?" she asked.

"Jenny, just come home."

She started crying on the phone. Her dad resisted telling her at first, but he finally broke at her insistence.

"Ben got shot in the leg," he said.

Jenny hung up. She was terribly upset, but as she processed the news she thought, *Maybe this is a miracle. Ben could certainly survive a leg wound.* She also thought this would mean he'd get to come home early from his deployment. *Thank God, he finally gets to get out of there and come home.*

Fort Benning, Georgia

Word was spreading back at Ranger barracks as well. Shane Harris, Ben's close friend from RIP, got called into a room as part of the 3rd Ranger Battalion's Delta Company. About ten Rangers gathered. A sergeant had a message to pass along.

"Ben Kopp from Charlie Company was injured in Afghanistan," the sergeant started. "He suffered a gunshot wound to the leg. It's serious. He's alive, but he's in a coma."

Harris's heart sank. He thought back to when they first arrived at Ranger battalion. He remembered how tough Ben had been getting hazed over the Morgan Garrett situation. Harris knew how tough Ben was. He shared that with the other guys.

"If there's anyone who could fight this, it's Ben. And he's not gonna quit."

Harris felt a growing sense of hope. He knew others had been shot and survived. He felt positive Ben would be okay. He stayed glued to Ben's CaringBridge site for updates.

Chicago, Illinois

Also following closely on CaringBridge was Jill's first cousin, Maria Burud. Maria and Jill had remained close over the years, and even though Maria hadn't seen Ben since he was a boy of about seven, his deployment had weighed on her the last couple of weeks. Seeing the call for prayers, Maria started letting her friends know. She thought of one friend in particular: her old coworker Judy Meikle.

Judy and Maria had remained in contact over the years, and Maria knew how patriotic Judy was and how much love and respect she had for the troops. She called her friend with a plea. "Hey, I just want you to know, my cousin's over in Afghanistan, and he got shot in the leg. There's a CaringBridge site, check it out."

Judy agreed to check out Ben's site. They also discussed Judy's pending heart transplant. Judy told Maria it could be a matter of days or a matter of months. After hanging up, Judy logged on and started following Ben's plight online, having no idea their lives were on a spectacular collision course.

PART

IV

Walter Reed Army Medical Center

Ranger staff sergeant Phil Paquette paced back and forth outside the emergency entrance of Walter Reed. It was Tuesday, July 14. Four days before, Sergeant Paquette had gotten word that Charlie Company's Third Platoon had been in a hellacious gunfight in Helmand Province and three Rangers had been wounded. Paquette, a part of Charlie Company, had been at Fort Benning on rear detachment and had called his friend First Sergeant Greg Knight in Afghanistan. "Hey, I'm going to go meet Ben at Walter Reed," he said.

Knight agreed with the plan and told Paquette that whatever he needed, he could depend on the Regiment back at Fort Benning to back him up. Army Rangers have a code: a wounded Ranger is never left alone, even at a hospital, and a wounded soldier's family always receives Ranger support. The duty is referred to as a "liaison officer."

Paquette, a Newport, Rhode Island, native, had never performed this role before. As much as Rangers train for different scenarios, they receive no formal training to be liaison officers. Sergeant Paquette didn't know what lay ahead. He could be walking into a very difficult, emotional situation, and possibly facing a family angry with the Army and the Ranger Regiment. He prepared himself for anything.

Paquette was no stranger to tragedy after nine combat deployments, but he'd only seen one death on the battlefield. (He'd been with fellow Ranger Jimmy Regan in northern Iraq in 2007, when Regan's Humvee was hit by an IED.) Before leaving Fort Benning, he retrieved Ben's blue book, which contained Ben's final wishes in case of a serious medical situation or death.

Paquette was dressed in his multicam duty uniform and khaki boots that day. His tan beret sloped down neatly over the right side of his head. He waited just outside the delivery area where ambulances bring wounded servicemen and servicewomen, completing the last leg of their trip after flying in from overseas. He knew of Ben because they were in the same company, but they were in different platoons and were not close friends. As Paquette paced, he heard the rumble of what sounded like a big truck. He turned and saw a massive ambulance heading toward him. It was bigger than the typical ambulance, more like an RV. The Air Evac, as it was called, could handle multiple patients on life support in the delicate transfer from aircraft to hospital. It was a twenty-five-mile trip on I-495 from Andrews Air Force Base to Walter Reed.

Paquette heard Ben had been shot in the leg, but he didn't know much else. He wanted to make eye contact and wave to Ben to let him know he was here for him. He waited for the crew to roll his fellow Ranger out. He anticipated Ben would be sitting up on the stretcher and looking around at his new surroundings. Paquette watched as the doors swung open. Ben's stretcher was rolled out, but it wasn't what Paquette had envisioned. Ben was unconscious and on full life support, his body shrouded in a thicket of tubes. A crew carefully carried him and his connected machines off the ambulance and into the hospital, leaving Paquette frozen in shock.

Just inside the hospital doors, another Ranger was waiting on Ben, though Paquette didn't know it. Command Sergeant Major Rudy DelValle was the ranking enlisted man at Walter Reed. DelValle served as the adviser to the hospital commander. He had noticed a Ranger on the manifest of the incoming wounded today and wanted to be there to greet him when he arrived.

DelValle, a native of Moscow, Idaho, grew up in the Ranger community in the First Ranger Battalion in Savannah, Georgia. He saw it as his mission to check in on all the wounded, but he always took special notice when a Ranger or other special operator arrived at Walter Reed.

DelValle had come on board at Walter Reed after the Building 18 controversy broke in early 2007, revealing poor conditions and a failing and complex bureaucracy. While DelValle wasn't part of that administration, he desperately wanted to turn the reputation of the old Army hospital around. The hospital was home to injured service members coming in from Iraq and Afghanistan, veterans, retirees, and members of Congress. DelValle helped lift the spirits of so many who came through Walter Reed on his watch. He had met people like Brendan Marrocco, wounded earlier in 2009—the first quadruple amputee to survive, get prosthetics, and become an inspiration to countless others. The hospital also took care of CIA agents injured in the field. Even ABC News reporter Bob Woodruff went there after he was severely injured by an IED in Iraq in 2006.

DelValle went up to the third floor to see Ben in the intensive care unit. It broke his heart to see him in this condition. He couldn't quite comprehend it. *How could this have happened from a gunshot wound to the leg?* DelValle spent about thirty minutes with Ben after he first arrived in the ICU. He talked with the medical staff and told them he wanted regular updates on Ben's condition.

Moments after DelValle left, Phil Paquette walked in and tried to talk to his fellow Ranger. "Hey, Ben, how's it going, buddy?" he said softly. "I hope you're getting better." He wasn't sure whether Ben could hear him or not. His thoughts turned to Ben's mother, who was just landing in Washington. He was feeling nervous about meeting her. What would she be like? A single mother coming to be with her only child, who was clinging to life—this was going to be tough. After sitting with Ben for a while, Paquette went down to the lobby to wait for Jill.

A man and woman dressed in military uniform greeted Jill and her mom, Mary, at the airport. The mother and daughter followed them out and climbed into a van. They drove across the Potomac River and through DC to Walter Reed. The buildings of the nation's capital were a blur as Jill thought about her son, longing to lay her eyes on her precious Ben once again.

Pulling into the five-story parking ramp at Walter Reed, they got out and proceeded to the third floor and the ICU. After a short jaunt through the hallways, Jill spotted someone who looked like a Ranger and approached him. It was Phil Paquette.

Paquette had a New England bluntness that would sometimes serve him well in his new duty and sometimes not. "If Ben could speak, he'd probably tell you I'm an asshole," he told Jill within minutes of meeting her.

"It doesn't matter now," Jill quickly replied, surprised by his words.

Paquette was trying to explain that he had come into the Ranger Regiment when discipline was doled out through intimidation. Early in his Army career, he'd been on the receiving end. When Ben came into the battalion five years later, Paquette was on the giving end. He'd just wanted Jill to know it was nothing personal.

"My job is to get you whatever you need, no matter what," he told her, as they walked toward Ben's room.

"Thank you," she said. She had no idea at the time the lengths Paquette would go to do so.

They walked through the hustle and bustle of the military hospital—doctors, nurses, and orderlies rushing to their next patients. But when they got to Ben's room, Jill and Mary had to wait in the hallway. A combination of veterans and active-duty service members, most in their fifties and sixties, were crowded around Ben. Jill had flown halfway across the country and hadn't laid eyes on her son yet. These men now turned to her to introduce themselves. She remained patient. The men were very respectful and offered their good wishes and prayers. One even gave her his military coin, which had a display of three stars. But Jill desperately wanted to fight past them to see Ben.

After they'd left, Jill and Mary went in to see Ben. He was hidden behind an octopus of tubes, cords, and wires. His eyes were taped shut, and he was covered with a sheet and blanket. He looked surprisingly good, Jill thought, muscular, healthy, and strong. His color was good, and his hair was short. Jill went to her son's side, never taking her eyes off his face. She put her hand on his head. He was warm. His closely cropped hair felt soft, like it had when he was a child. It meant the world to her to see him, even like this.

Her hand went from his hair to his hand; she noticed how strong it felt. She was grateful to be touching him. She thought of families meeting flag-draped caskets at air bases around the country, or still others with service members who came home physically healthy, but because of PTSD and the mental anguish of combat, later took their own lives.

A perpetual chorus of machines breathed and beeped, all of it keeping her son alive. Despite the wound to his leg, there was no injury to his face or upper body. The medical personnel told her his leg would be fine, and she took their word for it. She had no desire to look at the wound herself. The doctors told Jill they would be running tests during the day. They would all meet the following morning and let her know what they'd found.

Ben's CaringBridge page was exploding with messages, prayers, and well wishes from all over the country. Jill printed out the messages and put them on Ben's bed. After spending the rest of the afternoon at her son's side, Jill and Mary left that evening, drained from the flight and an emotional day. They returned to their hotel to rest for the next day, which would be one of the most difficult and trying of their lives. They needed a miracle, and they prayed they would get one.

Camp Leatherneck

Four days after Ben was injured, the mail for him in Afghanistan was piling up. At mail call, one of the sergeants wandered in with a handful of envelopes. It was clear from the swirling script and return addresses that most of Ben's mail was from young women. The sergeant called out the various names in the platoon, handing out envelopes filled with love, fear, concern, and good wishes. When Ben's pile of mail came up, the sergeant ran his thumb across the edges of the letters like a deck of cards, then shook his head incredulously. "He must be a pimp," he joked.

While the hearts of most of the guys in Third Platoon remained heavy over Ben's grave condition, there were a few chuckles. It was comforting to them that even in his current state, Ben was still a ladies' man.

Walter Reed Army Medical Center

On July 15, visitors started showing up. When Jill walked into Ben's room that morning, a command sergeant major and his wife stood on opposite sides of Ben's bed. Jill walked forward and stood next to the sergeant major, dressed in his duty uniform.

He turned to face her. "I'm Jeff Mellinger. This is my wife, Kim." He put his arm around Jill's shoulder, pulling her closer as they looked down at Ben. "I'm really sorry about your son," he said.

Jill felt a sudden sense of love and compassion emanating from two people she'd never met. It was a feeling she would soon get used to, the heartfelt love and empathy of total strangers.

Jeff Mellinger had an interesting claim to fame. He'd been drafted during the Vietnam War on April 18, 1972. While he never actually went to fight in Vietnam, he was the last continuously serving enlisted soldier drafted during the Vietnam era. He had also served in some impressive leadership posts, including a thirty-three-month deployment in Iraq as the CSM for Generals George W. Casey and David Petraeus. Mellinger and Rudy DelValle were close friends. DelValle had called Mellinger and told him about Ben, asking for his support and prayers.

Mellinger was a frequent visitor to Walter Reed. His big heart went out to wounded guys. He was now the Army's Materiel Command Sergeant Major. He lived in the DC area at Fort McNair and traveled to Fort Belvoir for work. But when it came to wounded warriors, he always wanted to know how he could help. He hosted barbecues at his house for injured service members and their families, feeding them chicken and ribs whenever he got the chance.

Mellinger looked at Ben Kopp, the young Ranger lying in the bed. He thought about his condition, and the strength and toughness he must've had as a Ranger. He looked up at Jill, who was now sitting across the room from her son. He admired how cool and collected she was considering all she was going through. *This is really an unusual woman*, he thought. Mellinger would continue to check in on Ben and Jill.

Later that day, Jill, Mary, and Sergeant Paquette shuffled into an empty room down the hall from Ben's for a meeting with the doctors. Jill was fixated on the doctors' faces, trying to read their expressions for some sign of hope. She didn't see anything positive. As they sat down, the doctors bluntly told her they believed Ben was brain dead. They came to that conclusion after performing manual stimulation tests on him—needle pricks to the feet and palms and light shone in

Jill's brother JT was hit by a car on July 15, 1982, at the age of eleven near his St. Louis Park, Minnesota home. He died days later. The family made the decision to donate JT's organs. Jill got the news that Ben would not survive on July 15, 2009, exactly twenty-seven years later.

the eyes. A person who wasn't brain dead would still react to these, even if unconscious, the doctors told her.

The doctors also said the time had come for her to start considering donating Ben's organs. Jill felt a surge of anger. Her thoughts immediately went back nearly three decades to her younger brother, JT. The eleven-year-old was on his way home from baseball practice in St. Louis Park, Minnesota. He'd decided to take a shortcut across a very busy Highway 100. While crossing, he was hit by a car. He was rushed to a nearby hospital and remained on life support for ten days before the family learned he wouldn't survive. Together, the Burud family decided to donate JT's organs in an era when that was a new concept. The day JT was hit was July 15, 1982, exactly twenty-seven years to the day. The coincidence sent chills up Jill's spine.

The anger she'd felt tearing through her moments before exploded. "How could God do this to two mothers in the same family?" she blurted out. She picked up a box of tissues on the table in front of her and threw it across the room. "How could God do this to two mothers in the same family?" she repeated, thinking of her little brother, her mom, and now Ben. Jill was filled with rage and disbelief. She looked up at Mary, who was crying. Jill knew she was reliving the death of her own son in what appeared to be the imminent death of her grandson.

And then something came over Jill Stephenson. She suddenly realized that this wasn't all about her, and that Ben's death would affect a lot of people.

She turned and looked into her mother's teary eyes and saw survival and hope. Over the years, her mom had worked through the pain of losing her son. Jill was comforted knowing a shining example of how to deal with this excruciating sadness was sitting right next to her. She would somehow get through this, and she wasn't alone.

Jill decided that she was not yet ready to pass along this news. She knew that many people were praying for Ben all across the country, and she didn't want to tell those people to stop. She turned back to the doctors to address their question about donating her son's organs. "Yes, of course," she offered, her voice now calm. But despite Jill's approval, Ben was now twenty-one years old. They told her they would have to consult his Army blue book to review his wishes. And there were other hurdles to clear. Doctors needed to administer a test required by law to determine whether there was any brain activity. They warned Jill and Mary that the instrument used for the test wasn't readily available, and it might be a couple of days before it was. While most families might anguish over the delay, Jill realized that this bought her more time with Ben, a small reprieve.

Hastings, Minnesota

Jenny Boll walked into her family's kitchen and found her mom standing at the sink crying.

"Mom, what's wrong?" she asked.

"Nothing," her mom replied, concerned about her daughter's fragile condition fresh out of treatment. But Jenny pressed her.

"There are more complications with Ben than we thought," her mom said. She broke down crying.

Jenny stood there, stunned. When she recovered she said, "I need to go! I need to get on a plane right now!"

Jenny found her dad in his office and made the same plea. She needed to be with Ben as soon as possible. It was now about 11:00 p.m. Dave Boll went online and tried to find her a flight; there was nothing until the next day.

"We need to go right now," she insisted.

Her dad told her he didn't want to push this on Jill, that he needed her permission first. Dave Boll called Jill and told her how badly Jenny wanted to be there for Ben. "She's determined that her presence will make a difference in Ben's survival," he offered.

"Jenny is welcome to come out here," Jill said. "I can't help her at all, though. I can't pick her up at the airport, and I can't get her to her hotel. But she's welcome to be here."

Dave told Jill he understood. He would come with his daughter, and they would try to get on the next plane to Washington.

Walter Reed Army Medical Center

Sergeant Paquette quickly became invaluable to Jill. She was overwhelmed by the emotion of the life-and-death decisions she had to make nearly every hour. If Paquette saw her in distress, he was right there to back her up. Paquette became the buffer Jill needed between herself and the many doctors, nurses, and others who demanded her attention. He would protect her, physically standing in front of or beside her, and he wouldn't let anyone do anything without his permission. He also rarely left her side. To some it might've seemed overbearing, but Jill found his presence and counsel comforting.

Jill and Paquette started going to Walter Reed's chapel each day to pray. Sitting side by side, they held hands as Paquette offered prayers aloud. He spoke extemporaneously, praying in a way Jill had never heard before. Her prayers had always been silent and more formal. Phil opened a Bible and read some passages, and they talked about the meaning. She told Paquette Ben hadn't grown up in the church, but in the last few years he'd been on a faith journey. She also said she'd always believed in God, and she would sometimes share a prayer at home with Ben. Paquette suggested that Ben be baptized as soon as possible. Soon after, a chaplain came to Ben's room and performed the ceremony. For Paquette, a Catholic, sharing this time at Walter Reed with Jill was also a spiritual journey for him.

"There is a purpose behind all this," Paquette offered during one of their prayer sessions. "You can't think that this is all for naught. You have to find something in this."

Jill couldn't yet see what that purpose was, but she began to call

Paquette her "Ranger Angel." For his part, Paquette's anxiety about dealing with a grieving family and a distraught mother was gone. He was now completely comfortable with Jill and felt he owed her everything he could give.

On Ben's recommendation, Jill had bought two copies of *The Road to Unafraid* by Jeff Struecker. She had given one to Mary and was reading the other herself. She and Mary had brought their copies to Washington to pass the time as they waited with Ben. She told Paquette that just before Ben was injured, he had called her and told her he was reading the book.

"Really?" Paquette asked. "You know Struecker's in the Regiment, don't you?"

Jill's face lit up on hearing this. It wasn't that Jeff Struecker had displayed remarkable courage during the Battle of Mogadishu, or that he was one of the characters made famous by the Hollywood blockbuster *Black Hawk Down*. It was that he was someone Ben idolized. "The back of the book says he's retired and lives in West Virginia," she said.

"Well, he's still in," Paquette replied. "You want me to call him?"

"Are you kidding me?"

"No, we can go call him," Paquette said. "Jill, I'm gonna call him and get him up here."

Paquette made the promise without first checking with Struecker because he knew the character of Rangers, particularly in a situation like this. It never occurred to Paquette that Struecker might *not* come.

"You can do that?" Jill asked.

"I will for you," he replied.

Paquette retreated to a phone and called the staff duty desk back at Fort Benning. He asked for Chaplain Struecker's number and dialed him up. Struecker happened to be on vacation with his family in his hometown of Fort Dodge, Iowa. When he answered, Paquette wasted no time explaining Ben's situation. "When can you be here?" Paquette asked.

"Hey, I'll be there tomorrow," Struecker said without hesitation.

Paquette came back into the room.

"He's on vacation, but he said he'd cut it short to see Ben." Jill was overwhelmed with the support that seemed to come from every corner of the Ranger Regiment.

That night, Jill and Mary lay in their hotel beds talking in the dark.

"I have a vision," Jill said. "When it's our time to go, God reaches down and plucks us up off the earth, like this big arm that comes down and says, 'Now it's you.'"

Mary mulled this over in silence.

"No, that's not quite how it is," she started. "God doesn't just pluck us up when it's our time. We reach up to him too, so we meet in the middle."

Jill lay there, thinking about what her mom had just said. It created a beautiful image in her mind. "Mom, that's the most profound thing I've ever heard you say. Why does it have to take a situation like this to realize something like that?"

Mary Barnes pondered the question for a moment. Knowing they were facing another incredibly difficult day, she didn't answer the question. But as a mom who had laid a child of her own to rest, she offered her daughter some advice. "You need to tell Ben it's okay to go. It's important for him to know he has your permission, and that you'll be okay. I told your brother that."

"Okay, Mom, I will."

Walter Reed Army Medical Center, July 16

Jenny Boll walked as quickly as she could down the hallway at Walter Reed, her dad trailing her. She was certain her presence at Ben's bedside would be enough to wake him up.

She rounded a corner and spotted Jill right away, standing just outside Ben's room. Jill turned to see Jenny moving with great purpose toward her. Jill managed a smile, and Jenny hugged her.

"Are you ready for this?" Jill asked.

"Yeah," Jenny said, taking a deep breath. Her tone revealed some doubt.

"Are you sure?"

"Yes!" Jenny said impatiently, wanting to see Ben immediately.

Jill directed Jenny into Ben's room. Jenny's mind and heart were ready for anything. She laid eyes on him and was surprised Ben looked so good. She thought he looked healthy, like he was just taking a nap. Then she noticed the tubes and wires. She felt as if she was in a dream. *This couldn't possibly be happening.* Tears started to roll down her face.

Ben's grandmother, Mimi, who was sitting in the room, suggested, "He likes kisses."

This brought a little smile to Jenny's face. She sat on the bed next to Ben. A machine hooked up to Ben displayed a number that correlated to the pressure on his brain. A nurse explained to Jenny what the number meant, that it was now too high and needed to drop. The nurse pointed to a line on the monitor where Ben's level needed to be. The nurse explained that they were trying to control his brain pressure with medication but were having trouble. Jenny sat on the bed and held Ben's hand, watching the brain pressure machine and willing the number to drop.

Later in the day, family and visitors took a break outside Ben's room. A slow, creeping realization came over all of them—Ben wasn't getting better. He wasn't even holding steady. They were silent and somber, unsure of how to react in this limbo.

Mimi finally broke the silence. "We're all a little mad at God right now," she said.

Jenny nodded, knowing what she meant, then she and her dad left to go back to their hotel.

As the night came to a close and visitors filed out, Jill went to her son's bedside. She was emotionally and physically exhausted. She remembered the conversation she'd had with Mary the night before.

"Ben, I'm okay with your decision, whatever it is," she said. "There are a lot of people praying for you. You need to decide: Do you want to keep the prayers and the miracles being asked for in your name, or do you want to give them away? It's up to you, Ben. And I want you to know I support whatever decision you make, and I'll be okay if you choose to give them away."

Walter Reed Army Medical Center, July 17

Jill arrived at Ben's room early that morning. As she passed through the doorway, she looked down at Ben and something immediately struck her. She could see a marked difference in him, even from the night before. She instantly had the feeling his soul had left his body. She turned to Mary. "He's not here . . . He's not here."

Minutes later, Ben's medical staff backed up her assertion. They told her Ben had had a rough night, and they were having trouble controlling the swelling in his brain. Ben was suffering from cerebral hypoxia, a lack of oxygen to the outer portion of his brain.

Jill thought of all those people who were praying for Ben. She knew the prayers and the pleas for a miracle would soon flow in different directions, toward other people in need of their own miracles. People like Kenzie Postlewait, who lay in a bed just across the hall from Ben. Kenzie was just four months old but needed heart surgery. Her very young mom and dad, who weren't much older than Ben, were at her bedside constantly. Both of them were in the service. Late at night her dad, Kenneth, would drift from Kenzie's room into Ben's. He'd heard the commotion and had seen some of the high-profile visitors coming and going. He also learned of the heroic way in which Ben had been wounded. He'd spent a few nights at Ben's bedside, talking to him and praying for him in the middle of the night. He had even written Ben a letter, which he handed to Jill.

I know you don't know who I am or what I do. But I know who you are and what you have done with your life. You're an Army Ranger, something most people could never become or even think of trying to become. You're not an average man. You are much more! To some you are a dream, a wish, a want to be. To some you are a little boy out in the backyard. To others a friend and a beautiful smiling face, a person to talk to. Someone we wish we had the guts to become. But to me and my family you are someone to be admired and held in our best regards. You are a HERO, and you are the American Dream, a true protector of America and its freedom. We would like to extend our prayers and our best regards to you and the ones closest to you. Thank you for what you have done and the sacrifices you have made.

Sincerely,
Kenneth Postlewait & Family

Jill was overwhelmed. She thought of little Kenzie and prayed she would be okay. She also thought of the people who would soon receive Ben's organs. Deep inside, Jill knew Ben had made the choice to give them away, one more sacrifice by a Ranger who had already sacrificed so much.

It was now Friday, one week after Ben had been shot. It was also a day filled with visitors. In some ways, things at Walter Reed were happening so fast, and in other ways the days dragged on as they waited for information and tests.

As Paquette had promised, thirty-six hours after the initial phone call, Chaplain Jeff Struecker was at Walter Reed. When he walked into Ben's hospital room, he glanced at the young soldier, but he went right up to Jill.

"Hello, I'm Jeff Struecker," he said. "I'm here for you, and I'm here as long as you need me."

Jill had heard so much about him from Ben, and she knew her son was inspired in the last days of his life by his book. Struecker was handsome and about forty. Within minutes they were praying over Ben's bedside.

In one of the only times Phil Paquette left Jill's side, he hopped in a car and drove to Andrews Air Force Base. He'd gotten word that Captain Krueger had arrived back in the States and was being treated at Andrews. Krueger was making a fast recovery from his gunshot wound. Paquette picked him up and, on their way to Walter Reed, explained that Ben's condition had worsened, and there was little chance for recovery.

When Krueger walked into the room, he didn't say much. To him, Ben looked lifeless, and it hurt to see him that way. Krueger and Jill prayed together. He told her he was sorry for what had happened to her son, and he appreciated serving with him. Krueger wanted to comfort Jill and was stunned by her concern for him while her son lay on the brink of death. He also assured Jill that everything possible had been done for Ben in the field after he was wounded. Still, Krueger felt guilty about the way things had played out. *Why should I be perfectly fine while Ben isn't?* After about thirty minutes, Krueger returned to Andrews to continue his recovery.

Walter Reed Army Medical Center, July 18

The final tests conducted on Ben's brain confirmed what Jill and her family feared all along: he showed no sign of brain activity. Eight days after courageously fighting against the enemy and being shot during battle, Ben Kopp's passing was now paradoxically quiet and clinical. A doctor's signature at exactly 1:00 p.m. on a piece of paper confirmed it was over. Ben was dead.

Ben still looked the same. He wasn't unplugged, and no one was coming to take him off life support. The machines that had been keeping him alive for the last four days kept working even after the death certificate was signed. As Ben had fought so bravely to save others in his last act in life, his body was now being prepared to save the lives of even more people in death.

Doctors called Ben's family together to talk about which organs the medical team could recover. Jeff Struecker remained at Jill's side, helping her through the meeting as he had helped dozens of Army and Ranger families during times of loss.

At one end of the table sat a group of doctors in white coats—a neurologist, a transplant surgeon, members of an organ recovery team, and the doctors who'd been taking care of Ben since he arrived. When a transplant surgeon began to explain the donation process, Struecker sensed that the doctor was being more clinical than he needed to be.

"You can cut the spiel and get right to the chase with her," he advised.

The doctor understood. The medical team made it clear they could take all or none of Ben's organs, or even just some. After the lead doctor was done speaking, Jill asked for a few minutes alone to talk things over with Mary outside the conference room.

A short time later, the women returned. "Take it all. Take everything," Jill said.

The medical staff also told her a little-known fact about organ donation: if she wanted, she could designate organs to anyone waiting for a kidney, liver, or heart. Jill told them she didn't know anyone who was waiting on an organ.

The doctors warned Jill that they might not be able to use Ben's heart because his medical records from Afghanistan indicated he'd suffered a cardiac arrest. They also advised that they couldn't take his eyes because of an eye disease he may have been exposed to in southwestern Asia. And because Ben was now twenty-one, they also needed some evidence of his final wishes.

Jill remained composed. Struecker was amazed at her strength, considering what she was hearing. The meeting ended, and the doctors filed out. "How did you just pull that off?" Struecker asked Jill. "I don't think I could've done that."

"I know where Ben is, and he's not here anymore," Jill replied.

Meanwhile, Paquette had returned from his hotel room with Ben's blue book. It stated that Ben wanted to be an organ donor, and under the question "Which ones?" Ben had written, "Any that are needed."

Ben had also requested that in the event of his death, his high school sweetheart, Brittney Doran, be called. Brittney, who was back in Minnesota, knew Ben had been wounded, but she didn't realize the seriousness of his condition. In her mind, Ben was strong and would pull through. That afternoon Jill called Brittney with the news.

Brittney was at work at a cell phone retail store when she got the call. She immediately broke down and left. Despite their awful fight in Georgia the last time they'd seen each other, Brittney was devastated. The man she'd considered her soulmate was gone. It hurt even more that they'd left things on bad terms.

Back at Walter Reed, Jenny got to spend some time alone with Ben. She realized she needed to work up the nerve to say good-bye. She looked down at him. *He still looks so handsome*, she thought. She held his hand and thought of all the good times they'd spent together. She also thought of how supportive Ben had always been, despite her struggles with drug addiction. With tears streaming down her face, Jenny whispered,

"I love you. I'll see you later."

She walked out of the room and into her dad's waiting arms.

Camp Leatherneck

The news of Ben Kopp's death hit First Sergeant Greg Knight hard. He had never lost a guy before. He and the rest of the leadership now had to inform the company and Ben's Third Platoon.

Battalion Commander Dan Walrath, Company Commander Don Kingston, and Battalion Surgeon Jay McKenna choppered from Kandahar to Leatherneck to break the news. The Rangers of Third Platoon filed into the operations center. Their mood was grim, many sensing the pending announcement.

When Knight shared the news, grown men—America's best and bravest warriors—broke down and cried. Others took the news quietly and somberly. McKenna assured the Rangers that the medical system in place to save their lives still worked. In fact, Ben's was the only case he could recall in which a Ranger should've survived his injury but didn't. He'd seen Rangers survive far more catastrophic injuries. As a result, Ben's death deeply troubled McKenna and would for years. He felt that everything had been done under his and the medics' care in the field to save Ben, and yet something happened out of their hands that took his life.

Company Medic Michael Melvin, who had worked so valiantly under enemy fire to save Ben's life, was overcome. He immediately left the operations center, went straight to his tent, and covered his head with his pillow. He lay there all day and cried. He had been through this with Jimmy Regan in Iraq. Now it was happening again. *Not again!* He had told himself after Regan's death he would *never* let it happen again. *Why?* The pain cut so deep. For years to come, Melvin would struggle with the inexplicable circumstances and pain surrounding Ben's death.

Captain Sandifer, as responsible as any in Charlie Company for helping Ben develop his faith, was also devastated. He had spent so much time in the last week praying and asking for God's help to heal Ben. His death suddenly had him questioning everything. He knew Jesus said in the Gospel of Matthew, "Ask and it will be given to you." Sandifer had been asking God for Ben's survival and recovery during hours of prayer. *Why weren't our prayers effective?* People looked up to Sandifer as a person with deep faith, but Ben's death had left that faith shaken. He went back to his tent and cried. *This doesn't make any sense! This isn't the way it was supposed to go!* Sandifer later invited anyone who wanted to talk and pray to join him. When the sun came up the next morning, about fifteen guys showed up to pray with Sandifer and ask for God's guidance. They prayed for Ben and his family and Sandifer shared with them Psalms 13 and 145.

Kandahar Air Base

Nick Irving and Mark Pendleton were standing just outside their quarters when one of the sergeants from Headquarters Company approached them. Irving sensed bad news from the expression on the sergeant's face.

"Hey, I need to talk to you guys," the sergeant said. "Ben Kopp died today. If you guys need anything, let me know."

The sergeant walked off. A few other Rangers who knew Pendleton and Irving were with Ben when he was hit walked up and offered their condolences.

Irving felt sadness welling up inside him. It pushed at his throat and eyes, and he desperately needed to let it out. But there was nowhere to grieve in private, so he bottled up his feelings. He and Pendleton didn't talk about Ben's death for days. It would be months before Irving let his feelings out. And when he finally would, they'd come out in an epic burst.

Chicago, Illinois

Maria Burud returned to her home on Chicago's Northwest side that Saturday after a graduation party. It was hard to celebrate; all she could think about were her cousins, Ben and Jill. Before going to bed, she logged on to her computer and checked Ben's CaringBridge site. She knew his condition was critical, but reading that Ben was now officially dead was gut-wrenching. She also read that Ben's organs would be donated.

It was late, even later on the east coast where Jill was. Maria couldn't call her, but she still wanted to type something heartfelt on the site. As she sat in front of the computer screen, she couldn't think of the right words. She decided to sleep on it.

When Maria awakened the next morning, July 19, the horrible reality of Ben's death consumed her. Her emotions swirled from sadness to anger and back again. After a while, her thoughts turned to Jill and what she could do for her. *What can I possibly say?* Maria knew she would have to find the words, but reaching deep inside to do it was painful. Knowing Jill had already lost a brother made it even tougher. She was unconsciously resisting. *Be a big girl, Maria, and say something!* Eventually she sat down at the computer and found these words:

Words cannot express my admiration for your amazing show of strength, hope, and grace throughout this time. Ben paid the ultimate sacrifice for our country and you, as his mother, were right behind him. I look at Ethan, only eleven, and cannot even imagine for you it was a mere ten years ago. I'm so sad—I had such hope Ben would make it. I have a girlfriend waiting for a heart here in Chicago. Your and Ben's decision will give her or someone else life. It really is so beautiful that he will live on through someone else. It's one gift that is priceless—besides his life.

Much love and prayers continuing,
Maria, Marielle, Isabelle, and Ethan

Walter Reed Army Medical Center, July 19

"I've got some really great news!"

That was the claim from the twenty-seven-year-old organ donation coordinator. Jill and Mary weren't prepared for his unbridled enthusiasm, considering her son had just died. They looked at him like he was crazy.

"Your son is a beast!" he continued. "We can use his heart. This is unheard of!"

The donation coordinator explained that normally anyone who's had a cardiac arrest is eliminated from being a heart donor. But because of Ben's status—twenty-one years old, healthy, with a high level of fitness—his heart held up to the testing and was more than good enough to donate. (This was also likely a sign his cardiac arrest at Camp Dwyer hadn't been caused by a problem with his heart, but something else.)

Jill and Mary now saw the reason for the coordinator's excitement. In the next twenty-four hours, Ben's heart might save someone's life. Both women were moved to tears.

Jill and Mary arrived at Paquette's hotel that afternoon for a meeting with two Army casualty assistance officers who had been assigned to help with funeral arrangements and other logistics. When one called to say she was running late, Jill decided to pass the time on the hotel's public computer checking Ben's CaringBridge page for new messages.

Since arriving in Washington five days earlier, Jill gained strength from all the tributes people had posted online. She had read dozens of prayers, good wishes, and declarations that Ben was an American hero. As she sat in the hotel lobby and scrolled through the messages, her eye caught part of a post her cousin Maria had written:

> I have a girlfriend waiting for a heart here in Chicago. Your and Ben's decision will give her or someone else life.

The message buzzed like a neon light in front of her. She immediately recalled what doctors had told her about designating Ben's organs. Jill had said at the time she didn't know anyone, but now she did. She jumped up and ran back to the hotel meeting room, telling her dad they needed to call Maria right away. Jill decided right on the spot to offer Ben's heart to Maria's friend, knowing full well it was a long shot. Jill grabbed her phone and called Maria.

"Maria, I don't know how to say this," Jill started. "But God pulled my eye to your post. I see you have a girlfriend who's waiting for a heart."

"I can't believe you saw that, Jill. I didn't know what else to say," Maria said, as she drove southeast down Chicago's Kennedy Expressway. She was with her mom and sister on their way to a baby shower.

"Yesterday the transplant team asked if we knew anyone waiting for any organs, and we said no. Then this came across. I just want you to know I can designate Ben's heart to your friend. If she's a match, she can get Ben's heart."

"But we're in Chicago," said Maria. Judy had told Maria she was limited to receiving a heart within a very specific radius around Chicago, including several Midwestern states.

"Well, I don't know. I can tell the transplant team here," Jill replied. "But first, I need your girlfriend's information—her name, the hospital, and her phone number. She's on the official list, right?"

"Oh yeah, she's on the official list for sure," said Maria. "She's been tracking Ben, Jill. She's been keeping up with his situation and caring about him the whole time."

"Okay, well, let me know," said Jill.

They hung up. Maria, still driving, immediately dialed Judy Meikle.

"Judy, I know this is crazy, but Ben, my cousin Jill's son, died and his organs are available. Jill knows about you, and she says they can designate his heart to you if you're a match."

"What?" said Judy. "But he's in Washington, DC."

"They think they can do it. I just need your information."

As Maria drove and talked, her mom wrote down Judy's information. Maria felt a sudden sense of irony. They were on their way to a shower for a cousin who was about to enter the world as they made plans for the heart of another cousin who had just left it.

Back in DC, the tardy casualty assistance officer arrived at the hotel and apologized to the group for her lateness. Jill assured her it wasn't a problem, realizing that if the woman hadn't been late, it might've been a day or two before she looked at Ben's CaringBridge page again. And that might have been enough time to prevent what she hoped would be a serendipitous connection.

Chicago, Illinois

That afternoon Maria was back on the phone with Judy, who was concerned about the long odds of a match.

"Maria, this isn't going to work out," Judy said. "I just want you to know. Don't get your hopes up."

"You're closer, Judy," Maria encouraged. "You're getting closer to something."

"I'm not getting my hopes up. One, it's too far. Two, the possibility of a match is so remote."

"Well of course, don't get your hopes up, sweetie, but hey, it's something good that's happening. You're closer now than you used to be."

"It's a million-to-one shot," Judy said.

A few hours later, while Maria was shopping for dinner, her phone rang. It was Judy.

"I'm in the car. I'm on my way to Northwestern. I'm getting your cousin's heart!" Judy said. She was crying and her voice shook as she announced the news.

"Oh my God, Judy, that's wonderful!" Maria said.

"Please call your cousin, let her know there are people everywhere like me getting a second chance at life. Ben's donation is helping people live, and everyone is elated. She's making so many people so happy right now. It's not just me."

"I'm so happy for you, Judy."

"I can't believe this, Maria, I cannot believe this."

"Are you sure it's *his* heart?" Maria asked.

"They can't tell me, but I asked them, 'Is this the designated heart?' And they said yes. So I know it's your cousin's heart."

Maria hung up and stood still for a long moment, reflecting on the whirlwind of activity. *This day has been like an opening in the universe*, she thought. So many confluent things were happening, and now this miracle. It had come together improbably, and she was a big part of it. She felt a swirl of emotions somewhere between sorrow and joy. Judy had just used the word *elated*, but Maria knew Jill was as far from elated as she could be. She couldn't possibly call Jill and express her elation over the match. Then she told herself, *Maria, this is a God thing. Just shut up and do what you're supposed to do.*

Washington, DC

Jill suggested that the crew that had been standing vigil at Ben's bedside needed a break, and that they should go get a beer along with dinner. Phil Paquette was relieved. He had been suggesting that all week. He had eaten nearly every meal with Jill and thought a beer or glass of wine might do her good.

Their small group headed to a nearby restaurant. The humidity of mid-July in Washington, DC, grabbed them as they walked down the busy street. Jill led the way, wearing a summer skirt of various blues and browns with a navy blue t-shirt. She also wore the rosary that had been wrapped around Ben's hand the entire time he had been at Walter Reed. She thought about burying Ben with it, then decided against it. It had touched Ben's skin in his final moments, and she wanted to keep it.

She walked with her dad, Jon. Paquette trailed, keeping pace with

Marcus Engebretsen, another Ranger who'd just arrived from Fort Benning to stand guard over Ben's body and escort it back to Minnesota. Engebretsen was also assigned to Charlie Company's Third Platoon. He and Ben had served two deployments to Iraq together. But Engebretsen had stayed back at Fort Benning during Charlie Company's Afghanistan deployment to train for the Best Ranger Competition, a grueling test to determine the best Ranger-qualified buddy team in the Army.

As they marched along the Washington pavement, Jill's phone rang. It was Maria.

"Jill, you're not going to believe this," she said, "but I have really great news. This is a miracle. This is an absolute miracle."

"What?"

"They're a match! Judy and Ben are a match!" Maria said. "I know this is really hard for you, but I just want you to know that Ben's heart is going to my friend Judy."

"Oh my God, oh my God, oh my God!" Jill exclaimed.

She couldn't contain herself. She stopped in her tracks in the middle of the sidewalk to continue the conversation.

"My mom said this is a first-rate Catholic miracle!" Maria said.

"It *is* a miracle!" Jill shouted, her face alight with joy. Dabbing tears from her face, she handed the phone to her dad and turned to explain what had happened to Paquette and Engebretsen.

Jill felt a wave of bittersweet emotion. It was as if she had wings and could fly, but her feet were encased in cement. *This has to be what a miracle feels like,* she thought, *equal parts joy and sorrow at the same time.*

Northwestern Memorial Hospital

Heart transplant surgeon Dr. Edwin McGee talked over the phone with his hospital's transplant coordinator. The coordinator told him the family of a soldier who had just died at Walter Reed Army Medical Center had designated a heart to one of *his* patients, Judy Meikle. McGee had performed more than one hundred heart transplants, but even he had never heard of a heart being specifically designated.

"Well, how can that happen?" McGee asked. "Is that possible? Can we even do that?"

"Yeah, it's definitely legal," replied the coordinator, informing the surgeon that he had fully vetted the donation.

Dr. McGee then called Dr. Umraan Ahmad, his thirty-two-year-old protégé. He told Dr. Ahmad he needed to board a private organ donation jet to Washington, DC, to procure a heart and bring it back.

Walter Reed Army Medical Center

When they returned from dinner, Jill realized it was now time to say good-bye to Ben. She had allowed many of his friends and family to say their farewells earlier, but she would be last. She walked into his room and sat down on his bed, tears streaming from her eyes. It had been a long and tiring journey. This was the sixth day at Walter Reed, and the tenth since receiving the news that Ben had been shot. Jill and Mary had arrived praying for a miracle. And now this is what was left, her beloved only son kept alive by machines. Twenty-one years of work, twenty-one years of love and dreams and hopes, had now come down to only a few more minutes with him.

She held his right hand, leaned forward, and kissed the bridge of his nose, the same spot she'd kissed when he was a baby and little boy. Her mother's lips always fit perfectly there and still did. The tears flowed faster now.

"I'm really proud of you, Ben," she said. "I love you very much, and I'm going to miss you. You've changed a lot of people's lives. You've saved lives. You've made me more proud than I could even imagine I could be as a mom. And I will see you again. I'll see you in heaven. I'll see you when I get there."

She stared at her son, still on the ventilator, his body oxygenated for organ donation. He looked peaceful. She kissed him one more time, tears rushing down her cheeks, then got up and walked out of the room.

Just before she left the hospital, she saw Engebretsen in his Ranger duty uniform, his tan beret pulled down over his forehead. She knew he would stay with Ben. Paquette had told her Engebretsen wouldn't leave her son's side until he was back home in Minnesota. Jill was struck by Engebretsen's resemblance to Ben. No one would mistake them for brothers, but perhaps cousins. They were both handsome with the same fair complexion, blond hair, and blue eyes. Jill was grateful for his presence.

She checked in with him one last time, and Engebretsen made her a promise. "Ma'am, I'm not going to leave your son. He will never be alone."

And with that small bit of comfort Jill and Mary walked out of Walter Reed Army Medical Center.

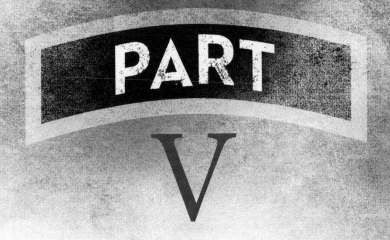

PART

V

Walter Reed Army Medical Center

About 11 p.m. the night of Sunday, July 19, Rob Mac Seain showed up to work to learn that the second autopsy of his career would also include organ procurement. Mac Seain, an Air Force pathology technician, had never seen this procedure before. He picked up the patient folder and looked at the register:

NAME: Kopp, Benjamin Stephen
DOB: 1/20/1988

Mac Seain was struck by the age of the young soldier, a year and a day older than he was. *This could be my brother.* He felt a chill, then closed the folder.

By the time Mac Seain entered the basement room where the procedure was taking place, he was about five minutes late. About a dozen people in the room surrounded the table, ready to go. He shuffled in and found an opening at the table where Ben lay connected to a ventilator, his chest still rising and falling, his heart still beating. Mac Seain was now directly across from Dr. Ahmad, who had just arrived from Chicago to remove Ben's heart and return it to Northwestern Memorial.

There was Ben Kopp before them. Someone who had been spectacular in life, living on the edge and challenging others to take that ride with him, was now on a table in a room full of strangers. Mac Seain impulsively reached forward, something in him wanting to touch this soldier. He placed his hand on Ben's hand. *He shouldn't be here*, he thought. *This shouldn't be happening.*

Across from him, Dr. Ahmad prepared to remove Ben's heart. The cardiothoracic surgeon was honored that he'd been sent here. He understood the gravity of the situation because directed donations were very rare. He also knew the soldier before him was a hero who had sacrificed for the country, and he wanted to make certain his death wasn't in vain.

Dr. Umraan S. Ahmad had grown up in St. Louis. His father had emigrated from Pakistan in the sixties, and his mother traced her ancestry to the Continental United States before the American Revolution. One of his ancestors had fought in the Revolution, and he had friends and relatives currently serving in Iraq and Afghanistan. He had a patriotic streak, leading some of the nurses he worked with to call him by his initials: Dr. USA.

Before going any further, there was a call for a moment of silence. The dozen or so medical professionals surrounding the Ranger bowed their heads in unison in respect for the hero who lay before them. After a few seconds, they went to work.

Using a small power saw, Dr. Ahmad cut straight down the heavy bone of the sternum to open Ben's chest. When he had sawed through the connective bone of the rib cage, he placed a retractor between his cutline to further open the ribs. With the retractor now in place, he could see Ben's heart which was wrapped in a semitransparent sac called the pericardium. The young doctor opened the sac, exposing it with some sutures. Ben's heart was now fully visible, yet still beating strongly in his chest. All eyes in the room now focused on this spectacular sight—a human heart still full of life, pounding right before them. Watching it beat, Dr. Ahmad judged that Ben's heart looked strong and functioned well. He looked for any abnormalities and found none.

He asked the heart transplant coordinator who had traveled with him from Chicago to call Dr. McGee back at Northwestern Memorial. When McGee answered, the nurse held the cell phone to Dr. Ahmad's ear.

"The heart looks good," he said. "We're going to cross clamp. We're good to go."

The organ procurement team administered a dose of blood thinners so clots wouldn't form in or around any of the key organs after they stopped the heart. Dr. Ahmad put a clamp across the aorta, the big artery just above the heart. He had already inserted a small catheter just below that clamp to administer high-potassium cold fluid, which would stop Ben's heart. As the cold liquid flowed into Ben's heart, Dr. Ahmad watched carefully, waiting for it to "relax" and stop. Using scissors, he cut some of the veins that brought blood back to the heart so the returning blood wouldn't warm the organ, and the heart could depressurize. Dr. Ahmad was mindful that excess pressure on the heart now would stress it. Suction tubes in Ben's chest drained the returning blood flowing from the cut vessels. The surgeon watched and waited, letting the cold potassium solution do its job. He reached into Ben's chest and felt the heart with his hand, waiting for it to soften and relax. Ben's heart was slowing, showing just faint signs of activity now. Ahmad then packed Ben's open chest with ice, pouring it around the heart to cool it down. Every couple of minutes, Dr. Ahmad felt the heart to make sure it remained soft and relaxed.

Ben Kopp's heart was now completely at rest. It no longer beat like it did when he sprinted on the football field at Rosemount High School, when he kissed Brittney Doran for the first time, or when he opened fire in combat in the last hours of his conscious life. Ben's death had been recorded on paper more than twenty-four hours previously. But in the very late hours of July 19, Ben finally no longer had a pulse. The heart of a Ranger was still but alive and awaiting its next mission.

Dr. Ahmad continued to work. Other surgeons who had come to retrieve Ben's liver, kidneys, and other organs now worked alongside him. They operated simultaneously and with purpose as they removed key organs to get them on their way to patients in the DC area.

When it came time to remove the heart, Dr. Ahmad made a cut across the inferior vena cava, the vessel that returns blood to the heart from the lower half of the body. He was careful to leave enough of the vein segment for Dr. McGee to install on the other end.

Dr. Ahmad then cut the superior vena cava, the vein that returns blood from the upper body. He took the clamp off the aorta, making a cut there and leaving plenty of extra length. He then cut the veins at the back of the heart, then the pulmonary arteries. When he was finished, he slowly and gently slid his hand underneath the heart. Without closing his fingers, he raised it straight up out of Ben's chest. He looked down at it, inspecting it one more time. Ben's heart looked very good.

Across the table, Rob Mac Seain was fixated on the heart in the doctor's hands. He had never seen anything like it. Mac Seain felt a sense of admiration looking at it. Here was a human heart that had just been beating in the chest of a Ranger and was now heading to some fortunate lady in Chicago. He felt a pang of sadness for the soldier in front of him, whose life had been cut short.

Ben's heart was carefully placed into a clear plastic bag and filled with cold saline solution. That bag was then sealed in a clear plastic canister, which was put into two more bags of cold saline to keep a sterile seal. That whole package was put into an unremarkable red and white Igloo cooler, the same kind Ben had pulled hundreds of beers from in his short life. Dr. Ahmad also removed some lymph nodes from Ben's abdomen that would be used for testing Ben's white blood cells against Judy's, a cross match to further ensure they were compatible. The cooler was strapped to a rolling suitcase; Ben's heart was ready for transport.

The clock was ticking. Dr. McGee insisted on having the heart in the chest of the recipient within four hours of its removal. Dr. Ahmad and the coordinator he'd traveled with rushed to the ER, where Ben had arrived only five days before. They met a waiting ambulance, climbed aboard, and raced—sirens blaring—toward Dulles International Airport.

Northwestern Memorial Hospital

Late that Sunday night, Judy waited in her hospital room with her closest friends, PD Weatherhead and Ruthie Marion. The heart was now on its way from Washington, DC, and would arrive at the hospital a few hours after midnight. The mood in the room was cautiously optimistic. Everything had fallen into place. Nervous small talk was all they could muster, as PD tried to ease Judy's concerns and assure her everything was going to be fine.

Judy joked that after getting a twenty-one-year-old heart she might be attracted to twenty-one-year-old men. PD reminded her that the incoming heart belonged to a young man, and that maybe she would soon be looking at twenty-one-year-old women differently. They all chuckled, easing the tension of the looming surgery.

Judy's phone rang. It was Maria checking in. "Good night. Good luck. See you on the other side," she said.

A nurse entered the room and shampooed Judy's hair. PD remarked that at least Judy was getting her money's worth out of the stay. "That heart better be a good match, though," he quipped. "Otherwise, this is going to be one damn expensive trip to the beauty parlor."

As the clock approached midnight, PD told Ruthie to go home and get some rest. She would want to be there to see Judy as soon as she awakened from surgery. She left, and PD said he would keep her updated.

Washington Beltway

"We're on our way to the airport. The organ looks good. Everything went fine, no surprises," Dr. Ahmad reported over his phone to the waiting medical team back in Chicago.

It was a thirty-one-mile trip from Walter Reed to Dulles International Airport, a trip that would normally take up to forty-five minutes without traffic. But in a speeding ambulance just after midnight, the trip was cut to thirty. They crossed the Potomac River and headed west into Virginia toward Dulles.

Their preferred plan had them flying into Reagan National,

but under post 9/11 rules, all flights into Reagan had to have an air marshal. They had tried to get one aboard their organ donation flight, but in the end could not and had to settle for Dulles. That cost them precious time.

The organ team had cleared security earlier, and entering the area that handled private and corporate aircraft, the ambulance rolled right up to the waiting Aerocare Air Services Lear 35A. Dr. Ahmad and his coordinator jumped out, pulling the rolling case with the cooler containing Ben's heart. They climbed the stairs of the small jet and turned the cooler over to the pilots, who secured it so the heart wouldn't be damaged in flight.

Dr. Ahmad once again called the transplant coordinator and let him know they were about to take off and should be touching down in Chicago in about two and a half hours.

The aircraft taxied, accelerated, and lifted off the runway. The jet climbed then banked west toward Chicago. Ben's heart, still very vital, was airborne and flying across America on one more critical mission.

Northwestern Memorial Hospital

Heart transplant surgeon Dr. Edwin McGee was just arriving at NMH. For a transplant surgeon, time is critical. Dr. McGee had transplanted hearts from local donors within ninety minutes, and even thirty minutes when the donor and recipient were in the same hospital. But this case was different. The logistics would be pushing McGee's preferred four-hour limit to the brink, and that had him concerned.

Edwin McGee, the son of a general surgeon, had grown up in Florence, South Carolina. He discovered early on that he had a talent for fixing things. When he was in high school, he worked as an orderly at the local hospital. He tolerated the job because it gave him the opportunity to watch operations. After attending Washington and Lee University, he enrolled at Vanderbilt University for Medical

School. Dr. Bill Frist, a future US Senator, was his medical school adviser. Working alongside Dr. Frist, McGee went on several transplant runs. He marveled at the ability of human beings to transplant organs and save lives. He found himself bitten by the transplant bug and had worked in the field ever since.

By 2:45 a.m. on Monday, July 20, the medical team was rolling Judy into the operating room. McGee had met Judy before and sized her up as a good candidate for a heart transplant. They had scheduled the surgery so they would be ready to remove her failing heart the moment the jet carrying Ben's heart landed at Midway Airport on Chicago's Southwest Side. It was a precise and delicate dance. Dr. McGee couldn't start removing her heart too soon. He could go as far as opening her up during air transport, but he wasn't willing to cut the heart out until he had word the aircraft had landed safely. By that time the incoming heart would be about twenty minutes from the operating room. The last thing McGee wanted was for Ben's heart to sit in a cooler while the team was still working to open Judy up and get the old heart out. They simply didn't have the luxury of extra time.

The surgical team in Chicago went to work. In the operating room were two nurses, an anesthesiologist, a physician's assistant, an observing fellow, a perfusionist (who ran the critically important heart-lung machine), and Dr. McGee. The team had about thirty minutes of work to prep Judy before Dr. McGee could start to "cut skin."

Once the prep work was completed, Judy needed to be connected to the heart-lung machine, which would keep her alive after her heart was removed. Standing on Judy's right side, Dr. McGee, his surgical mask covering his graying goatee, went to work opening her chest.

Once her rib cage was pried open, her failing heart was exposed. McGee, his blue eyes peering down through glasses, carefully connected the tubing from the heart-lung machine to the blood vessels extending from Judy's heart. One by one, he inserted the tentacles of the machine into small slits in the aorta, the superior vena cava, and the inferior vena cava, just above where he would soon cut her heart out. But he would not transfer her vital functions to the machine until the moment he was ready to remove her heart.

While Dr. McGee worked inside Judy's chest, the transplant coordinator kept in contact with the approaching aircraft, giving periodic updates to the team as they awaited the heart's arrival.

Aboard Lear 35A

"Thirty minutes out."

The organ transport aircraft passed over Indiana, nipping the southern tip of Lake Michigan, the lights of Chicago's spectacular downtown skyline in view. They dropped altitude and aligned the Lear with the now-quiet runway at Midway. As they touched down, Dr. Ahmad let the team in the operating room know they were close. "We're on the ground. We're at Midway. We'll call you as we're getting close," he reported.

A special organ donor agency SUV driven by an off-duty Chicago firefighter waited for them at Midway. The SUV was equipped with flashing lights and sirens. Dr. Ahmad wheeled the precious cargo to the SUV and secured it inside. He hopped in with the nurse coordinator.

"Okay, we're going to run hot and loud," Ahmad announced.

It was the same phrase he always used when he climbed into a vehicle carrying an organ, but this time speed really was of the essence. The clock was ticking at about three hours and twenty minutes since Ben's heart had been removed. Forty minutes remained until the four-hour deadline, and they weren't even at the hospital yet.

The off-duty firefighter negotiated the streets of Chicago's Southwest Side, crossing Archer Avenue and Forty-Seventh Street before rolling onto the Stevenson Expressway and heading northeast toward downtown. The time of day—the wee hours of a Monday morning—couldn't have been better. Chicago expressways can back up at nearly any hour, but this was about as good as it got.

When the SUV pulled up to Northwestern's ambulance arrival area, Dr. Ahmad and his assistant scrambled out. They sprinted into the hospital and toward the elevators.

Six stories above, the heart-lung machine had taken over for Judy's heart. The machine detoured blood from her body, oxygenated it, then returned it to the vessels just outside her heart, pumping it back into her system.

Minutes earlier, Dr. McGee had looked at Judy's heart and determined that the time was right. After fifty-seven years in her chest, the failing organ was coming out. He made a cut at the left atrium, cleanly severed the aorta and pulmonary artery, and cut the superior vena cava and the inferior vena cava to remove it. For a few minutes on that table Judy Meikle was a woman without a heart, a machine the only thing keeping her alive.

Judy's long frame was covered by surgical sheets, her chest open and awaiting its new inhabitant. Dr. McGee knew Ahmad was in the building and on his way up with the heart. He was ready for installation. Their timing was nearly perfect.

The recovery team burst into the operating room with the Igloo cooler and its priceless contents. Their medical marathon was over. With nearly a thousand miles behind them, they crossed the finish line in respectable marathon time, about three hours and thirty minutes after Ben's heart was removed at Walter Reed. It was now time for Dr. McGee to finish the job.

A few procedural items had to be completed first. Paperwork reconfirmed the identities of the donor and the recipient. They also confirmed the blood types. Dr. Ahmad opened the cooler and took out Ben's heart, removing it from the layers that had protected it. As Dr. McGee stood by, Ahmad performed one last inspection and, knowing Dr. McGee's preferences, tailored the length of the new heart's protruding arteries and veins so it would fit into place.

The four-hour window was closing. Disaster wouldn't necessarily strike minutes after the four-hour mark, but McGee was always determined to beat that timeframe. He now had just twenty minutes to do it, about the same amount of time it took Ben to change a car's oil when he worked at Jim Cooper's Tire and Auto Service.

As the veteran of one hundred heart transplants, Dr. McGee knew he could mitigate the time pressure by getting blood flowing to the heart before all five blood vessels were reconnected. With just two connections, he could start blood flow back to the heart. But he would have to install the organ in a different order than he usually did.

Dr. McGee held Ben's heart and carefully lowered it into the empty cavity in Judy's chest. He had five connections to complete. He started at the left atrium, sewing the connection with medical-grade monofilament, similar to fishing line. The left atrium receives oxygenated blood from the lungs, which drains into the left ventricle and is pumped out to the body through the aorta. Normally, McGee would fuse the inferior vena cava second. But in this case, he opted to connect the aorta and start the blood flow immediately. McGee sewed Ben's aorta to Judy's using a stronger monofilament. The blood vessels would regrow, though the monofilament sutures would always remain.

Once McGee finished those connections, he removed the cross clamp from Judy's aorta, allowing her blood to flow to and from the new heart. What happened next was as good as any surgeon could hope for. As soon as the blood surged in, Ben's heart jumped to life, beating right away. The pressure of the four-hour window was off, as the new heart was now getting precious oxygenated blood. *Man, that thing is jamming away. This is the heart of a highly conditioned athlete,* McGee thought as he watched it work. The pumping heart would wash out the potassium solution applied at Walter Reed, allowing it to recover and "warm up" even further.

Normally, a newly installed donor heart might have to sit in place while the heart-lung machine continues as a surrogate, and the new heart regains its rhythm. That might take twenty or thirty minutes. A more sluggish heart might need an electro shock to get it going. But

McGee, through his years as a surgeon, had observed that the human heart generally wanted to go to work. The organ has its own intrinsic pacemaker and would contract on its own. The heart is connected to the nervous system, but, as Dr. McGee knew, it didn't have to be connected to start beating.

Ben's heart was clearly strong, and Dr. McGee now realized that Judy was a very lucky lady. A donor heart showing up at Northwestern Memorial might more commonly belong to a sixty-two-year-old car accident victim who'd spent a lifetime gorging on fast food. Getting the heart of a twenty-one-year-old Ranger in the best shape of his life was like winning the lottery.

It was a little harder for McGee to connect the inferior vena cava with the new heart beating so strongly. After making that connection, he focused on the superior vena cava. He fused it, then moved to the pulmonary artery, which in minutes would be taking Judy's spent blood back to her lungs. McGee finished his last connection and looked at the clock. He had installed Ben's heart in time, narrowly beating the four-hour window. Dr. McGee continued to watch the activity inside Judy's chest. Ben's heart was beating like a drum. McGee now believed the time was right to wean Judy off the heart-lung machine, a process he described as the surgeon's equivalent of landing a plane. McGee watched Ben's heart closely as it started to take over the work of pumping blood through Judy's body. Over the next several minutes the machine's process was decreased, converting from fully circulating Judy's blood to allowing Ben's heart full power.

The medical team administered drugs to ensure Judy's body wouldn't reject the new heart. McGee kept his eye on the echocardiogram and the transesophageal echocardiogram, a probe in the esophagus that gave him real-time data on the new heart.

Dr. McGee concluded Ben's heart was functioning very well. He started the process of closing Judy up, taking out the retractors, bringing the sternum back into line, and wiring her breastbone back together. After he'd finished the last suture, McGee stepped back, satisfied with how the surgery had gone. Ben Kopp's heart—very much alive—now belonged to Judy Meikle.

Camp Leatherneck

News of Ben's death stunned and devastated the Rangers who had served with him. Even days after getting the word, the sting hadn't gotten any better. Some couldn't sleep, some couldn't eat. However, when they heard his heart went to save another person's life, there was a small but uplifting sense of hope. For Captain Lane Sandifer, it was redemption for his doubt. His faith had been rocked just a couple of days before, but he now saw and understood God's plan. Someone out there had new life, another heroic act by Specialist Kopp.

Ben's closest friends in the platoon were allowed to travel home for the funeral. Erick Innis, Ryan Lundeby, and Chase Vanderhule had packed up and were already on their way back to the states. A memorial service at the base was being prepared for the soldiers who couldn't travel stateside for the funeral.

Company Commander Don Kingston was having a hard time coming up with something to say about Ben. He suddenly realized he hadn't known Ben as well as he should have. He felt terrible that he didn't have a single personal recollection of Ben to share during the memorial service.

This epiphany would forever change Kingston as an Army officer. He realized he hadn't taken the time he should have to get to know the guys who served under his command. When he'd taken command of the company in February, he'd been focused on training them for Afghanistan, not on building relationships with the men he held dear.

A chaplain at Leatherneck gave Kingston Ben's diary. That helped the officer get a better idea of who Ben was, but deep down Kingston felt this was a terrible way to get to know one of his own guys. He vowed to never let this happen again. In the future, he would build relationships, trust, and his team by getting to know his guys before it was too late.

Northwestern Memorial Hospital

Judy remained unconscious under the powerful anesthesia that had kept her sedated during her transplant operation. She'd been rolled out of surgery to a recovery room, her chest held together by wire.

Hours later, her motionless sleep started to give way to dull consciousness. She slowly awakened and looked around the room without lifting her head. There were no nurses, no doctors, no friends; not even PD was there. She was alone.

But she also didn't see Saint Peter waiting at the gate. There was no bright light at the end of a tunnel, just a plain and empty hospital room. Judy felt incredibly sleepy, but she fought the anesthesia, trying to keep her eyes open. She realized she had survived her operation. She was alive. She closed her eyes and drifted back into darkness.

Reagan National Airport

After a five-day vigil at her son's bedside—a week that began with hope for a miracle and ended with her son's death and organ dona-tion—Jill was physically and emotionally exhausted. She was sitting at an airport gate waiting to get on a flight to Minneapolis. As her mind replayed the events of the prior week, she realized that for the rest of her life, no days would ever mean more to her than the five she'd spent with Ben at Walter Reed.

She now faced making funeral and burial plans. This was compli-cated by the fact that Ben's funeral would be back in their hometown of Rosemount, but his burial would be at Arlington National Ceme-tery. Ben's body, still at Walter Reed, would have to make the same trip she was now making home and then fly back to Washington. The one thing that buoyed her in her grief was that her son had died doing what he loved. He had been struck down defending his country, and had died a Ranger, a warrior, a patriot.

Near Jill sat Sergeant Paquette, who was talking to his wife on his cell phone. He could've gone home to his family in Georgia, but he had asked Jill if she still needed him during the funeral planning. "If you want me to stay with you, I will," he'd offered.

"Yes, please," Jill replied without hesitation, knowing full well that Phil's wife, Heidi, was pregnant with their first child. Jill understood the sacrifice he was making, and his support meant the world to her.

Jill had spent the week unsettled and deeply sad, but a sense of peace had come over her. Ben's life, his service to his country, his death on the battlefield—it all fit neatly yet painfully together. She was finally beginning to accept it and focus on what was ahead: planning a funeral and burying her son. And then her phone rang. "Jill, this is Jay McKenna."

Captain McKenna was calling from Kandahar. He explained to Jill that all the details surrounding Ben's death didn't make sense to him. He told her he had traveled to Camp Dwyer to check things out for himself and to interview those at the hospital who had been involved with Ben's care. He told Jill there had been a problem with a defibrillator and another with a respirator. Those alone may not have caused Ben's death, but McKenna believed some combination of complications at Dwyer did.

Jill started to take notes, until Dr. McKenna told her something that completely rocked her: in his view, Ben shouldn't have died, and his death should have been preventable.

Jill knew Ben had suffered his cardiac arrest at Camp Dwyer, but she thought it must've been directly related to being shot. McKenna now said he didn't believe that was the case. The stunning news distracted Jill from the announcement at the gate that it was time to board the plane.

Jill hung up with Captain McKenna feeling as though she'd been punched in the gut. She had just started to come to terms with her son's death only to find it might've been negligence or some other preventable complication. She felt as if she was sinking into a black hole, the same feeling she'd had when she first learned Ben was shot.

As she crossed from the jet bridge into the plane, Jill looked around and realized the flight was nearly empty. That helped, because she was now having trouble breathing after getting McKenna's news. *Why did it have to happen this way?* she wondered.

Jill explained everything to Paquette, who saw she was clearly distressed. The news made him angry, but as the jet took off, he urged her not to overthink it, to just let the news settle. They also prayed together, telling God that they trusted in His plan and knew that in time He would help them share this news the right way.

It was after dark, and the lights on the aircraft were low. Jill moved to her own private space in the cabin to get some rest. She decided that no one needed to know this information right now, and that there would be a time and place to examine all of it. She didn't want to blame the Army for her son's death, and she certainly didn't want to blame the Rangers. Right now, her son was a hero, and she wanted to get home and give him the hero's good-bye he deserved.

Northwestern Memorial Hospital

PD hung up his suit jacket behind the door of Judy's recovery room. His tie around his neck was loosened. He sat in a chair, kicked his feet up onto Judy's hospital bed, and went to work on his laptop answering e-mails and dealing with other business. Next to him, Judy's chest rose and fell as the respirator helped her breathe. He would normally be in his downtown office on a Monday morning, but instead he was standing guard to give Judy the good news that her surgery was a success, although it was hard to tell looking at her now. Despite Dr. McGee's assurances that the surgery had gone well, PD thought Judy looked like she'd just crashed to earth.

The nurses told PD they believed Judy would likely regain consciousness around midafternoon, but even then she'd remain groggy for quite a while. About an hour later she started to stir again, and this time she opened her eyes.

"Hello, sleepyhead," PD greeted her, a teasing tone in his voice. He put down the laptop and stared into her eyes. As close as Judy and PD were, they didn't have a touchy-feely relationship. There were no hugs or embraces to celebrate her successful surgery. Their eye contact was enough to show that this was a very big moment. Judy had made it.

Judy had a breathing tube down her throat and couldn't speak. As she regained her strength and awareness that afternoon, she started signaling that she wanted the tube taken out. PD, ever the prankster, ignored her. He liked the power he had over her in her forced silence, a rarity for Judy. Smiling the entire time and pretending not to understand her gestures, he got a white board and marker pen and gave it to her.

"Tube out!" she wrote.

"What are you talking about?" PD said. "This is the quietest you've ever been. I'm not sure I'm going to tell anyone to take the tube out!"

He laughed at her predicament and egged her on. When a nurse came in and saw Judy's continued motions for the tube to come out, PD said, "Judy's quite the talker. You might want to leave that tube in for a while."

The nurse didn't see the humor in the situation and began making preparations to take Judy's breathing tube out. PD gave up his quest for a silent Judy and instead began to reach out to some of her friends to spread the good news. He called Maria first.

"She's resting; it went well. Everything's a success."

"Oh, that's wonderful news, PD, thanks for the call."

When they hung up, Maria pondered the whirlwind of events

that had played out over the last few days. The next time she talked with Judy, it would be like she was talking to Ben as well. Maria couldn't wait to see her friend and feel the beat of her new heart. She was excited, though still very sad over Ben's death. Maria also felt conflicted about her serendipitous involvement as the go-between for Jill and Judy, a role even her mother questioned.

"Maria, don't you think someone else should've gotten that heart?" her mother had asked. "I mean, how old is Judy? What if a kid needed that heart?"

Her words were a punch to the gut, and left Maria feeling like she had interfered with the natural order of things. But finally she'd said, "Mom! I can't help it. It's out of our hands. It's a God thing now."

"Yeah, that's true," her Italian mother said, coming around to see her daughter's point of view.

Like most of Judy's friends, Maria had tried to set Judy up on dates in the past, all without much success. But in the end, Maria became Judy's ultimate matchmaker when she linked her friend with her cousin, the handsome young soldier who saved her life.

Camp Leatherneck

Just outside Rangers' quarters within the sand-filled walls of their secured compound, a memorial was being set up for Specialist Ben Kopp. A small wooden platform sat on the sand and gravel. Ben's khaki boots were placed at the base, his rifle propped muzzle down into the top of the box. His silver dog tags hung from the rifle's forward hand grip, and his helmet sat on top of the butt. Behind the memorial flew a gold-trimmed American flag.

When the Rangers started to gather, many were surprised at the number of Marines who had come for the service. There were also Navy Seabees filtering in.

It was heartening to Ben's friends and fellow Rangers to see all the forces coming together to remember Ben and his sacrifice. By the time they were ready to start, a couple hundred service members had shown up. Among them were First Sergeant Greg Knight, Captain Lane Sandifer, Sergeant Stephen Shipe, and the medics who had taken care of Ben in the field, Michael Melvin and Ryan Walker. Most of the rest of Charlie Company's Third Platoon were there as well. A chaplain said some words, then Walker stepped forward to give his eulogy.

Having a memorial service is a hard thing to prepare for. You're expected to sum up the life of someone in the matter of a short period. What can you say about Ben, other than he was a ball of fire, just the intensity with which he lived life. No matter what he did, he couldn't sit still. He could be in the gym cleaning ninety-five pounds and drop it like it weighed over two hundred. The way he told stories, so energetic, like the time he was convinced he saw Bigfoot at some golf course in Minnesota. I always remember his smile. Never a serious face, unless it was at the gym or that twenty-nine-kilometer walk at NTC. You can ask Scappaticci, always telling him to take a knee so he could drink his Camelbak. But then again, no one was smiling that day.

There are a lot of stories to tell about Ben, but [it's] so hard to decide which ones. Everyone who knew Ben has funny stories, some not suited for a memorial. When we got back from last deployment, I ran into him and a couple other guys in downtown Savannah on Halloween weekend. He was trying to chase this one girl all night. We bounced around from club to club. Of course I was trying to do the Ranger buddy thing and dance with her larger friend. Well, due to Ben's ability to dance like a teenager at a middle school dance, the better looking of the two wanted to swap. I remember leaning over to him and saying, "I'm sorry," trying my best to get her back with Ben. I told her I was married and that just backfired on us, because they just left. Instead of being mad, he just brushed it off. Then we just spent the night dancing by ourselves like fools. At the end of the night, we both concluded that all you need are great friends to have a great time.

Ben was an ambitious individual. We always talked about the future when we got out. I was going to wait until next summer when he got out and both buy a house together down in sunny Tampa, Florida. He wanted to go to college and become an athletic trainer, and I a nutritionist. We had this big dream of eventually opening our own gym and during our time off just hanging out at the beach and having a few brews and enjoying the sun. Well, Ben, I hope the sun is shining in heaven and you're finally able to enjoy life once again. You will be missed as a Ranger and most importantly as a dear friend.

When Walker was done, the group recited the Ranger Creed. Then it was time to line up and pay respects at the front of the memorial they had created. One by one, Ben's fellow Rangers stepped up. Some stood and saluted, others knelt and prayed. Everyone acted tough, trying to keep their emotions in check.

Ben's former roommate, Stephen Shipe, moved forward and knelt. He told himself to pull it together. When he looked up, staring back at him was the biggest group of badasses he had ever known. He saw tears streaming down their faces. Some were openly sobbing. That's when Shipe lost control of his emotions. He stood and gave way to another. As the line moved forward, one by one the Rangers and Marines offered Ben the best and only thing they could—a slow, deliberate, final salute.

Platoon Medic Ryan Walker salutes his friend. Walker worked hard to keep Ben alive, both at the Alamo compound and on a Black Hawk medevac to Camp Dwyer.

Northwestern Memorial Hospital

Judy was becoming more lucid. But by Tuesday, July 21, more than twenty-four hours after coming out of surgery, she was having a tough day. She was experiencing a lot of discomfort and nausea.

The nurse came in and took her blood pressure which had always been notoriously low. The nurse announced the new number: 130 over 80—a big improvement over her pre-surgery typical 100 over 60. PD took notice.

"You've never had a heart that pumps this well. Now you do," he told her. "Your hands and feet will finally feel warm."

Judy managed a smile. Ruthie appreciated seeing that.

Judy was able to do a few simple tasks. She got on her laptop and visited Ben's CaringBridge site. She found a picture of her heart donor posted on the page. She stared at the screen for a long time, studying his face.

"What a great-looking kid," she murmured.

PD and Ruthie leaned over and looked at her screen and nodded in agreement. Ruthie could see now that Judy was starting to regain not only her strength but her wit. She was ready for a little ribbing. "You've got a twenty-one-year-old heart. I just hope the rest of your body holds up."

Judy smiled. "Well, I'm going to outlive you all, because I have the heart of an Army Ranger!"

Judy wasn't the only one to receive an organ from Ben. Curtis Brantley, a husband and father of three, got Ben's liver. Fifteen-year-old Devaun Mason received one of Ben's kidneys, and sixty-six-year-old Fred Thurston, who'd been on dialysis for five years, got the other. A fifty-seven-year-old woman from Pennsylvania received Ben's pancreas.

Judy realized Ben's funeral was fast approaching, and there was no way she'd be able to go. "Listen, PD," she said, "you have to go. You need to do this." Coming from Judy, it was less a request than an order.

PD was swamped with work, but he agreed it would be an honor to represent her at the funeral of the young American hero.

Rosemount, Minnesota

When Jill arrived home, she had so much on her plate she didn't know where to turn. She had to plan her son's wake and funeral, then wait a week for another service and burial at Arlington National Cemetery. To top it off, Ben's body wasn't home yet. There were some complications getting it released from Walter Reed.

Despite the chaos, Jill decided it was time to reach out to Judy Meikle, the woman who'd received her son's heart. She knew Judy was still recovering and probably couldn't talk yet on the phone, so she put her thoughts in an e-mail.

Hi Judy,

You and I have been brought together by circumstances that represent events of our humanness completely out of our control. Most call them unfair and say they beg the question "Why me?" or "Why the only child of a single mother?" "Why a young brave soldier?" While these are all valid questions, what holds me up is the truth that there is another side to this story. This is your story, Judy. I know very little about you. I know you are a fifty-seven-year-old woman whose heart was going to cut short your life. You live in Chicago, and are a longtime friend of my cousin, Maria. You have a good friend named PD whose sense of humor I love. Where I rest my belief in this story is that you were chosen to receive Ben's heart.

It started with Ben choosing to be an organ donor, my honoring those wishes after learning he would not survive his injuries, Maria's message on the CaringBridge site, and my forwarding your information to the transplant team at Walter Reed. The order and the outcome of these events are a MIRACLE. A true-blue, good as it gets MIRACLE. Judy, I have no question you were meant to get Ben's heart and that he picked you to receive it. When I realized Ben would not survive his injuries, I thought about all of the prayers that had been said and miracles that had been asked for. I know that no prayer ever goes unanswered, and that it may not always be answered in the manner in which it is asked. I knew we had thousands of prayers and an enormous amount of love being offered. I whispered to Ben that it was up to him to decide if he wanted them for himself or if he wanted to give them away. It was his decision. Of course we know he chose to give them away because he was too proud to live a life of people taking pity on him for having a body that was less than desirable.

Ben was very proud of his accomplishments and the independent spirit it took to have as many as he did at such a young age. Again, I can only believe he saw this in you. Maybe I'm wrong about that, but I believe with all of my heart that Ben's heart has plans for you. I feel blessed that we will get to know one another and that you will know where Ben's spirit came from and what he was like and [that] I get to see how this will live on in you.

Words cannot adequately explain how this feels—to have so much sorrow and joy at the same moment. I suppose this is what a MIRACLE is, and no question it's God's work at its best. I will continue to pray for your recovery as I know you are not out of the woods yet and can't begin running around Lake Michigan tomorrow. I will pray that Ben's spirit has not just added years to life, but, more important, life to your years. I look forward to reading your progress, staying in touch, and meeting you in person. I am going to get a New Year's trip planned soon so we can ring it in together in Chicago. I'd say we have much to celebrate!

In God's love,
Jill

Northwestern Memorial Hospital

By the middle of the week, it had become clear Judy had made it through her surgery with flying colors. Her nurse friend, Cary Tyler, stopped by to check up on her.

"Are you having any pain?"

Judy shook her head no. Cary was surprised. In fact, Judy was now out of the ICU and into a room on the cardiac floor. She was up and out of her bed. The nurses encouraged Judy to get a little exercise, so she walked the hallways. But she had one great fear. It was not that her heart would give way during these first tests of the new equipment. It was that someone would catch a glimpse of her bare rear end through the flimsy hospital gown as she trudged down the hallway.

"I don't want anyone to see my butt," she told PD and Ruthie.

"How would they even find your butt? You don't have one," Ruthie countered.

Ruthie was right. Judy had lost a tremendous amount of weight. She was down to around 120 pounds, a big drop from her usual weight of 150 pounds on her five-eleven frame. But protecting the eyes of the public became Judy's top priority. She made her friends steal doctor's scrubs from medical carts, asking them to get the longest pair of pants they could find. Eventually Judy did the dirty work herself. She'd rifle through the supply cart, refusing to wear just the gown itself.

Her cardiologist, Dr. William Cotts, showed up for a visit. He explained to Judy and her friends that even when transplant surgery goes well, there is sometimes rejection later on. But Judy's tests showed that everything looked great, and rejection wasn't likely.

"Doc, we can't recall the last time Judy rejected any man, much less a good-looking Ranger," joked PD.

Everyone broke into a chuckle. Dr. Cotts told Judy that with continued good progress, she might be able to go home the following week. By late that week, word was beginning to spread that Judy might be in record territory at Northwestern for fastest discharge after a heart transplant. They told her she might get out as early as Monday, July 27. Up to this point, the standing record at Northwestern was seven days from surgery to discharge. However, Judy still needed to have a procedure done that couldn't be completed during the weekend.

In PD and Ruthie's estimation, she was "looking good." Judy still got tired easily, but she couldn't wait to get home to see her cocker spaniel, Lacey. She predicted that by Sunday she'd be "going bonkers" at the thought of staying in the hospital any longer.

PART

VI

Saint Paul, Minnesota

The Mississippi River flows to the northeast as it rolls by downtown St. Paul, passing the modest skyscrapers of Minnesota's second-largest city. Once past downtown, the river bends again to the south. On the inside of that turn is St. Paul's Holman Field, a small urban airport that services the corporate jets of the Twin Cities, as well as the Minnesota National Guard's Black Hawk helicopters assigned to the 34th Combat Aviation Brigade.

Jill and Phil Paquette arrived just before lunchtime to meet her son's body as it touched down on Minnesota soil. It wasn't the homecoming she'd hoped for when she hugged him good-bye back in May.

The Patriot Guard was there as well, at least twenty of them holding American flags just outside the building. Patriot Guard volunteers escort fallen soldiers' caskets by motorcycle. Jill sat in a waiting room with her parents and Sergeant Paquette, hoping the flight would arrive soon. Jenny Boll was there as well.

The door opened to the waiting room. Two women, both with long manes of blond hair, peeked in. One was in her mid-forties, the younger in her twenties.

"Jill?" the younger woman inquired.

"Yes, I'm Jill."

"It's Jen," she said, her tone suggesting that Jill should recognize her.

"I'm sorry?" Jill replied, not recognizing the woman.

"Jenny Larson. I lived across the street from your sister."

"Yes! Oh my God, Jenny." Jill suddenly remembered they had once gone camping together.

"This is my mom, Linda. We're in the Patriot Guard, and we're here to escort your son." She handed Jill a Patriot Guard pin. Jill twisted the pin around to look at its inscription: "Mission Complete."

Just outside, a white twin-engine Falcon 20 touched down on runway 32. Ranger Marcus Engebretsen stayed strapped in the jet's jump seat while the two-man crew brought the aircraft to the edge of a huge retractable door on the backside of the terminal. Ben's flag-draped casket was secured in the cargo hold of the small jet. As the plane taxied, the welcoming party watched somberly. Inside the bay door was a waiting hearse, its rear door facing the hangar's open door. On the driver's side of the vehicle stood seven soldiers in dress blues, an honor guard detachment from the Minnesota Army National Guard. Funeral Director Tom Schultz stood at the back of the hearse. About two dozen Patriot Guard members holding American flags formed a circle from the plane to the hearse, surrounding Ben and honoring his homecoming.

Jill emerged from the waiting room in time to see the aircraft roll to a stop. Nearby was Paquette, who watched her every move. The engines, still loud enough to drown out conversation, started whirring down from their high revolutions. When the plane's cargo door opened, Jill spotted Engebretsen, the young man who promised her at Walter Reed that he wouldn't leave her son's side. He had held true to his promise. Jill also saw a corner of the flag-draped casket containing her son. A scissors lift rolled forward to the edge of the aircraft. The casket was gently pushed onto the lift. As the casket was lowered, the honor guard stepped forward in unison to take control of it. Six National Guardsmen grabbed hold and under the orders of a staff sergeant, reversed their course and carried Ben's body to the back of the waiting Cadillac. He was twenty-one miles from the funeral home. What would normally be an uneventful drive would prove to be anything but.

Once Ben's body was secured inside the hearse, the honor guard saluted and the welcoming party made their way to their vehicles. Without traffic, the ride to the Henry W. Anderson Mortuary in Apple Valley would normally take no more than twenty-five minutes. A St. Paul Police officer on a motorcycle led the procession, his blue lights flashing. Behind him rode the squadron of Patriot Guard volunteers. Paquette drove Jill in a rented SUV behind the hearse. As they entered

I-494 and headed west, Jill could see the stripes on the flag covering her son's casket inside the hearse.

Some drivers saw the Patriot Guard and the hearse and pulled over out of respect, which warmed Jill's heart. But the lack of respect from other drivers was startling. One tried to cut between their SUV and the hearse. Paquette honked the horn, and the guy flipped them off.

"You have got to be kidding me!" Jill said.

Other drivers tried to cut in on the procession; several even cut off the motorcycles in the process. Jill sat in disbelief. *If only they knew we were bringing home someone who lost his life fighting for this country.*

They approached the busy 494/35E interchange and took the right-hand ramp, routing them to the south. They had to merge onto southbound 35E with traffic also coming in from eastbound 494. As they approached the merge, Jill saw a maroon sedan to her right, just out of the corner of her eye. She was struck by the vehicle's speed. The woman driving wasn't slowing down to accommodate the merge. Ahead of their procession there were cars on the shoulder that had pulled over, respecting the blue police lights and the oncoming motorcade. But the maroon sedan kept barreling into the merge. The driver first clipped one of the cars that had pulled over, then bounced into the Patriot Guard motorcycles, knocking them over like dominoes. Jill and Paquette watched in horror as four motorcycles went down on the interstate entrance ramp.

"Oh my God! . . . Oh my God!" She yelled.

One of the blond women Jill had talked with earlier rolled onto the pavement. The rider tumbled three times head over heels, then, incredibly, popped up to a standing position like a gymnast. She hesitated a second, stunned and vulnerable on the roadway, then stepped onto the shoulder and out of the way of oncoming traffic. *Motorcyclists must practice that,* Jill thought.

The whole motorcade screeched to a halt. The maroon sedan came to rest at an awkward angle between Jill's SUV and the hearse, nearly hitting the black wagon carrying her son. That the driver nearly hit the hearse both horrified and infuriated Jill. She now realized those motorcycles took the fall to protect Ben. They truly *were* the Patriot Guard.

Sergeant Paquette noticed the woman in the maroon sedan appeared to be injured. He got out of the SUV and ran to help. Inside, he found a woman in her late fifties. She was bleeding steadily from her arm, which had been sliced by something during the crash. Paquette immediately took his belt off and used it as a tourniquet.

Police soon arrived on the scene. After some assessment it was clear the motorcycle riders were shaken, scraped, and bruised, but not seriously injured. Jill and Tom Schultz, the funeral director, decided to continue on to the funeral home. Jill's nerves were shot. *How much does a mother who just lost her only child have to deal with?* she wondered.

Northwestern Memorial Hospital

On Tuesday, July 28, eight days after having Ben's heart installed in her chest, Judy was going home. It was hard to say good-bye to the doctors, nurses, and staff who had taken such good care of her. Still, Judy hoped she was leaving Northwestern Memorial for good. She'd spent nearly two months total here over the last year, and she was ready to be home in Winnetka with her dog, Lacey.

Judy left the hospital in a wheelchair. As she rolled out the sliding glass doors to the turnaround drive in front of the hospital, she was struck by the fresh summer air blowing off Lake Michigan. The sun rising over the lake filled the gaps between the tall buildings with light. It was one of those absolutely perfect and priceless July days Chicagoans dream of when January temps plunge below zero.

Judy's new lease on life gave her a heightened appreciation of everything around her. As her friend steered the car onto Lake Shore

Drive, Judy remarked at how blue and beautiful the lake looked. She pointed out joggers and bicyclists along the water's edge. When they reached North Avenue, she commented on the beach volleyball games and the pedestrian bridge over the drive, and the Lincoln Park Zoo. Judy had lived within twenty miles of downtown Chicago her entire life, but today everything seemed new to her. She remembered the one-hit-wonders Aliotta, Haynes, and Jeremiah, and their song "Lake Shore Drive," which described exactly how she felt:

> There ain't no finer place to be than running Lake Shore Drive
> And there's no peace of mind or place you'll see
> Than riding on Lake Shore Drive

Judy was all smiles when they pulled into her driveway. Ruthie was there, waiting and waving outside. She had stopped by the neighbors' house to pick up Lacey. As Judy exited the car and headed toward her front steps, the little brown cocker spaniel charged to meet her. They were so excited to see each other—Judy squatted down, while Lacey jumped up.

Judy learned that PD and Ruthie had taken care of hiring a caregiver. The service had sent two, but one, seeing Lacey, quickly announced she was allergic to dogs. The other, Joanna Zyzniewska, was from Poland and had been in Chicago for about ten years. She too was on her knees playing with the dog. Judy noticed, and it meant more to her that her new caregiver would get along with Lacey than with her. "Congratulations, you're hired," Judy said.

PD dropped by after work that evening to check on things. Ruthie and PD were so elated to see their friend alive and in her natural habitat that they stayed until midnight. As they left, both felt comfortable that Judy was in very good hands.

Rosemount, Minnesota

The funeral was just a couple of days away, and there was still work to be done. Phil Paquette desperately wanted a Black Hawk flyover, one of Ben's dying wishes. He called the Minnesota National Guard, but had no luck there. He finally called the pilots directly in St. Paul. This being the eleventh hour, he was beyond asking gently. "Hey, you've *got* to do this. This *has* to happen," he pressed.

He described exactly what they were looking for—a Black Hawk escort over the hearse as it traveled from the funeral home to Rosemount High School. The commanding officer at the Guard's 34th Combat Aviation Brigade agreed to honor the request.

Meanwhile, Jill was adjusting to life back at home. When she'd arrived a few days previously, the first thing she noticed was that her house seemed really empty. She was used to Ben being away from home, but the knowledge that he'd never return left her feeling so lonely.

Jill needed to busy herself. Fortunately, she had plenty to do in the near term. She went shopping for both the funeral and the wake. *What am I going to wear to my son's funeral?* It was a question she couldn't believe she was asking. But she needed to find something, so she went with her sister and niece to the Macy's in Burnsville. Jill dreaded the trip, but she knew it would be a good diversion. She picked out a colorful dress for the wake and a black one for the funeral.

Not long after returning home from the store, Jill decided she also wanted a necklace with a crucifix. She returned to the same store, where a pleasant-looking woman seemed eager to help her.

"Is it for a graduation?" the woman asked.

Jill didn't want to burden the woman with the story of what it was for, so she simply said, "No."

"A wedding?"

"No."

"Is it for a family member?"

"Yes, my son."

"Okay, let me help you."

By now the clerk had noted Jill's somber tone and seemed to understand no further questions were needed. She was kind and accommodating and gave Jill a generous discount on the necklace.

Winnetka, Illinois

The day after returning home, Judy was already restless inside her house. The weather was perfect again, and she wanted to get out and walk. It was about five blocks to Lake Michigan from her house, a walk she'd made without effort hundreds of times. She convinced Joanna they should try, and together they put the leash on a very excited Lacey. They headed out the door and walked up to Elder Lane, then turned east toward the beach.

Ben's heart recipient Judy Meikle with her caregiver Asha and her new dog Lacey.

As Judy, Joanna, and Lacey strolled along, Judy reflected on how much had happened in the last ten months. She thought back to that walk on the Green Bay Trail the previous fall and the feeling of struggling to breathe. She sure didn't feel like that today. As her long legs covered the Winnetka sidewalk, she sucked air into her lungs and took pleasure in how full they felt. She could feel her heart pound faster as they picked up the pace. She felt as good as she had in years.

Judy could hear the waves on Lake Michigan as she and Joanna crossed Sheridan Road and headed toward Elder Lane Beach. After letting Lacey run around and wear herself out, Judy and Joanna turned around to head home. But Judy realized now that she was tired from the short walk. Dr. Cotts had warned her it would be a while before she was at full strength. Fortunately, Judy had a friend who lived a few houses down Sheridan Road. They dropped by and sat on the patio while Judy caught her breath and rested. On the trek home Judy's breathing was easy, but her legs grew weary. The five blocks home felt more like five miles. But the heart recipient was determined to do it.

When they finally made it back, Judy collapsed onto the couch in her front sunporch and fell asleep. Hours later, she awakened to find PD sitting in her living room. He had come by to say good-bye as he was heading out the next day for Minnesota. He would represent her at Ben's funeral service.

"It sounds like it's going to be quite a moving experience," he said.

"I'm sure it will be," Judy replied.

Apple Valley, Minnesota

At the funeral home, Ben lay in his casket in his crisp green uniform. But Paquette and Engebretsen had a problem. They wanted to ensure every pin and medal on Ben's uniform was meticulously placed according to regulation. However, they were missing a major component: his boots.

Rangers dress a little differently than other soldiers. Along with their dress greens they wear polished black boots, with their pants tucked into the footwear. Jill said she didn't care if he had boots or not. The lower half of the casket would be closed anyway, so no one would know. But Paquette and Engebretsen wouldn't hear of it. Their brother's uniform, especially the one he'd wear for eternity, had to be perfect. Jill saw their passion and understood.

Over the next few hours, they managed to track down a pair of black Army boots. But there was also another issue to deal with. In Ben's blue book he'd asked to have a case of beer and a tin of chew placed in his casket. Jill and the Rangers wanted bottles of beer, because that's what Ben liked. But a full case wouldn't fit. They finally managed to find a twelve-pack of Michelob Golden Draft Light, Ben's favorite, and a tin of Copenhagen. They placed both near the newly acquired black boots.

"I'm just going to pretend this isn't happening," said funeral director Tom Schultz. With the front half of the casket closed, anyone attending the wake or funeral wouldn't see the items.

On the afternoon of her son's wake, Jill arrived to the funeral home about 3:00 p.m., an hour early. She walked up to Ben's casket and gazed down at him. Ben had been dead now for more than ten days.

Engebretsen stood sentry by Ben's casket, a duty he'd performed for more than a week. Other Rangers had arrived from Fort Benning to give him some relief. Chaplain Jeff Struecker was also there, preparing for the funeral service the next day and offering support and counsel to Jill and any of Ben's Ranger brothers who sought him.

Picture boards displaying Ben's life from childhood through high school were spread around the chapel. Some of Ben's girlfriends, including Jenny Boll, had helped create the mementos. A video looped on a TV screen showed more photos of Ben set to Kenny's Chesney's "Don't Blink."

People started to come through the door, just a few at first, then a steady stream of mourners, well-wishers, family, and friends.

Before Jill knew it, there was a line of people out the door, and she was trapped. Everyone wanted to pay their respects and tell her how sorry they were over the loss of her son. But it was overwhelming. She felt the physical and emotional crush and her stress started to grow.

Seeing Jill struggling, Erick Innis and Chase Vanderhule came over and stood guard on either side of her. Jill kept looking at the line, which wasn't getting any shorter. Her knees got weak, and she started to feel queasy. She motioned for Innis to come closer. "Hold me up."

Eventually, some family friends took Jill by the arm and pulled her into an empty room. Once the door was shut, Jill slumped into a chair, relieved to be out of the press of well-intentioned people.

She didn't know what to do. She couldn't just leave everyone who had come to see her and Ben and pay their respects, yet the thought of facing everyone now seemed impossible. After a while a few well-wishers and relatives, including Mary Barnes, made their way to the room. Mary tried to get her daughter's mind on something else. "Have you seen the flags outside?"

"No."

"Well, you need to look out the window."

When Jill got up and looked outside, she was taken aback by the sheer number of flags out front. They were everywhere, dozens of them. But Jill didn't have time to fully appreciate them. After finishing a bottle of water, she desperately needed to relieve herself. She got up and made a beeline for the ladies' room.

Meanwhile, Jenny Boll walked over to the casket and looked at her dear friend. *This doesn't look like my Benny,* she thought. Even back at Walter Reed he had looked just like he always had.

Jenny was overwhelmed by the turnout. Her emotions were about to burst. She turned and locked eyes with Paquette, who could see she was struggling. When he approached her to see if he could help, Jenny started crying.

"Do you want to see Jill?" Paquette asked.

"Yeah," Jenny said over her sobs.

Paquette pulled out an engraved metal bracelet that had Ben's name, rank, birth date, and date of death. He put it on her wrist and looked straight into her tear-stained eyes.

"Don't ever take it off."

"I won't," said Jenny, wiping away tears with the palm of her hand.

Two Gold Star mothers showed up to pay their respects. Gwen Olsen was the mother of Marine Lance Cpl. Daniel Olsen of Eagan, Minnesota. He had died in Iraq in 2007. Sandy Masterson's son, Army Corporal Conor Masterson of Woodbury, Minnesota, was killed in Afghanistan the same year. The two women were among Jill's first contacts with other Gold Star moms. They had a simple message for her: she wasn't alone now, and she never would be again. Jill was deeply touched by their presence.

Chaplain Jeff Struecker greeted and comforted many of the mourners, especially the Rangers. He noticed an old Army veteran who had shown up in his dress greens. Struecker studied the man's patches and pins. He was about eighty years old, but Struecker realized that he too was a Ranger. The chaplain fought through the jam of people to engage the veteran. When he introduced himself, the older man told Struecker his name was John Roy, and that he was a veteran of both Korea and Vietnam. He had served in both Special Forces and the Ranger Regiment. Roy said he had also helped found Camp Merrill in Northern Georgia and had once been an instructor there.

"John, did you know Ben real well?" Struecker asked, figuring there was some sort of local connection.

"Never met him before in my life," Roy said. He explained that he'd been reading the newspaper and saw a local Ranger had died. He wanted to come and pay his respects.

Struecker could see that Roy was now in tears over a young man he didn't know.

"If you don't mind my asking, why are you so emotional?" Struecker asked.

"It took me a long time to be man enough to show my emotions.

I lost a lot of friends in Vietnam. I still see a lot of warriors and their families when they pass away, and it took me until just a few years ago to be able to show my emotion when somebody dies. And now, I'm not embarrassed to cry."

The message hit Struecker right in the heart. It was something he would later share with his three sons and two daughters.

Linda, the Patriot Guard motorcycle rider who had crashed on the interstate as they brought Ben's body home the day before, came strutting into the wake on crutches. She displayed a big road rash on her knee. Jill took a look and decided it was the most horrific scab she'd ever seen.

Jill wanted to know more about how Linda had rolled into a standing position after she was hit. "How is it that you had such forethought to stand up and get off the road?" she asked. "Do you practice that?"

"What are you talking about?"

"Well, you stood up," Jill reminded her.

"No, somebody picked me up."

"What?"

"Yeah, when I was done rolling," Linda said, "I felt somebody put their arms under my armpits, and they stood me up."

"Linda, I was watching the whole thing. There was nobody there."

They looked at each other for a moment, each in disbelief at the other's take on the story. They both then concluded it must've been Ben who'd lifted her to safety.

Eventually, the chapel cleared out. Just a few family members and several Rangers were left. As they took down the pictures and carried out the TV, Mary walked toward Jill with Erick Innis. Innis had been stoic throughout the afternoon, but now he was crying a flood of tears. Jill reached out and hugged him and they cried together, Erick still sobbing, inconsolable at the loss of his best friend.

Winnetka, Illinois

Judy's caregiver was standing at the kitchen stove blanching some green beans for dinner. Joanna, nicknamed Asha, was still getting to know Judy's likes and dislikes. She was also learning that if Judy Meikle had an opinion, it was either very strongly for or strongly against.

Judy, seeking sunshine, was sitting on the front porch when Asha brought her a tray. She had prepared a dinner of baked chicken and rice with the green beans on the side.

"Oh, don't bother with the green beans, I can't stand them," Judy announced.

"They're the only fresh vegetable in the house right now," Asha replied.

"Well, I don't like green beans."

Asha didn't flinch.

"I don't care, you're going to try them," she said.

"Well, you can serve them, but that doesn't mean I'll eat them."

Judy started to eat, ignoring the beans in protest, but Asha pressed her. Finally, Judy agreed to try one. As she bit down, she expected the bitterness she'd disdained since childhood. But now she tasted something very different. They were delicious. She polished off the entire plate. Weeks later, she would learn from Jill that Ben's favorite vegetable was green beans.

Rosemount, Minnesota

Jill returned home late that night after meeting Ben's Ranger friends at a bar in Minneapolis. As she pushed open her front door, she flicked on the light. A pure white moth rested on the stair rail in front of her. It looked delicate, like if she reached out and touched it, it would turn to dust. As Jill watched, the moth started flying and circling toward the light.

"Oh, you're one of those light chasers," she said.

She watched the insect for a moment, then turned off the light and went upstairs to get ready for bed. She was facing another long day in the morning—Ben's funeral at Rosemount High School. As she settled into bed, what appeared to be the same moth from the stairs came flying into her room.

"Oh, hello there," she said. "What are you doing here?"

Jill later came to believe the moth was a sign from Ben. She saw the moth as a creature of transition. So too she thought Ben was transitioning, and this was his way of telling her he was on his way to heaven.

Rosemount High School

Beth Kingston, the wife of Ben's company commander, arrived at the high school well before the funeral's 11:00 a.m. start time. She and her husband had decided years before that if he was deployed and one of his men was killed, she would represent him at the funeral no matter where it was. Captain Kingston had lost three soldiers before Ben. One of the previous Gold Star parents had told Beth how much it meant for her to come. While they were still filled with grief, that made the Kingstons feel a little better. An officer deployed overseas isn't required to send his wife to one of his soldier's funerals. But for that officer who can't be there, it's the next best thing.

Beth Kingston, with her wide smile, cropped blond hair, and outgoing charm, could put anyone at ease, even at an event like this. She had brought a large bag of Ranger pins to hand out. An hour before the service, she noticed the incredible turnout by the Patriot Guard, most of whom were Vietnam veterans. There were a couple dozen standing in a line outside the school, each holding a flagpole with the Stars and Stripes perched in front of them. She felt grateful for their presence, so she and another Ranger approached them individually and thanked them for coming. She also handed each one a Ranger pin. Several of them told her no one had *ever* thanked them before. That stunned her, and she suddenly found herself shedding a few tears. Many of the Patriot Guard, seeing her tears, shed their own in return. Ben's funeral was now less than an hour away.

Holman Field, St. Paul, Minnesota

Lieutenant Colonel Greg Thingvold and Major Jeff Merricks of the Minnesota National Guard's 34th Combat Aviation Brigade arrived at Joint Force Headquarters on Airport Drive a couple of hours early that Saturday. Thingvold was commander of the Guard's 2-147th Air Assault Battalion. Merricks was the operations officer. The two guard officers had spent a year in Balad, Iraq, together flying assault missions for conventional forces. Their deployments overlapped both of Ben's tours in Iraq, though they had never met him. Today's "Hero Mission," as they called it, would be less dangerous than their flights in a war zone but more somber. It wasn't their first Hero Mission; they'd done it all too many times before in Minnesota and Iraq.

They walked into a briefing room for a crew and mission brief. Everyone at the brigade knew what the two pilots were doing, and those involved with the support and maintenance of the Black Hawks wanted to make sure this mission ran perfectly. They picked out the best and most reliable chopper but still made contingencies for a backup. They knew a Black Hawk flyover was one of Ben Kopp's dying wishes, and they were determined to make this mission perfect in his honor.

Thingvold and Merricks put together a basic flight plan. They studied Google Earth in advance and got a site picture of Apple Valley and Rosemount and key landmarks like the funeral home and high school. They completed some paperwork, attended a briefing, and about twenty minutes before take-off walked out to the Black Hawk to go through their preflight checks.

They climbed inside and checked the instruments, the communication equipment, and made some hydraulics checks. Once everything was in place, Merricks pressed the chrome ignition button and fired up the bird. They completed another series of checks, then taxied to the runway and contacted the tower.

"St. Paul Tower, guard two-three-seven-five-nine, at the guard ramp. VFR southbound, ready for hover taxi."

"Roger guard two-three-seven-five-nine. You're clear to take off with a left turn to the south."

The Black Hawk lifted off, St. Paul's humble skyline to the northwest, the adjacent Mississippi River to the east. Once airborne, Merricks steered the bird to the south, using the river as a navigational guide.

It was a ten-minute flight to Apple Valley and the funeral home, where they would escort the procession to Rosemount High School. They headed downriver toward the Pine Bend Refinery, where the Mississippi curls to the east and heads toward Hastings at its confluence with the St. Croix River. Once the refinery came into view, Major Merricks steered the chopper to the west, away from the river. The Black Hawk soared over Ben's hometown of Rosemount.

The pilots steered the chopper to the "University Lands," unaware that the soldier they were honoring that day had spent much of his youth directly below, snowmobiling with friends, exploring on bikes, or playing war games. The sprawling expanse of agricultural lands was the perfect place for a conspicuous Black Hawk to wait before making its way to the nearby funeral home. They were deliberately early, and now "loitered" using the sand pits at Biscayne Avenue and 170th Street as a landmark. They waited for their cue from a guardsman on the ground at the funeral home.

After about fifteen minutes, the crackle over the radio told them they were wanted in place over the funeral home. The chopper dipped forward and ate up space quickly, making the trip in a matter of minutes. Lieutenant Colonel Thingvold spotted the funeral home and the hearse outside. Their orders were to hover above the lead car and follow 4.8 miles down 150th Street toward Rosemount High School. They'd hold back from the school grounds, then fly over once the hearse was in place.

There were more than a dozen Rangers who had come from both Afghanistan and Fort Benning for Ben's service. They were in a series of vehicles behind the shiny black hearse, which lead the line. From the air, Merricks and Thingvold were stunned by the sheer number of people in Apple Valley and Rosemount who had gathered along the route. People held American flags and waved at the hearse going by. Some saluted, and some held their hands over their hearts. As they approached the high school, the crowds lining the streets grew bigger. The pilots, even ten football fields up, could sense the emotion below.

Rosemount High School

The hearse pulled into the high school parking lot; hundreds of people stood silently outside, all eyes fixed on the black Cadillac. The vehicle turned and drove around the side of the building, coming to a rest in front of some cargo doors on the east side of the school. About two hundred yards from the polished black wagon was the Rosemount High School Fighting Irish football field where Ben had distinguished himself years earlier. At the edge of the school, a lone bagpipe wailed "Amazing Grace." Ben's closest Ranger brothers got out of their vehicles and approached the hearse. Jill had come straight from home to the high school and watched as Ben's best friends prepared to take the flag-draped casket from the car. She stood next to Sergeant Paquette.

It started like a fast and distant drumbeat, an unmistakable roll coming from beyond the tree line to the west. That quickly grew to a roar that reverberated in the chests of those gathered outside the school. All eyes followed the noise coming from the horizon. The Black Hawk appeared low over the tree line. The sky was clear blue except for a few high wispy clouds, and the sun was strong. At just five hundred feet now, the Black Hawk was deafening as it approached. By the time it came to a hover over the hearse, the crowd gathered below could feel the rotor wash blowing down. The site of the chopper over her son's flag-draped casket took Jill's breath away. She was overwhelmed not only by the power of the display, but by the thought that Ben's greatest dying wish had finally been granted.

Six Ranger pallbearers slid the casket out of the vehicle. Their polished black boots shuffled on the pavement in unison; their distinctive tan berets pulled crisply to the right side of their heads. They stood, casket in hands, and paused. The Black Hawk dropped a bit lower, as if it were coming down to get Ben. It then slowly rose and broke off into the sun, disappearing in a matter of seconds.

Jill felt the chopper had just picked Ben up and lifted him skyward. She leaned over to Paquette, who was standing next to her.

"Ben just went into heaven," she said with a mother's certainty.

Paquette too was overwhelmed. He whispered back.

"You can't tell me there isn't a God. That's the most perfect thing that could've happened."

When the Black Hawk was gone and the roar from its engine had faded, the six Rangers gently moved with Ben's casket toward the cargo doors on the school's brick wall. As they moved up the concrete walkway, another line of Rangers stood waiting shoulder to shoulder. Their flattened right hands moved slowly and deliberately toward their tan berets. They held their pose as Ben was carried past.

There were no wheels or carts to place the casket on. Ben's Ranger brothers—Ryan Lundeby, Marcus Engebretsen, Chase Vanderhule, Shane Harris, and two others—bore the weight. They carried Ben just as Derrick Ball and Suarez had in the ditch back in Afghanistan. Just a couple of months earlier, Harris had attended the funeral of Ranger Ryan McGhee. He and Ben had gone through Ranger Indoctrination with the affable McGhee. Now, Shane was dealing with the second painful death of a close friend in just a matter of weeks.

Rangers carry Ben into Rosemount High School, where he'd graduated just over three years previously. Still more Rangers salute their brother. The Ranger saluting on the right is Major General Joseph Votel, a native of nearby St. Paul, Minnesota.

The Rangers carrying Ben disappeared past the doors and into the underbelly of the school. Lundeby felt the strain of carrying the casket and suddenly remembered it was a twelve-pack of beer and a can of dip heavier than it would've been with just Ben inside.

Many dignitaries arrived, including Minnesota Governor Tim Pawlenty and US Senators Amy Klobuchar and Al Franken. Jill was whisked inside to a private room, where she met with both Pawlenty and Klobuchar. The governor presented her with a proclamation honoring Ben across Minnesota that day. Words were exchanged, along with condolences and formalities, hugs and handshakes. Jill felt their presence was kind and honorable, but in the moment, her attention was elsewhere. Her heart and focus were on Ben.

Jill walked out of the room and down the hallway toward the gymnasium. When she got inside, the first person she saw was

Brittney. They embraced in a long, warm hug. Brittney told Jill she'd had a dream about Ben the night before, and in the dream he'd whispered to her, "Don't waste your life."

Jill found her seat in the front row of folding chairs set up on the basketball court. She picked a seat on the end of a row next to the aisle because her grandmother, Marian Rogers, was in a wheelchair. Jill loved her dearly and wanted to sit next to her for comfort. They held hands throughout the ceremony. In the seat directly behind Jill sat her first cousin, Maria. Also in the crowd was PD Weatherhead, who had come from Chicago to pay respects on Judy's behalf.

The bleachers were rolled out, and about seven hundred people were filing in. Atop the packed bleachers on either side were balconies, and Patriot Guard riders now lined the railings above the gathering, American flags in hand. Jill looked around and was blown away by the turnout.

Ranger Chaplains Mike Shellman and Jeff Struecker were busy up front getting ready to co-officiate. Struecker would serve as emcee, and Shellman planned to deliver the message. They stood at a podium at gym floor level directly under the retractable glass backboard and basketball hoop that for some reason had been left down for the service. Behind them were five different flags, including the American flag, the state flag of Minnesota, and the flag of the Order of the Purple Heart. One of Ben's blue book requests was for no flowers at his wake or funeral. Ben had nobly written "support mother instead." People either didn't know or didn't listen; there were stacks of floral arrangements around the podium.

Rangers Innis, Vanderhule, Krueger, and Lundeby had come from Afghanistan. Most of the other Rangers had come from Fort Benning. Throughout the ceremony, there were always two Rangers at the head and foot of Ben's casket, their presence saying, *He's still our brother. We are not leaving his side.*

So many familiar people were walking in to honor Ben. His pals from high school, like Josh Maldonado, Kyle Hildreth, and Tyler

Nelson. Tyler's sister, Desirae, found her seat. She'd always urged Ben to pursue his faith. Eric Pittlekow, who had mentored Ben in the Rosemount weight room and told him what to expect during basic training, was going over his notes. (Jill had asked him to say a few words about Ben.) Noticeably absent was Richard Rivera, who was deployed and unable to come home. Jenny Boll sat and waited for the service to get under way. Having the funeral at the high school seemed surreal to her; it was the very place she and Ben had spent four happy years together.

Ben's grandpa Jon looked around at the hundreds who had gathered to remember his grandson. *This is something. This is a special kid,* he thought.

Chaplain Struecker welcomed everyone to Rosemount High School, then Chaplain Shellman got up to speak.

"Greater love hath no man than this, that a man who would lay down his life for his friends." Shellman used this passage from the Gospel of John as a theme for the service. He thought it fit Ben to a tee. He talked about how much Ben loved being a Ranger and how passionate he was about it.

"God loves us, and God loves Ben, and God knew what Ben was doing on that mission. God was there. And in that moment when Ben passed into eternity, God was there. And Ben reached out and was a recipient of God's love."

Chaplain Shellman looked out at the sea of mourners. His eyes came to rest on Jill, who looked like an angel to him. He saw her tears, but he also saw radiance. He saw sadness, but also a vision of hope. He thought of her sacrifice and what she'd given to the country—her only son. He went back to the Book of John.

"For God so loved the world that he gave his only son so that everyone who believes in Him might not perish, but have eternal life."

There were many speakers, all of who wanted to say something about Ben. Major General Joseph Votel, a Ranger who had grown up twenty minutes away in St. Paul, praised Ben's courage. Senator Al Franken shared a few words. And finally, Ben's fellow Rangers were given the stage.

Captain Krueger walked to the podium and looked out.

"Over the past year, I have had the distinct privilege to serve with the men of Third Platoon, Charlie Company, 3rd Ranger Battalion," he said. "Throughout this time, I was able to see Ben Kopp distinguish himself daily. Even as a relatively young Ranger leader, he consistently led the way with a calm, directed demeanor that clearly commanded the respect of those around him. . . . Ben was a warrior, a patriot, a leader, and, most important, a friend. His dedication to service and to others was remarkable. I pray that he continues to inspire us in our daily lives and decisions so we can all seek to live for a higher purpose."

Chase Vanderhule also spoke and got choked up, shedding tears as he recalled fighting with Kopp in Afghanistan. "I said I would never have to wear a friend's name on my wrist," he said, raising his right wrist to reveal a metal bracelet that now bore Ben's name. "Well, now I do. My buddy, my friend, my brother. I'll see you on the other side."

Jill tried to focus on the words, but she was numb. She had shed so many tears over the last twenty days, there were none left for the funeral. She felt more shock than anything else; the reality that Ben was gone was settling in.

Jill had fretted over what music to use during the ceremony. She knew Ben wouldn't want the music to be morose or heavy. She had asked his pal Tyler Nelson to find a song he thought represented Ben. He came back with Randy Houser's "Boots On." The hard-driving country song started to pump through the gym's overhead speakers. When Jill heard the lyrics, she thought, *Yep, this is Ben.*

> In my dirty ol' hat
> With my crooked little grin
> Granny beaded neck

And these calloused hands
In a muddy pair of jeans
With that Copenhagen ring
No need to change a thing, hey y'all
I'm going out with my boots on

Jill had felt heavy and overwhelmed earlier but now found herself tapping her feet to the rhythm. *It's the way Ben would've wanted to go out,* she thought. For Jenny Boll, the words triggered too many familiar images of Ben, and she broke down crying. Even the reverent Jeff Struecker liked the unorthodox touch. *Only a Ranger mother could pull off that song,* he thought.

Shane Harris walked up and looked out at the hundreds of people there, their somber faces. He saw Ben's mom sitting in front of him. *I don't want to cry on this stage,* he thought, fighting back tears. Harris thought he needed to be as strong as Ben would've been in the same situation, and as strong as Ben's mom was being right in front of him.

He started to speak, trying to hold himself together. He reflected on how much Ben had changed in the short few years he'd known him since they met during Ranger Indoctrination. Harris remembered the rough and tumble kid with the tats and gold chains who had evolved into a proud and disciplined Ranger. He described Ben as a person who made everyone around him better and who had willingly died for his country.

Ryan Lundeby talked about how Ben never seemed to slow down and was always the life of every party.

"He was always stuck on full throttle," he said. Lundeby went on to explain that Ben never hesitated. If there was a chance to have fun, they'd have fun. He talked about their trips to Auburn University, and how Ben had coyly and calmly pulled him out of the way of a jealous boyfriend.

Eric Pittlekow was the only Rosemount friend who spoke. He

had served in the regular Army and had deployed to Iraq, but he was out of the military now. He shared memories of Ben, but by the time he was back in his seat, he'd fallen into shock. While it was a great honor to be the only local guy to speak, it was something he wished he'd never had to do.

Josh Maldonado was there, but he didn't speak. Ben was the first person close to him he'd ever lost, and his death hurt him deeply. It would throw Maldonado into a personal slump that included too much drinking, something he would later be forced to seek help for.

"Ranger . . . son . . . grandson . . . friend . . . defender of freedom. Go ahead, march on. May you rest in peace," Mike Shellman said. The service ended with an acoustic cover of the Allman Brothers song, "Soulshine."

But the sendoff for Ben was far from over. Because so many young service members were coming home in caskets from both Iraq and Afghanistan, Ben's burial at Arlington wouldn't be for another week. Ben wouldn't spend that week alone. After the Rosemount funeral, his body was prepped to be flown back to Washington, DC, and Engebretsen would again accompany him.

Jenny Boll was so shaken by Ben's death that the day after his funeral, she relapsed. But while the loss led her back down the wrong path, it was also ultimately what led her to quit for good. After a few weeks, she realized what she was doing wasn't making the pain any better, and that Ben wouldn't have wanted this for her. She knew that even in death he was always in her corner. She got help, and with Ben as her inspiration, she turned her life around for good.

Arlington, Virginia

Jill flew to Washington, DC, on August 5, the day before the Arlington burial, and checked into the Sheraton Pentagon with Mary. Ben's body had already been flown back from Minnesota. As the minutes ticked slowly by inside her hotel room, she realized his body was sitting in a funeral home nearby. She had just one more chance to see her son, and this was it. She drove to the funeral home with her dad, Jon.

Once inside, they were escorted to a private viewing room. The funeral director opened the casket. Jill thought Ben looked even more like himself than he had just a week before back in Rosemount. He looked so good, in fact, that she pulled out a digital camera and started taking pictures of him. They were pictures she would never share with anyone else, but in that moment she felt compelled to take them. The thought of taking pictures of her dead son was so crazy that she started nervously laughing. *He's going to smack me somehow for doing this—"Mother! Stop taking pictures of me!"* Her dad started laughing too. What a rare thing, she thought, to have a glimpse of joy in this moment. But the burst of one emotion soon turned to another, and their laughter transitioned to tears. For Jill it was the hard and heavy cry, the big one she had been avoiding since getting the call from Afghanistan. She let it all come out in front of Ben and her dad.

When she'd recovered, she asked her dad for a little time alone with Ben. During those precious minutes, she talked to her son and told him how much she loved him. She touched the bridge of his nose again as she had at Walter Reed and when he was a baby. Finally she kissed him, said good-bye, and left. She and her dad had to get ready for what they knew would be another emotional challenge: burying Ben the next day.

Arlington National Cemetery

Arlington National Cemetery, a sprawling expanse of emerald turf, towering oaks, and evergreens, dotted by thousands of white marble slabs, is the most somber and hallowed place in America. It is the final resting place of American presidents, astronauts, and of course the nation's greatest war heroes. There are about four hundred thousand graves in all, and each one has a story. It is home to the Tomb of the Unknown Soldier and the Eternal Flame at the Kennedy family gravesite.

The gathering for Ben's burial started in a small basement room at the administration building. Major General Votel asked for the attention of those arriving for the burial. Votel, like Ben, was a Minnesota native and a Ranger. He wore his dress greens, black boots, and a tan beret. In the twenty-eight days since Ben was wounded, he had received several Army awards and medals. He had also been promoted posthumously from specialist to corporal. They would present the awards here. Another Minnesota native, US Senator Al Franken, walked forward and found his place as General Votel began to speak.

"As you heard last week when we memorialized Ben up at the high school, he was a quintessential Ranger," General Votel started. "The strength and the spirit of our Rangers is carried on the backs of men just like Ben, who rise to the occasion and do exactly what their nation asks them to do, unquestioning and with complete willingness and always without regard for themselves, thinking of their fellow man and their fellow Ranger." Votel turned toward Jill.

"And certainly, this was the case with your son. And so this morning we are going to present you with three different awards. The first award that we will present you with is the Purple Heart." General Votel took the medal and walked it over to Jill, kneeling down to present it to her. A chaplain then stepped up and read the description for Ben's Bronze Star:

> For exceptionally valorous achievement as a machine gun team leader for a joint task force in support of Operation Enduring Freedom. Corporal Kopp led a machine gun team against many heavily armed enemy combatants, braving heavy enemy fire from close range. Corporal Kopp placed accurate suppressive fire on multiple locations, allowing the recovery of a reconnaissance team that had been decisively

engaged and unable to maneuver. His actions contributed to the destruction of twelve enemy fighters. Corporal Kopp's ultimate sacrifice undoubtedly saved the lives of multiple Rangers. Because of his distinctive accomplishments, Corporal Kopp reflected great credit upon himself, this command, and the United States Army.

General Votel presented the Bronze Star (with valor) and later the Meritorious Service Medal to Jill, who fought back tears. He then handed two folded American flags to Jill and her family, further mementos of Ben's commitment to his country.

The indoor ceremony paused before they headed to Ben's final resting place. Sergeant Paquette used the time to quietly introduce Jill to a representative from the federal agency whose agents had been along on the YETI 4 operation. The gentleman knelt before Jill and thanked her for her son's service and sacrifice. He then presented the family with commendations from the agency.

Outside, the sun was now nearly overhead, and faint cirrus clouds brushed the bright sky. It was just the kind of day Ben loved to spend at the lake with Ay-Yi, or with his Ranger buddies on the beach. The lushness of Arlington in August enveloped the mourners as they filtered outside. Some of the trees had stood there longer than Arlington itself, and their leaves fluttered gently in the slight breeze.

The black hearse containing Corporal Ben Kopp's body pulled up and came to a rest. An honor guard of Arlington's Old Guard fell in behind; they would march to the gravesite and complete their duties graveside. The rest of the vehicles lined up behind the hearse.

A small Army band marched forward, approaching the assembling motorcade. Captain Struecker walked to the front of the line, a lone Ranger leading the way. The band broke into a somber and muted version of "The Battle Hymn of the Republic" that grew in power as they played. Behind the Army band were twenty-one rifled soldiers, a color guard, and the rest of the vehicles.

There was a growing unrest among some in the burial party. Ben was being carried to his final resting place in the back of a Cadillac. He'd clearly stated in his blue book that he wanted to be buried at Arlington with "full military honors," something he had certainly earned. To many of the uniformed service members here—especially Ben's Ranger brothers—that meant being taken to his gravesite by horse-drawn caisson. But in the summer of 2009, Arlington was booked solid and couldn't meet the demand for caissons. Jill wasn't happy about it; when she'd called Arlington to set the date for Ben's interment, she was told a caisson would be a three-week wait. Without one, the wait would be ten days. She pondered what to do with his body during that extra time and reluctantly decided it would be better to bury him sooner, without the caisson. The slight to Ben would become a catalyst at Arlington for change.

In lieu of the clip-clop of horse hooves, a lone drummer beat out a slow and deliberate rhythm—*"bump . . . bah bah bump bump bump."* They walked past towering trees and the tombs of men who had served their country honorably. Some had died in combat like Ben; others had returned home to tell their war stories, raise families, and spoil grandchildren, before being brought here to rejoin those they had fought with decades earlier.

The band then broke into "The Army Goes Rolling Along." The music was glorious, and it brought to Jill a vision of Ben and his great-grandfather, LeRoy Rogers, standing proudly side by side at Arlington in their Army uniforms.

The procession turned east onto Bradley Drive and paraded down a gradual hill flanked by willow oaks, the trees so massive they provided a full canopy over the drive. Section 60 was to their left. Ben's final resting place, grave number 60-9088, was nearby and in view of the Pentagon. The massive structure peaked over the trees just ahead and to the right.

Jill now realized they had reached the place where her son's body would spend eternity. *Oh my God, what a beautiful place this is,* she thought. Jill had no choice in picking where Ben would be buried, but she now saw that this was a noble location, and that meant a lot to her. She knew Ben would approve as well.

Arlington's own soldiers serve as pallbearers. They're known as the Old Guard. Ben's Ranger brothers and best pals were forced to stand back and watch. Historically, the Ranger Regiment had never allowed any other unit to provide military honors for one of their own. It had always been Rangers taking care of Rangers. The only exception was here at Arlington. The Regiment now grudgingly allowed the Old Guard to take care of Rangers here. This was a reasonably new policy at the time, and there were still people within the Regiment unhappy about it.

Secretary of Defense Robert Gates and Army Secretary Pete Geren were expected to attend Ben's burial. They had called the Ranger Regiment and asked permission, which Jill had granted. Chaplain Jeff Struecker would be conducting the graveside services. He had performed, to this point, more than thirty Ranger funerals for those killed in action.

When the hearse could take Ben no farther, it rolled to a stop on Bradley Drive. Some seats had been set up under the row of oaks, and green all-weather carpeting was rolled out around the gravesite to cover the area still raw with dirt. A marching formation of Rangers— about a platoon strong—found a place just across the drive from the gravesite. Snipers Christopher Watkins and Mark Pendleton, side by side on crutches, limped as best they could down Bradley Drive. Watkins was recovering from the gunshot wound to the foot. Pendleton had fallen down a well in Afghanistan, injuring his leg badly enough to earn a trip home. Dozens more people poured out of tour buses to witness a hero's burial.

Jill, in a sleeveless black dress and sunglasses, stood on the roadway with General Votel, her hand clutching his elbow. They waited about thirty feet behind the hearse. She turned and looked behind her and couldn't believe how many people were swarming in.

Secretary Gates arrived and looked on somberly, the Secretary of the Army, Pete Geren, behind him.

The driver of the hearse, a woman in her fifties, went to the back of the vehicle. She opened the tailgate, revealing Ben's flag-draped casket. The Old Guard pallbearers in their dress blues removed Ben's casket from the hearse. They all displayed blue cords around their right shoulders, signifying they were trained infantryman and had completed infantry school at Fort Benning, as Ben had three years before. Once clear of the back of the car, the honor guard shuffled sideways with the casket, then carefully and in perfect step walked from the road and onto the grass. They passed through facing walls of eight Rangers, four on either side, who saluted as the casket moved past. The pallbearers then positioned the casket over the grave. Bending gently, the eight handlers placed the walnut-colored casket, flag draped over the top, down on green straps, suspending it over the grave. The flag was now slowly and meticulously pulled from the casket. The pallbearers, each with a portion of flag in their hands, then rose in unison and held the flag in place above the casket.

Captain Struecker came forward and began to speak.

"Jill, family friends, fellow Rangers, and friends of Corporal Benjamin Kopp. We've brought his body now as far as we can take it," he said. "We've brought him to his final resting place. The Bible says that God created all of us out of the dust of the earth, and one of these days into the dust of the earth our bodies shall return. And it's only fitting that Corporal Benjamin Kopp should be buried here in this honored place, writing a new chapter in Ranger history. He's buried among Ranger brothers from Omaha Beach and Pointe du Hoc, from Cisterna and Anzio (where Ay-Yi had served). He's buried among brothers from the long-range reconnaissance patrols of Korea and Vietnam, from Point Salines, Rio Hato, and Torrijos Tocumen. He's buried among brothers from Iraq and Afghanistan. And here among some of our nation's greatest patriots at Arlington National Cemetery, Corporal Benjamin Kopp will in just a moment be laid to rest."

Arlington National Cemetery's Old Guard carries Ben to his final resting place in Section 60 as Jill and his Ranger brothers look on. Note Ben's dog tags on the end of the casket.

Shane Harris took a deep breath and looked at Secretary Gates. He knew Gates didn't go to most burials at Arlington. Harris wondered why he had chosen Ben's. The Ranger looked at the secretary's face and studied his demeanor. Harris got the impression this wasn't some kind of PR stunt; Ben's death seemed to have a genuine impact on him, and he was "wearing it like the rest of us," Harris later noted.

Harris had just been to Arlington for his friend Ryan McGhee's funeral a few months earlier. Now he was here to see another close friend buried. He looked at Jill—she was so poised through all of this, especially now. *That's the strongest woman I've ever met,* he thought.

"The Bible says this is not the end of the story," Struecker continued. "It says for a man of faith, there is still another chapter after death. In the book of First Thessalonians, chapter four, the apostle Paul writes these words: 'But we do not want you to be uninformed brothers and sisters about those who have died, so that you may not grieve as others who have no hope. For since we believe that Jesus died and rose again even so, through Jesus, God will bring with him those who have died. For this we declare to you in the word of the Lord that we who are alive who are left until His coming will by no means precede those who have died. For the Lord himself will command a cry and with the archangels and the call and sound of the trumpet of God will descend from heaven, and the dead in Christ will be raised first. And then we who are alive who are left will be caught up in the clouds together with them to meet the Lord in the air, and so we will be with the Lord forever.' And then the Bible says therefore encourage one another with these words. Because of Ben's faith in Jesus Christ this is not the last chapter. And one of these days, all men and women who share his faith will one day spend eternity with Him. We brought him to his final resting place; this is where his body is being laid to rest. But right now, upon Ben's faith in Jesus Christ, his soul is with God in heaven, and those who have faith will spend eternity with him there. Ben was a great warrior. He was a patriot who loved his country, loved the Ranger Regiment, and loved his family and friends. With Ben's life, he honored this flag, and now in his death, this flag will honor him."

After Captain Struecker stepped away, there was silence. The eyes of those who had gathered drifted beyond the casket to seven other Old Guard soldiers in white gloves. In crisp perfection, they fired their rifles, returning the weapon to a rest position after each shot and using the bolt action to eject the shells in unison. They repeated this three times, twenty-one shots, each round reverberating across the cemetery.

A trumpeter played "Taps." Tears flowed, soldiers saluted, and mourners stood with hands over hearts. The Army band followed with "America the Beautiful." The honor guard, still holding the flag above Ben's casket, now folded it into a crisp triangle. A staff sergeant at the end of the line took hold of the flag, pressed it, and passed it to the man across from him. The flag was passed down the line of pall-bearers and presented to the captain in charge of their detachment.

"To my right, face!"

They marched away from the casket, which was still suspended above the grave. Their captain presented the flag to General Votel. He moved to where Jill was seated, kneeled, and presented it to her. "Thank you for your sacrifice," he said. "Your son will never be forgotten."

Jill thought his voice seemed so kind. She held the flag now, and she wanted to hug it. It felt like the last piece of Ben she could hold on to.

The service was over, and a line of people started forming to pay their respects. A middle-aged, white-haired woman was at the head of the line. She represented the Arlington Ladies, an organization that attends all funerals at the cemetery to make sure no service member is buried alone. That certainly wasn't an issue today. She shook Jill's hand.

Secretary Gates then stepped forward in a dark suit and dark tie. He approached Jill, who was now pressing the flag that had just covered Ben's casket against her body. Gates leaned over and shook her hand. "My condolences, and President Obama sends his personal condolences to you."

"Thank you," Jill replied.

The Secretary of the Army squatted down and gripped Jill's right hand with both of his.

Ben's Ranger brothers then greeted Jill. Ryan Lundeby could feel himself tearing up as he approached.

"I'm sorry. I'm sorry. I'm sorry. I'm sorry." It was all Lundeby could think of to offer.

He bent down and wrapped his arms around her, tears streaming down his face.

Rudy DelValle, the command sergeant major who had watched over Ben at Walter Reed, had managed his emotions through the whole service. But as Ben's Ranger buddies embraced Jill, he too let his tears flow. It was one of the most heart-wrenching things he had ever seen.

Rangers share condolences with Jill Stephenson moments after Ben's graveside ceremony at Arlington National Cemetery. Ben's friend Ryan Lundeby said all he could think of to say at the moment was, "I'm sorry. I'm sorry."

It was now time to say good-bye once and for all. Jill walked up to her son's casket, suspended over the open grave. She knelt down before her only son, her only child. She kissed her left hand, placed it on the casket, and gave the wooden top a motherly caress. She then pulled out a small bottle filled with dirt from under the big maple tree in their front yard in Rosemount. She sprinkled some of it on top of the casket and more into his grave. Then she got up and walked away.

Some of the Rangers returned to the casket to pray and to offer slow, deliberate salutes. Lundeby, Krueger, Nathan Bell, and Innis laid flowers down, and Innis placed a Ranger coin on top of the casket.

Then a familiar yet imposing figure in a dark suit made his way to the gravesite. Some of the Rangers watched in disbelief. Ben had always claimed he was related to pro wrestler Sgt. Slaughter, but most hadn't believed him. Sgt. Slaughter, his ex-wife, and their daughter placed some red roses on the casket. Slaughter then knelt, said a prayer, and kissed the casket's wooden lid. He reached around to the end of the casket and grabbed Ben's dog tags, which were affixed to a handle at one end. He looked briefly at the dog tags then got up.

People also left tokens and mementos on top of the casket. An older veteran left a military coin. It read, "Merrill's Marauders, Oct. 3, 1943 China, Burma, India, Korea, Vietnam, Panama, Somalia. *Sua Sponte.*" Another left dog tags that read, "I will be strong and courageous. I will not be terrified or discouraged; for the Lord my God is with me wherever I go. Joshua 1:9." Another coin bore the flag and read, "United States of America. One Nation Under God."

Kim Mellinger, who had visited Ben at Walter Reed with her husband, was there for the Arlington service. Command Sergeant Major Jeff Mellinger couldn't make it because he was deployed. She walked up to the casket and recorded its exact GPS coordinates to send to her husband.

Then they all turned away. It seemed that for the first time since he was struck by enemy fire, Ben was being left alone. But he wasn't. Buried to his left was David Turner, a Korean War vet. To his right were five men killed in action in North Korea in 1953. Behind him six men were buried together, all killed in a downed helicopter in Vietnam. Kitty-corner to his left was William Stocking, who died on December 5, 1942, while serving in World War II. And two rows behind and two graves to the left lay his friend, Ryan McGhee, his marker stone adorned with red roses and a tan Ranger beret.

Ben wasn't alone. He was in very good company indeed.

Springfield, Virginia

A reception followed at the home of Stan and Sharron Dreyer, Beth Kingston's parents. The narrow, hilly roads that led to their quaint home were lined with cars. A charter bus dropped off about a platoon of Rangers, completely blocking the road.

The first person to greet Jill when she arrived was Greg Tobin, the father of another Ranger. The elder Tobin had taken special operators for tours to Ground Zero in New York. He presented Jill with a large heavy cross made from rustic steel. He explained that it had been made from a beam from the World Trade Center. Jill was deeply affected by the gesture; Ben had first pledged to become a Ranger after watching reports on the 9/11 attacks. She would come to cherish that cross.

Rangers came marching into the backyard. Jill was struck by how young they looked, even younger than Ben. Some who had come up from Fort Benning for the interment were new to Charlie Company, had never deployed, and hadn't even met Ben.

While hearts were still heavy over Ben's death, this was the first time that many who'd followed his decline started to loosen up. It now was over—the medevac, the field hospitals, Germany, Walter Reed, the organ transplants, the funeral, and burial. It would take Jill weeks to process everything. But right now, on this sunny afternoon in Virginia, she felt a measure of relief.

The church ladies from Grace Presbyterian in Springfield, the same ones who had supplied seven hundred dollars of chewing tobacco to Charlie Company, had prepared a magnificent spread for the mourners. It gave them incredible pride to help in a situation like this.

So many lives converged here—Judy's friend PD had come from

Chicago. Sgt. Slaughter arrived and was the hit of the reception, posing for pictures with the young Rangers and putting anyone who asked in his trademark "Cobra Clutch." Among the Rangers present was Sergeant Morgan Garrett, who'd been thrown out of Ranger Indoctrination after his run-in with Ben. He watched Jill and saw her pain, but he also saw her strength. He kept trying to work up the nerve to talk to her, but as soon as he got the courage, someone else would walk up and engage her. In the end, he held on to the words he so greatly wanted to express.

New York, New York

Ben's story was gaining steam in the national media. The *Washington Post* included a story on the front of its metro section, and before Jill could get on a plane to go back to Minnesota, ABC News called inviting her to New York for an interview.

ABC put her up at the Helmsley Hotel. While she was there, Fox News and CBS also called to ask her to come in for live interviews. Jill wandered around Central Park and as she sat in front of the Plaza Hotel her phone rang. It was Judy Meikle.

It was the first time they had ever talked. Judy expressed how grateful she was for Ben's heart. She was upbeat and gracious, and it comforted Jill to talk with her. But the pain from Ben's death was still very raw, making the conversation bittersweet. Jill and Judy agreed to try to meet in person in the near future.

On Monday, Harry Smith interviewed Jill in studio for the CBS morning show; Judy joined remotely from Chicago. Even when they weren't on the air, Jill couldn't look away from the monitor that showed Judy. Here was the woman who now had her son's heart. It was all so overwhelming.

Jill later appeared on *Fox and Friends* before making her way to Central Park to meet an ABC News producer and photographer.

Meanwhile, another ABC crew in Chicago had driven up to Winnetka to interview Judy. During their evening newscast that week, Charlie Gibson reported the story.

"And finally, tonight we have a story that centers on the heart of a hero," Gibson said. "Twenty-one-year-old Corporal Benjamin Kopp was buried at Arlington National Cemetery last Friday."

In the report, Judy said she was going to use her gift to bring attention to organ donation. "I have the heart of a twenty-one-year-old Army Ranger beating very strongly in me. I go up to people and ask to see their driver's license, and if they're not a donor I say it's time to be one, sign right here. I'll be the witness. And no one denies someone who's just had a heart transplant. So it's working very well. I'm getting one a day."

In the same news report, Jill shared her hope that somehow Ben would see the incredible impact of his sacrifice.

"He cared a lot about people, helping his friends any way he could at the drop of a hat. I know he's looking down with pride. I know he is."

Columbus, Georgia

About five weeks later, Jill arrived at Fort Benning for the Battalion Memorial. They honored Ben and Ryan McGhee in what is called a "Last Roll Call" ceremony. During the ceremony, a sergeant from the company stepped forward in front of those assembled and began to bark the roll. He rattled off name after name of the men Ben had served with, and each Ranger shouted in response.

"Specialist Innis!"

"Here, Sergeant!"

"Private Scappaticci!"

"Here, Sergeant!"

"Specialist Lundeby!"

"Here, Sergeant!"

"Specialist Vanderhule!"

"Here, Sergeant"

"Corporal Kopp!"

There was silence. The wind blew, the flag flapped, and birds chirped. There was no answer.

"Corporal Benjamin Kopp!"

The second call was followed by more silence.

"Corporal Benjamin Stephen Kopp."

More silence followed, followed by "Taps" and a recitation of the Ranger Creed. Hearing that was all Jill could take. All around her were men Ben had loved like brothers, yet he wasn't here. He really was gone. She doubled over with grief and began to sob.

Ryan McGhee's family was present as well, and it didn't get any easier for Jill hearing his name called. The Ranger Regiment presented both Jill and the McGhee family with an etching from the 3/75 memorial that displays the names of Rangers who have been killed, including their sons.

Afterwards, Jill returned to Minnesota, but another big trip was now on her itinerary. She had been invited to a major national organ donation convention near Dallas. It would be there that she would finally meet Judy Meikle and, for the first time, feel her son's heart beating in another human being.

Grapevine, Texas

On September 29, Jill prepared herself for what she knew would be yet another emotional milestone. In a matter of minutes, she would finally meet Judy Meikle and be reunited with Ben's beating heart. She couldn't wait to feel it.

Jill had flown down to Texas with her mom. She and Judy had agreed to meet a local TV station at the hotel for a news story, but they wanted to talk privately first.

The American Society of Organ Transplantation's National Learning Congress kicked off the following morning at the Gaylord Texan Resort and Convention Center. Jill and Judy were scheduled to give the first speeches of the event to more than a thousand people. Jill was a bit nervous at the prospect. She had never been a public speaker, but she couldn't pass up an opportunity to share Ben's story.

Once Jill and Mary got settled, they exchanged texts with Maria, who had traveled with Judy from Chicago. After freshening up, Jill told Mary it was time to meet Judy. They navigated the vast hotel complex and eventually found the conference room they'd agreed to meet in.

When Jill walked in, she immediately recognized Judy from the TV monitor in New York. Judy was seated but now pushed herself back from the table and rose to her feet. The women locked eyes, knowing this moment had been a long time coming. The last twelve weeks had been so overwhelming for Jill, and now here they were face to face. So many thoughts and emotions flowed through her. First, she was grateful to be meeting Ben's heart recipient. It's not guaranteed that an organ donor's family will get that opportunity. But for the single mom who had suffered an unspeakable and heartbreaking loss, it was one more step toward healing, and a big step connecting Ben's story with the people who had made this miracle possible.

Judy towered over Jill, but they gave each other a warm hug as though they were old friends. Tears quickly turned to sobs, and the women held each other for a long time. When they finally broke from their embrace, Judy said, "Would you like to feel Ben's heart?"

Though tears still flowed down Jill's face, she couldn't help but smile. "Yes, of course!"

Jill reached her right hand forward and Judy grabbed it, guiding it toward her. Jill's palm came to rest perfectly over the heart, Judy's hand covering hers. Jill could feel it now, perfect and strong, *bump, bump, bump, bump.* Her palm absorbed the message from her son like Morse code. Jill's eyes widened—the rhythm felt familiar to her. It was the one she'd once felt from within, and the one she'd felt when her son pressed against her for good-bye hugs before heading off on deployment. Jill started to sob again. *What a wild ride,* she thought. *What a rollercoaster. How did I get here? How did this happen?* Through her sadness, she started to see what a blessing Ben's short life had been, not only for her but for so many others. *This woman is alive because of my son!* Through all her swirling emotions, Jill now felt joy.

Jill didn't want to let go, as though Ben was in there and trying to tell her something. As she felt the thumping of his heart, she realized the message was very clear: Ben, or at least a big part of him, was still alive. Her son was living on through Judy. In that moment, Jill and Judy each felt the same thing. Jill looked up at the caretaker of her son's heart and realized they both knew it. It didn't have to be said.

Columbus, Georgia

Nick Irving had been short-changed on any opportunity to grieve for Ben. While other Rangers were sent home early for the funerals and burial, Irving and others stayed behind in Afghanistan, finishing their deployments. He had wanted to cry the minute he heard the news about Ben at Kandahar, but he couldn't let it out in front of the other guys. Now, back on the ground in Columbus after returning from deployment, he waited for his wife to pick him up at Fort Benning. As family, friends, and loved ones joined their soldiers, some of the younger Rangers came out to greet the returning war fighters. Several of them recognized Irving. They had heard the stories about his record number of sniper kills. Irving had just embraced his wife, Jessica, when some of the young Rangers approached.

"Hey, Sergeant, it's an honor to meet you. I hear you killed a fuckload of people," said one young private.

Irving was stunned. These were things he didn't discuss in front of his wife. She stared at him, confused and disturbed by what she'd just heard. She never knew anything about his deployments. He always told her they worked out a lot, played Xbox, and watched DVDs. Irving and his wife quickly walked to their car and made the short drive off base to their nearby apartment.

Jess wanted to hang out with her husband at home, and after four months away, Irving wanted to relax too. But Ben's death had built up in his heart. Now, in the privacy of his home, he could feel the emotions inside him threatening to explode. But as he guarded his emotions in front of the guys on deployment, he also couldn't break down in front of his wife.

"Hey, Jess, I've gotta run to the gas station. Gonna get a six-pack," he told her.

He then raced outside and jumped into his car. But instead of a beer run, he drove to the other end of the apartment complex, found a secluded parking spot, and began to cry. He let out deep, heaving sobs for an hour straight, finally releasing all the pain and sadness he'd tried to suppress.

He thought about Ben's mom. *Would she be mad? Would she hate Rangers now? Would she hate the Army?* Irving had known other men who died. He had seen guys get shot and survive. But Ben was the only one he'd seen shot who had died. And the fact that it was someone who had rushed to save his life cut deep into his soul.

Grapevine, Texas

Judy and Jill arrived at Gaylord's cavernous ballroom with plenty of time to spare. The crowd of organ transplant professionals was just starting to trickle in. Jill had tweaked her speech all morning, writing it out by hand, making corrections, and penning jumps around the four pages of notes until she thought it was just right.

A stage rose from the center of the room; however, there was no podium to hide behind or rest notes on. And to make things even more complicated, the stage rotated. When the attendees had found their seats and quieted down, there was a brief introduction and welcome to the conference. The lights dimmed, and the production team rolled a video montage of Judy and Jill's TV interviews from the last couple of months. As the story was explained, Jill and Judy weaved their way through the darkness and took their places onstage.

When the video ended, the lights came up, and there sat Judy and Jill. The crowd broke into an enthusiastic round of applause even though the two ladies hadn't yet uttered a word.

Judy leaned over and whispered in Jill's ear, "Oh my God, there's no way our speeches will top that." Jill laughed, knowing she was probably right.

Judy was up first and started by thanking Maria Burud for playing matchmaker. "I am a very lucky and unique woman, as I have a designated heart from a genuine war hero: twenty-one-year-old Army Ranger Benjamin Kopp, who sacrificed his life in the name of our country. Ben saved six of his fellow Army Rangers on July 10, saved my life on July 20, and we're still unsure of how many others through Ben and Jill's generous donation of all of his organs, tissue, and skin."

She went on to explain that each day, eighteen people die waiting for organ transplants. In addition, while there were more than one hundred thousand people on the transplant list, only fourteen thousand received transplants in the first half of 2009 from just 7,200 donors. The numbers made Judy realize the odds really were stacked against her.

"I guess I always knew that someone would have to die in order for me to live, but I never realized how personal it would be. They prepare you to never hear from your donor's family. Ben's heart has truly changed my life in so many ways—all positive. Jill has become part of my healing process and support team. Knowing my donor's family is a huge blessing, and I can only hope our crusading for the cause will somehow be a partial repayment for the terrible and tragic loss Jill has suffered."

Jill stepped up next. She was nervous, but she composed herself and took a look down at her handwritten notes.

"Good morning," she said. "My name is Jill Stephenson, and I am Ben Kopp's mother."

The audience was silent, all eyes on her. Jill relayed the story of her brother, JT, and how her family had donated the eleven-year-old's organs decades before.

"I never imagined that I would lose a brother and then a son," she said. "Who would? Imagine my shock when I got the phone call July 10 that Ben had been shot in the leg during a firefight with the Taliban."

After talking about Ben's time at Walter Reed and her family's serendipitous connection to Judy, Jill closed with these words:

"We both agreed this was a miracle and God's handiwork at its best. I was lost in a whirlwind of emotion, enormous sorrow at losing Ben, and yet enormous joy in knowing he now has seven lives saved to his credit!" Jill explained that she and Judy were now just getting to know each other, and that she was grateful to feel her son's heartbeat. "Knowing her has given me hope that life always goes on and that love gives and gives and gives. Judy and I are forever connected by Ben's strong heart beating in her chest right now. I feel incredibly blessed to know Judy personally. To see the zest, feistiness, and compassion so alive in her gives me that enormous sense of joy. Most people who lose a loved one live with great sorrow in the days, months, and years that follow. I will too, but I count myself lucky—I know it sounds silly—but I also get to experience that joy, that great joy in knowing and seeing with my own eyes the life my son gave to Judy. Has this helped me heal? Absolutely. Every day I experience equal parts of joy and sorrow and believe in my heart this is what a miracle feels like."

When she finished, the crowd rose to its feet in thunderous applause. Jill looked out through the fluttering hands and focused on individual faces. She noticed that men and women alike—hundreds of them—were dabbing their eyes. Ben's story was spreading, and Jill felt its power.

As she stepped down from the stage, people rushed up to her, deeply moved by Ben's story.

"How did you get through that?" asked one incredulously.

"That was amazing!" someone else said.

"Thank you for your son's service," another chimed in.

"How could you say all that without breaking down?" asked another.

Not only did Jill not break down, she drew strength from the experience. Ben had been that source of strength to be brave in the face of fifteen hundred people. She realized she had a new mission in life: sharing Ben's powerful and selfless story, which would resonate with people all over the country. She felt it was his gift to her, to help her heal and move forward. To Jill, Ben was twice a hero, once on the battlefield and again as an organ donor.

Ben's death was Jill's sacrifice to the country. *Ben gifted me the ability to tell his story and to give people hope when they believe they are in hopeless situations.* She realized this was just the beginning.

At that very moment, amid a crush of people reaching out to touch and talk with her, Jill closed her eyes and made a pledge to her son: "For the rest of my life, I promise to honor your life, to never allow you to be disrespected, and to make you as proud of me as I am of you."

Jill Stephenson is an active Gold Star Mother. She visits Ben at Arlington National Cemetery at least twice a year, every Memorial Day and again before Christmas to take part in Wreaths Across America.

EPILOGUE

Even years after his death, Corporal Ben Kopp is a ray of light that still brings people together. The conduit for that connection is Ben's mom, Jill Stephenson, a tireless Gold Star mother who has built friendships with nearly all the people involved in Ben's story.

While being interviewed for *Heart of a Ranger*, Ranger Chaplain Jeff Struecker described Jill as a shining example of the Gold Star program. "I've seen a lot of exceptional Ranger families, but Jill is at the top of the list," he said. "No one has conducted herself better and represented who Rangers are and what Ranger families are all about better than Jill Stephenson. She's amazing."

Every summer, Jill hosts the Ben Kopp Memorial Ride, a motorcycle rally that kicks off in Apple Valley, Minnesota, near Ben's hometown of Rosemount. Ben's family, friends, fellow Rangers, and other veterans come from all over the country to take part. The ride is led by Ben's "Black Stallion" Chevy pickup, which Jill keeps and maintains. Each year, Jill picks two distinguished guests, one to drive Ben's truck and "lead the way" and another to carry the boots he wore on his last deployment. The Ben Kopp Memorial Ride attracts a big crowd and raises money for a variety of military and veteran causes.

For Jill, the connection she shares with Ben's Ranger brothers and the rest of the Ranger community means the world to her. She has traveled the country countless times to take part in their life milestones, and she's involved in many nonprofits, all of which were started by Rangers.

Hanging on to Ben's truck is one of the ways Jill maintains a connection with her son. Shortly after Ben's death, she tried to give it away to Ryan Lundeby, who declined the offer because he believed it would be too emotional for him to look at every day. Jill now takes pride in maintaining it. In fact, she had a chance to share the story of Ben's truck with country music star Lee Brice, whose 2012 hit "I Drive Your Truck" describes a young man driving his brother's truck who was killed in action while serving in the Army. The song resonated with Jill. Hearing this, Brice dedicated the song to her and Ben at a concert in Minneapolis while Jill was in attendance. On a similar note, country star Randy Houser gave Jill a handwritten copy of his song "Boots On," the tune that friend Tyler Nelson found for Jill to play at Ben's funeral service at Rosemount High School.

Ben Kopp touched so many lives both in life and in death that people have reached out to Jill to let her know how. In 2010, Alicia Pratt got in touch. She was the flight nurse who took care of Ben and held his hand on that brief trip from Camp Leatherneck to Camp Bagram. She couldn't get Ben off her mind, so she flew to Minnesota with another member of the New York Air National Guard who was on the same flight with Ben. Jill was so touched she put Alicia up in Ben's bedroom. Alicia and her colleague spent three days in Minnesota and attended one of the memorial events held in Ben's honor. She got to meet many of his friends and relatives there, which helped her find closure and a measure of peace.

Rob Mac Seain, the pathology tech who was present for Ben's heart procurement, was troubled by Ben's death for months. He had intense dreams about the fallen solider, including one where Ben lay on a couch with a baby girl on his chest. Mac Seain thought it was a vision into Ben's future, a future that had been stolen from him. After weeks of inner torment, he decided to reach out to Jill. He was terrified to contact her, but when he did, he found her to be warm and receptive. Mac Seain still lives his life with great reverence for Ben's heroism and remains close to Jill.

Judy Meikle is now a tireless advocate for organ donation. Years after Ben's death, she is in good health and remains the grateful care-taker of the heart of a Ranger. She still lives an active life from the same home in Winnetka where she grew up.

Judy's friend PD Weatherhead died suddenly in 2011. Jill flew to Chicago to attend the funeral. It occurred to Judy during PD's funeral that she and Jill had, over the previous twenty months, both lost the person they were closest to.

Judy and Jill have connected on many occasions, and Judy has gotten to know many of Ben's Ranger brothers as a result. Ross Ritchell, a Ranger that Ben met shortly after Ranger Indoctrination, hails from Judy's hometown of Winnetka. Ritchell and Meikle became friends, and Ben's buddy Shane Harris was the best man at Ritchell's wedding. After the ceremony, Shane got a chance to feel his friend's heart beating inside Judy. When he did, he broke down and started crying, releasing two years of pent-up emotion in the middle of the joyous gathering.

Captain Dan Krueger remembered Ben in a special way at his own wedding at West Point, which Jill attended as an honored guest. His bride, Lindsay, carried a bouquet that—among the flowers—contained small photographs of those close to them who'd been lost, including a photo of Ben. Krueger remains an Army officer and lives in the DC area.

Ryan Lundeby did end up going to Australia right after the Afghanistan deployment. Jill graciously gave him the $1,000 refund from Ben's airline ticket as a gift to use for the trip. Ryan and Jill still keep in touch regularly. In July 2015, he flew up from Texas to be part of the annual Ben Kopp Memorial Ride.

Erick Innis and Jill also remain very close. Erick now lives in the Tampa, Florida, area and works for a military/tactical training partnership.

Ben's death still haunts former company commander Captain Don Kingston, who now makes sure to form personal connections with all the soldiers under his command. Kingston has since been promoted to Major and remains an Army officer.

Chase Vanderhule married a girl from Ben's hometown. The pair began dating soon after Jill introduced them. In 2011, his daughter arrived three weeks early on Jill's birthday. Vanderhule is a police officer in South Dakota.

Ryan Walker is a father and police officer in Connecticut. In 2016, Jill attended his wedding as a surprise guest invited by his fiancée.

Michael Melvin remains a highly respected Army medic. He left the Ranger Regiment and is now assigned to a Special Forces unit.

Ron Kubik, one of the Rangers Ben hung out with in Panama City, was killed in Afghanistan in April 2010. Kubik was credited with saving the lives of five fellow Rangers, five Afghan soldiers, and nineteen Afghan women and children. He was posthumously awarded the Silver Star, the military's third-highest honor.

Jenny Boll attends the Ben Kopp Memorial Ride every year. She is a foreman on an ironworker crew in the Twin Cities, building bridges and high rises. She credits Ben for his encouragement to be tough in a world dominated by men. In the spring of 2016, she got engaged.

Brittney Doran and Jill remain close, so much so that Brittney's little girl calls Jill "Grandma Jilly." Brittney and Jill speak often and share many fond and funny memories of Ben.

Richard Rivera, who wasn't at Ben's funeral because of his own Army duties, felt immense guilt over the death of his friend. He recently left the Army after serving honorably for twelve years.

Dr. Jay McKenna made several trips to Camp Dwyer to investigate Ben's death. What the official investigation revealed is that a combination of problems that occurred at Dwyer were likely to blame.

As Ben recovered from his initial surgery, he remained on a ventilator connected to an oxygen generator and compressor. The investigation found that there was a problem with the compressor, and that it wasn't sufficiently powered to generate the oxygen saturation it should have. Also, at the time Ben went into cardiac arrest, the batteries in the defibrillator weren't charged. Instead of a quick shock back to rhythm, the machine needed to be plugged in and fired up. McKenna, while being interviewed for *Heart of a Ranger*, said those two problems alone may not have *caused* Ben's death, but they certainly may have contributed. He also noted that if Ben's cardiac arrest had stemmed from a hidden health problem, his heart wouldn't have been viable for transplant. McKenna believes something as yet undiscovered or undetected led to (or at least contributed to) Ben's death. The official report concluded: "Death may have been preventable with the equipment functioning properly."

Had these events happened to Ben as a civilian, a civil action might've been filed. However, under the Feres Doctrine, because Ben was actively serving in the military, all government employees are protected from legal action.

Ben's heroism and sacrifice have been noted nationally many times. Jill re-created his face in flowers and other organic matter on the side of the Donate Life America float in the 2011 Tournament of Roses Parade. And in May of 2012, Ben was honored during the opening ceremony of ABC's broadcast of the Indianapolis 500.

Ben's name is also associated with a spectacular phenomenon that occurs when a helicopter rotor slices through sand blown up off the ground by the downward rotor wash. The process produces a spark that is visible in low-light situations. Millions of sparks create a spectacular glowing halo around the spinning rotor. Journalist Michael Yon dubbed the occurrence the Kopp-Etchells Effect. He coined the term in honor of both Ben and Corporal Joseph Etchells, a young British soldier who was serving in Afghanistan and was killed the day after Ben died at Walter Reed.

Ben is laid to rest in the hallowed section 60 of Arlington National Cemetery. Ben gets frequent visitors from his brothers-in-arms and their families and friends who now know his remarkable story. Several classes of middle school students have had their photos taken at Ben's resting place. Families make special stops during their personal vacations. Jill visits ANC at least twice each year—Memorial Day weekend and in December to take part in Wreaths Across America. She receives a new photo about once per month from Ben's many visitors.

While Nick Irving couldn't attend any of Ben's funeral services or his burial, he did eventually visit Ben's grave. Irving says he now talks to Jill like he talks to his own mom. Irving has enjoyed much success after leaving the Ranger Regiment, including penning a *New York Times* best seller, *The Reaper,* about his 2009 deployment. "I wouldn't be here today if it weren't for Ben," he says. "We called in air strikes, and we couldn't get air strikes. We called for another platoon to come get us out, and they couldn't come. But Ben and his machine gun team came to get us, right in the middle of a hellacious firefight. I owe him everything."

ACKNOWLEDGMENTS

Thank you to my wife, Sheri, and my three boys, John, William, and Daniel, who put up with me during the two plus years it took to complete this project. I could've been a better husband and father during that time, but you all understood that preserving this story was important. Special kudos to Sheri for her insight, patience, and thorough review of the manuscript; and to John, a Minnesota National Guard infantry soldier, who helped review my basic training descriptions from Fort Benning, where he—like Ben—completed OSUT.

Without Jill Stephenson, this book wouldn't be possible. Her unending desire to share her son's story and her ability to connect with those close to Ben meant finding the next interview was just a text or phone call away. Her strength and resilience continue to inspire me. She calls that magic "Benergy." It's something I have witnessed on more than one occasion, that Ben's spirit is still working to influence things in this world.

Thank you to Ranger Chaplain Jeff Struecker, who encouraged me early on and assured me that this was an important and worthwhile project.

Thank you to all the Rangers who agreed to be interviewed for this story: Erick Innis, Ryan Lundeby, Chase Vanderhule, Dan Krueger, Sean Scappaticci, Michael Melvin, Don Kingston, Justin Johanson, Christopher Watkins, Nathan Lyons, Morgan Garrett, Shane Harris, Ryan Walker, Phil Paquette, Derrick Ball, Stephen Shipe, Nicholas Irving, Lane Sandifer, Jeff Mellinger, Rudy DelValle, Mike Shellman, and Jay McKenna. Thanks also to Air Force JTAC Stan House, who explained how air support works over a Ranger operation. Thank you to Army wife Beth Kingston, for her unique perspective as the wife of a Ranger company commander, and a witness to Ben's story.

I also appreciated my time talking with Carter Malkasian, a foremost expert on the local tribes, governments, and Taliban presence in Helmand Province. Malkasian's book, *War Comes to Garmser*, was an excellent resource.

I really appreciated talking with Ben's childhood friends, Jenny Boll, Josh Maldonado, Richard Rivera, Tyler Nelson, Eric Pittlekow, and Kyle Hildreth. It meant so much to me to hear the stories of Ben's teenage years. Thanks also to Brittney Doran for reaching into her heart to share stories of her romance with Ben during their high school years.

My aunt, Beverly Malatesta Temple, has nudged me on my grammar and usage my entire life. She got the final say on such points in reviewing the manuscript through countless revisions, and I'm forever indebted for her support.

Thanks also to my in-laws, Leonard and Monette Vazzano, for always encouraging me as a journalist.

My special thanks to Major Anthony Mayne with the 75th Ranger Regiment, who helped coordinate and clear interviews with Rangers still on active duty.

Thanks also to my friend David Arndt, author of the novel *Grimm Patriot*. We encouraged each other while writing books at the same time. I also appreciate my KSTP-TV colleagues, Dave Dahl and Leah McLean, who listened to endless updates on the book's progress.

Ben's great-grandmother, Marian Rogers, helped me with firsthand memories of her husband, LeRoy, and generously shared all the letters he sent home from World War II. In October of 2016 Marian died at the age of ninety-five. Her family members read her an advance copy of *Heart of a Ranger* in her final days.

Big thanks to Judy Meikle, who continues to be a champion for organ donation and was always available to talk and answer questions. Thank you as well to the remarkable cardiothoracic surgeons, Dr. Edwin McGee and his protégé, Dr. Umraan Ahmad, for carefully explaining the procurement and implantation of the human heart. (Dr. McGee's memory was so remarkable that he specifically remembered Judy's surgery, even though he had performed more than three hundred heart transplant surgeries by the time of our interview.)

Thank you to Amy Quale at Wise Ink Creative Publishing in Minneapolis, who handled this project with gusto. Thank you also to my editor Anitra Budd, who took my massive manuscript and skillfully honed it to a more efficient and readable story.

And, finally, thank you to Ben's brothers, all the men of the 75th Ranger Regiment, past and present, who volunteer to do remarkably brave things most people don't ever hear about. They are quiet professionals who risk their lives to keep our country free and safe. As I have learned: Rangers truly lead the way.

ATTENTION VETERANS

If you knew Ben or someone like him, his story may have deeply affected you and reawakened thoughts, feelings and emotions. Those can be difficult to deal with and may make you want to isolate. This is normal. The best medicine is talking with a comrade who has earned the right to listen to you and who understands.

Transition from the military is far harder than most expect it to be. Many veterans experience a profound sense of loss, regret, even survivor's guilt at the loss of a beloved comrade such as Ben Kopp. When they return home after service, or move to a new location for work or school, finding someone with similar experiences is difficult if not impossible. Many struggle with a sense of purpose, having gone from supporting and defending the Constitution of the United States, willing to lay down their life for their brothers and sisters, to a civilian community that seems disconnected and self-oriented. A career focused on making money seems obscene compared to their former life of service. These things combined can create obstacles to employment, harm relationships, and worsen when the veteran turns to self-medication often with alcohol or other substances.

It doesn't have to be this way. Ben's mom, Jill Stephenson, works with GallantFew, Inc. to help veterans get and stay connected. GallantFew is a national nonprofit that helps transitioning veterans connect with local veterans who have already successfully transitioned and are established in the community. GallantFew also helps veterans who have for years felt purpose and hope slip away by guiding them back through mentoring, counseling, and diagnosing needs and finding resources.

No matter where you are on this journey, get connected at gallantfew.org. If you are a Ranger veteran, GallantFew has a program specific to Rangers called the Darby Project. Learn more and get connected at darbyproject.org. If you need to talk to someone right now, call 817-600-0514.

KARL MONGER, EXECUTIVE DIRECTOR GALLANTFEW, INC.
MAJOR, US ARMY RETIRED RESERVES
1ST RANGER BATTALION, 1990-1993

ABOUT THE AUTHOR

Bill Lunn is an Emmy Award-winning anchor and reporter for KSTP-TV in Minneapolis, Minnesota. Lunn covers military and veterans' issues. His reporting has taken him into Special Operations Command in Tampa, Florida for a behind-the-scenes look at how special operators are trained, supplied, and deployed. He embedded with Minnesota Red Bull troops in the Mojave Desert during 2016 training at the National Training Center at Fort Irwin, California. He also emceed all major events for the national Medal of Honor Convention in 2016. He is a graduate of St. Mary's University in Minnesota and holds a master's of journalism from Northwestern University. He lives in Stillwater, Minnesota with his wife and three boys. *Heart of a Ranger* is his first book.